TAKE IT
FROM ME

TAKE IT FROM ME

An Agent's Guide to Building a Nonfiction Writing Career from Scratch

Alia Hanna Habib

Pantheon Books
New York

FIRST HARDCOVER EDITION
PUBLISHED BY PANTHEON BOOKS 2026

Published by Pantheon Books, a division of Penguin Random House LLC, 1745 Broadway, New York, NY 10019.

Pantheon Books and the colophon are registered trademarks of Penguin Random House LLC.

Grateful acknowledgment is made to publishersmarketplace.com for permission to reprint excerpts from "Ask an Expert: Vicky Bijur." © 2023 Cader Company Inc. dba publishersmarketplace.com

Library of Congress Cataloging-in-Publication Data

Names: Habib, Alia Hanna, 1977– author
Title: Take it from me : an agent's guide to building a nonfiction writing career from scratch / Alia Hanna Habib.
Description: New York : Pantheon Books, [2025] |
Identifiers: LCCN 2025002493 (print) | LCCN 2025002494 (ebook) |
ISBN 9780593700877 hardcover | ISBN 9780593700884 ebook
Subjects: LCSH: Authorship—Vocational guidance
Classification: LCC PN151 .H2125 2025 (print) | LCC PN151 (ebook)
LC record available at https://lccn.loc.gov/2025002493
LC ebook record available at https://lccn.loc.gov/2025002494

penguinrandomhouse.com | pantheonbooks.com

Printed in the United States of America

1st Printing

The authorized representative in the EU for product safety and compliance is Penguin Random House Ireland, Morrison Chambers, 32 Nassau Street, Dublin D02 YH68, Ireland, https://eu-contact.penguin.ie.

To my mother
For passing along her love of reading

And to Adrienne & Jackie
For getting me through

CONTENTS

WHAT'S IN THIS BOOK, HOW TO USE IT, AND WHY I WROTE IT

From my first encounter with Janelle's work, I knew I had to do everything possible to become her agent. I was helping a friend paint her new apartment during the dog days of a New York summer, and the place had no AC. Within minutes, we were dripping with sweat; within an hour, we were painting in our underwear. At some point, Janelle's voice came on the ancient radio we'd plugged in, and the story she reported made me put down my paint roller, sit on the bare floor, and just listen. Her piece embodied everything I love about narrative nonfiction at its best: the way it can move seamlessly between empathy and analysis, intimacy and rigor. My friend didn't have Wi-Fi yet, so I held my phone aloft in her empty apartment, trying to get a signal so I could figure out a way to track Janelle down. I remember finding her email at last, my message slowly rainbow-wheeling its way to her. While I don't believe all good deeds in life are necessarily rewarded, I'm so glad Janelle came into mine while I was in the middle of one.

When we finally met in person, Janelle reminded me of early computers, how their hard drives were so large they'd fill a room. Her intelligence and ambition were so immense they were palpable, a kind of physical presence. I was thus surprised when she told me she was skeptical about writing a book and even seemed overwhelmed by the notion. On paper and in terms of the quality of her work, she was fully "professionalized," and much further along than many of the writers I meet at conferences and workshops, through referrals from their writer friends or via MFA or journalism programs. Janelle had gone to journalism school and knew people who had published books. After many years of hard, ill-paid work as a freelancer, she had finally gotten her first job at a national media organization. Of course, she loved books and was a voracious reader. Like many writers, publishing a book was one of her most dearly held dreams. Yet as is often the case with those dreams that mean so much to us, she had no small amount of apprehension.

As I spoke to her in my part unlicensed therapist/part busybody way, I realized that yes, some of Janelle's reluctance was the usual writerly fear of failure, but even more than that: Despite already being highly professionalized, she was thoroughly mystified by the business side of the prospect, and that mystification was stopping her in her tracks. She wasn't sure how or if she'd make money on a book, particularly if she had to take time off from her hard-earned job to write one. She didn't know how much of the book she would have to write before selling it (All of it? Or if only parts, which parts? Would she need a sample chapter?), or how long publishers might give her to write the thing. Did she need to find all her "characters" before writing a proposal? And once the book was sold, what would be my role as her agent while she finished it, versus that of her editor?

These were just her first rush of questions. As is true for many writers who haven't yet sold a book, and even those who have, the publishing process was largely opaque to Janelle. Over the course of that first meeting, we talked houses and imprints, what the submission process typically looks like and how it functions for a book sold on proposal rather than on a full manuscript, how advances are paid out, and what kind of support she could reasonably expect a publisher to give her in terms of publicity, marketing, and editorial guidance. With every new piece of the publishing puzzle laid bare to her, I watched as transparency worked its magic; the more concrete the process, the more comfortable she became with the idea of writing a book-length work. It was clear that although Janelle knew plenty of writers and had even met with some agents and editors prior to our discussion, she hadn't yet been in a situation where anyone had addressed these questions, or—like many intelligent people feeling the pressure to perform knowledge and paralyzed by not knowing something they perceive they already ought to—where she felt comfortable asking them.

I bring up Janelle, a pseudonym, not because her concerns were unusual, but because she is one of the most confident and ambitious people I have ever met. I did sign her and she went on to publish bestselling books as part of her amazing and ever-growing career. But the fact that "Janelle" could be so daunted by the process despite everything going for her means that a nonfiction writer starting from scratch will be even more daunted. As an agent who also started from scratch, despite by now (at last!) having found my groove, I confess I closely relate to Janelle's initial intimidation, shared by countless would-be writers. Overcoming it is, in fact, the story of my career.

•   •   •

My father was a bartender, my mother a secretary in Wilkes-Barre, Pennsylvania. I arrived in New York City in 1997 as a first-generation, low-income college student. (Learning to decode the rules of the game at Barnard and Columbia on a full-ride scholarship after being educated at a Title I high school was my first, unwitting lesson in tackling a career in book publishing.) I'd been a bookish kid who'd grown up knowing precisely no one who worked in books professionally and thinking that the only employment option if you loved reading was to be an English teacher. That I got hired as an assistant to the director of cookbook publicity at Houghton Mifflin, then a large independent publisher, right out of college was nothing short of miraculous. I didn't know what a publicity assistant did (and I definitely didn't know how to cook!), but I knew I loved books and thought I'd like to work with them. As this was the first book-related job I was offered, I grabbed it. I probably would have tried to become an agency assistant instead if I'd had any idea what a literary agent was, but my path ended up being quite meandering. (Part of it involved spending the first couple weeks of my publicity assistant job confused about the nature of the "escorts" I was booking to accompany my authors on tour. Maybe publishing *did* have money after all!) Given the insularity and relative homogeneity of the publishing world, as I worked to build my career, I often felt I was in it but not *of* it—as if everyone else had been handed a guidebook, but no one would tell me where it was kept.

After a few years in the publicity department (and a lengthy detour to graduate school), I realized that I wanted to do work that was closer to the actual conceptualizing of a book, and to have more say about the kinds of books I worked on. I was desperate to transition to the editorial department, but I was a publicity manager and already over thirty. The only path for me by then would have been to start back at the beginning, as an editorial assistant, and no one was looking to hire a thirtysomething editorial assistant who'd spent years as a manager. (I know because I tried.) Ultimately, I became an agent thanks to a literary godmother named Julie Barer. Barer, then already a successful agent, now nothing short of a legend, took me out to lunch one day as a thank-you for doing a good job on one of her books. I shared my ambitions and my woes, and she looked at me and said, "You know, I think you'd be a really good agent. And that path is much more open to people from nontraditional backgrounds." I still wasn't entirely sure what an agent did, or how I'd become one, or even how they got paid, but Julie's suggestion struck me as an idea worth pursuing. I reached out to agents I'd admired from afar to ask if they'd do informational interviews so I could learn more about the job, and ultimately try to find a spot at an agency. Within a few months I had a desk and a chair and a commission-only contract at a small agency. For my first few years as an agent, I side-hustled as a freelance publicist to keep the lights on.

My path was challenging in part because it was unusual, and that too shaped how I think about the role of the agent and the publishing industry more widely. Most agents are trained "on the desk" of other agents; that is, they work first as an assistant to a well-established agent before taking on clients of their own. While that is hardly an easy road, being an agency assistant for a few years is a means to learn what an agent does while also earning an (admittedly modest) salary while you do so. Sometimes an assistant will start building their own list based in part on referrals from their boss or fellow agency colleagues or from the agency's slush pile—a route that wasn't on the table for me. Nor was a salary or a "draw"—i.e., a predetermined amount of money paid to some agents by the agencies that employ them, set against projected commissions. In building a client list while also building a base of knowledge while also building a base of income, I was starting from scratch in every sense.

Once I got that first agent's desk, the stakes of filling in my knowledge gaps were high. I was forced by economic necessity to get over any shame about asking the questions I'd normally pretend to know the answer to: What are the key components of a book proposal? What is a standard book payout? What's the typical timeline for a nonfiction book? Amazingly, I couldn't have answered any of these questions on day one of "being an agent," even though I had been working in publishing for half a decade. I take this as proof not that I was extraordinarily clueless, but that a lot us run around not knowing how major parts of our own industry work, because knowledge is shared in such a haphazard and siloed way (or treated as a zealously guarded commodity). There were countless times when I thought for sure I would never make it, which I defined at the time as reaching the salary I'd left as a publicity manager. Getting there took me five years. That early precarity left an indelible mark on how I approach my role as an agent and how, in turn, I guide my clients in building their own careers.

In practical terms, my list was initially created through reaching out to then-emerging nonfiction writers—Clint Smith, Nikole Hannah-Jones, Adam Serwer, Merve Emre, and Lauren Oyler, to name a few I cold-called when I was starting out—and pitching myself to them, often repeatedly. I thus know how important it is, especially when you're coming in over the transom, to have that pitch be undeniable, and how it feels to send it with fingers crossed and candles lit. I also know how it feels to spend years screaming into the void. When I meet a new writer trying to establish herself and get editors and agents to take her seriously, I can't help but think back to those first few tough years as an agent. I think that identification leads me to fight for my clients so doggedly. When I did manage to score a meeting with a potential client I wanted to sign, I couldn't, at least at first, offer years of experience. Instead, I worked with what I had; I brought in-depth knowledge of publicity and media and a hands-on commitment to my writers' success. I also brought a sense of urgency to my job because I was in a bit of a sink-or-swim situation myself—I was already in my early thirties, my checking account regularly dipped into the three digits, and I had no parental or spousal safety net. I think the writers who chose to throw in their lot with me did so because my hunger was apparent, and because my position as an inside/outsider was an appealing bridge. I now see that starting out with a lack of received wisdom can be a blessing in disguise. It made me unafraid to ask questions, good at anticipating the ones my writers might have, and willing to interrogate the way things were done. I also saw quite clearly how much assumed knowledge there was in the moment writers met publishing professionals. I understood that I had to get that knowledge quickly and make sharing it central to my work with my clients. This sharing of knowledge was empowering for both them and me.

I don't pretend I'm capable of telling my writers *everything*, but I try to be sure that by the time one of my clients meets with an editor, they have a fully conceptualized vision of their book, realized through writing and researching their proposal, a solid grasp of how book publishing works, the relevant timelines and rhythms for nonfiction, details about the editors and imprints in question (as well as the means to find out more), a strong sense of the competitive titles in their field, publicity and marketing capabilities and expectations, and the basics of publishing math—and what to expect in that terrifying editor meeting and how to excel in it. I want to equip them with a wealth of information about selling, writing, and publishing a book, both because I think that is my responsibility as an agent and because I've seen time and again that having such information is crucial to setting up a writer for a successful and fulfilling publishing experience—not to mention a pleasant relationship with their editor.

I know, though, that not all writers lucky enough to win an audience with a publisher are so well armed, including those who have already been sluiced through the process of acquiring an agent. I don't think other agents are asleep at the wheel—despite our sharky reputations, I firmly believe most of us *really* want our clients to do well and to feel empowered and are in this business for the love of authors and books. An agent's structural role, however, means that many writers view us as an impediment rather than a means to publication—another hoop to jump through, at a 15 percent charge, in a long series of hoops. When an author meets an agent, if they even get to that point, the author tends to feel the onus of simply impressing the agent in question. (By extension, meeting an actual book editor is that too, only more so.) Often, they ask only the questions they know enough to pose or feel comfortable asking. This is a sensible strategy if you assume, not irrationally, that the person you are talking to is primarily a gatekeeper rather than a guide.

In my work as an agent, I emphasize guiding as much as I do gatekeeping, in large part because I remember what it is like to be on the other side of a gate, as well as how many times earlier in my career I was desperate for clarification, context, and guidance that was hard to find. Even now, as a seasoned agent with numerous *New York Times* bestsellers and prizewinning works of nonfiction behind me, I keenly remember the stakes, for me, of not knowing. The purpose of this book is to create the kind of guidebook I once wished I had, a central place to find credible, contextualized answers about publishing nonfiction from an experienced source within the industry. I am candid about my own particular experiences and point of view throughout this intro, and I am just as candid throughout the book, an approach I take intentionally. I'm purposely informal on the page, in part because that's my default conversational mode, but also because I want to make the often inscrutable and foreboding world of publishing approachable and even welcoming, made of real, fallible people with a range of opinions, experiences, and methods of doing this work. There are some doorstops written about publishing; this book is not one of them. One school of thought on writing nonfiction idealizes the view from nowhere, the idea that in the interest of objectivity, a nonfiction writer should approach their subject with such neutrality that their personal experiences and beliefs cannot and should not enter into what they write in any way. I believe that the best nonfiction, even when prescriptive, is quite clear about where the writer is coming from, and that clarity is a strength, not a weakness. I also think a narrative approach to advice is more fun to read and makes information easier to digest and retain—I've focused on narrative nonfiction as an agent for a reason! As you read this book, I want you to feel you have a friend in publishing.

But the expertise here isn't just mine. I conducted over seventy in-depth interviews with authors, editors, publicists, and other media and publishing professionals to ensure the advice I'm giving doesn't reflect only my own opinions and experiences. Many of these experts are directly quoted; other times, their valuable input informed my explanations of best and most common practices as well as the most common points of frustration for nonfiction writers. Researching this book was often an exercise in humility—I once again discovered how siloed publishing can be, and often I realized I knew much less than I thought! While I now understand the finer points of a work-for-hire contract and how a book first sold in the United States ends up being published in China, I don't have direct experience in some areas, so in certain cases I turn the mic over to industry specialists for more in-depth Q&As. These appear as sidebars throughout the book and are more technical in tone than the primary text. I preserved them in all their wonky detail to make sure you are armed and ready when the time comes.

One of the great joys in reporting this book was getting to interview dozens of writers and fellow publishing professionals I admire. These conversations shaped so much of the advice I give. I've included longer excerpts from three of them—writers Chloé Cooper Jones and Andrea Elliott and agent Brettne Bloom—each of whom has had a singular career and offers an illuminating perspective on a writer's work. I spoke with Chloé Cooper Jones at the tail end of the interviews for chapter 2, on education. Jones would tell you herself that hers is an atypical path—she has multiple graduate degrees—but I was in awe of the voracity and creativity of her approach to school and how she used a rigorous, formal education to create her own rule book. Your education needn't be either formal or rigorous, but her story is a good reminder that a less direct route to publication can yield its own rewards. Jones also offers the best advice I've ever heard about how to have a positive publishing experience. She's not just brilliant; she's wise. Brettne Bloom is a fellow agent and a kind of memoir whisperer. Talking with her made me want to share her advice with every aspiring memoirist as she anticipated and answered the questions that come up again and again. I end the book with my interview with Andrea Elliott, the recipient of two Pulitzer Prizes in nonfiction. Though it was unintentional at the time, the interview manages to capture so many of the themes of this book. While *Take It from Me* isn't a craft book, and I don't offer much in the way of general guidance on how to get your book *done* (from personal experience, I can recommend living in a building with a vending machine), I hope you can draw from the particulars of how these extraordinary writers actually did it.

This book purposefully gives focused attention to a writer's career *before* landing an agent, which is particularly important, as having a publication track record of articles and essays is helpful even for debut nonfiction writers of books. By giving guidance for the period before a nonfiction writer starts pitching agents, I'll show how the slush pile isn't the only or even the best route to landing one, especially for nonfiction, and how to put yourself in the best possible position to do so when ready. Thus Chapter 1: On Pitching, or Starting Small focuses on pitching essays and articles, which includes (sometimes counterintuitive) advice from top editors from a range of media outlets and successful freelance writers, as well as sample pitches. I also share tips on becoming a pitch detective so you can avoid emailing contact@magazine.com and instead build a relationship with a real, living, human editor.

In Chapter 2: An Author's Education, I examine some educational options for aspiring nonfiction writers through case studies and conversations with successful practitioners who have pursued one of three educational paths: a creative nonfiction MFA, journalism school, and doctoral programs in the humanities and social sciences. The point of this chapter isn't "you need school to be a writer," but rather, what to expect if you do want to take the graduate-degree approach to building your writing career. This is the moment in a writer's career I have the least direct experience with, and thus the chapter in which I draw most heavily from the experiences of others. In that spirit, I conclude with compelling case studies of two writers who built extraordinary literary communities and careers for themselves outside educational institutions.

Chapter 2.5: What Is a Platform and How Do I Define Mine? is a mini chapter on the vexed term, which frustrates many aspiring writers while also confounding publishing professionals. (Don't believe me? If you work at a publisher, ask ten of your colleagues what platform means and come back to me with the twelve different definitions you receive.) I try to provide fresh and inspiring ways to think about your platform and use the tools and skills already at your disposal to bolster your writing career and impress potential publishers in the process.

In Chapter 3: The Book Proposal, or Don't Be Boring, I get into the essentials of one of my favorite parts of my job: crafting book proposals. I give you everything you need to know to write a strong proposal, and I'm frank about the useless stuff I see in proposal after proposal so you don't waste your time on fluff and filler. I share tips for making your proposal a good read in itself, which will generate more interest in the actual project, which in turn can result in more offers, a higher advance, a stronger editorial match, and best of all, a better book.

Chapter 4: What Is an Agent For? lifts the veil on how agents actually work. I explain how nonfiction agenting often functions quite differently from fiction agenting, and how you can use that knowledge in your search for an agent. I give advice on how to find the best agents to query as well as the most effective ways to do so when you are ready. I'm also frank about what an agent can and can't do for you—our powers are formidable but even we have our limits—and share best practices for working with the agent in your life to get the most out of your partnership.

Though I can't offer any assurance about what the end results of submitting your book for publication will be, I can make the process far less mysterious and overwhelming by giving you a sense of what you can reasonably expect and control. In Chapter 5: The Submission Process, or This Is Where It Hurts, I go into detail about submitting your proposal, from timing, to how to handle a meeting with an interested publisher, to the nitty-gritty of how books get sold (auction! preempt! none of the above!), to how payments are structured. And I lay out your role in the whole process. I also share a brief explainer on book contracts, courtesy of a trusted publishing lawyer.

In Chapter 6: The Publication Process, I detail everything that happens in the year (yes, it often takes a whole year, and sometimes even longer!) between turning in your manuscript and your book being published. I cover what actually happens in the sales, publicity, and marketing departments of a publisher, what should happen when, and what to do if it doesn't. As I say again and again in this book, book publishing is a team sport (an axiom repeated by people who likely never played team sports by choice), and you'll have a better experience as a published author if you know how to work with your team. I also make clear what you can and should be doing as an author to support your own book, with lots of advice from authors who have navigated this part of the process well.

While the chapters more or less follow the conventional arc of a writer's career, there are many variations on what is typical, and writers have different needs at different points in their careers. I planned this book so that you could get lots of useful things from it without reading it cover to cover. Not interested in doing an MFA? Not a problem at all; go ahead and skip that chapter. Bored by detail? The stuff on book contracts is there for you if you need it, but nothing in here is mandatory. Please dip into and out of the book as you please. One of the many delights of reading is that no one is watching over your shoulder.

A recurring theme of this book is empowerment through transparency. Often writers get stymied because they don't understand the ins and outs of the publishing side; in other cases, they simply don't know what to ask. Knowing that nonfiction books are sold largely on proposals and understanding how much research you need to do in order to write one will save you time and effort. Learning how book payouts are structured and timed will keep you from expecting checks that are months away from arriving. Understanding the difference between what is within a book publicist's powers and what falls outside it will help you advocate for yourself where and when it counts. Throughout this book, I share questions you can and should ask of the publishing professionals in your life and very hands-on insight to make the author-agent, author-editor, and author-publicist relationship one of mutual collaboration instead of a source of anxiety for writers. I'll help you understand what is normal, what is not, when you can ask for more support, and how to do so effectively.

My other theme: There is no one way to do things. In these pages you won't see anything like "Ten Steps to Becoming a Published Author!" or "The Five Secrets to a Million-Dollar Advance!" If such outcomes could be reduced to a formula or a recipe, we'd have a lot more millionaire writers running around—and I wouldn't object to that! I can't give any money-back guarantees, but I can promise that the advice here is honest, experience based, and yours for the taking (or leaving). I offer it up in the same spirit I give to my writers: There are lots and lots of ways to become a successful author, and one size doesn't fit all. I'll show you a variety of ways to do that, so that you, my writer-reader, can find your own.

TAKE IT
FROM ME

CHAPTER 1

ON PITCHING,
OR STARTING SMALL

Dorothy Brown is a professor of tax law. As she'd be the first to admit, it's not the kind of profession that makes people line up to talk to you at cocktail parties. (The opposite is true for literary agents, and it has nothing to do with personal charm. I once spent a party watching a young man work up the courage to talk to me, only to discover it was so he could pitch me his book idea: *What Cheese Are You?* Lest you think I missed out on an amazing publishing opportunity, he wasn't even able to tell me what cheese I am.) As a professor and now as a writer, Brown is determined to make her seemingly arcane body of research widely accessible. In doing so, she's working against the tide of her own profession. To Brown's great frustration, when fellow academics say "Your work is so accessible," they may well mean it as an insult.

Brown's research is on tax and race, a field she has essentially pioneered. Her long-term goal was to publish a trade book for a general-interest audience as opposed to an academic one targeted at fellow legal scholars, but her route to doing so wasn't to pitch agents, at least not at first. Brown set her sights instead on publishing Op-Eds in *The Washington Post* and *The New York Times*. She did this with several larger aims in mind: to get her work read by both the general public and policymakers—hence the choice of newspapers read by them—and to make herself more appealing to publishers when it came time to sell a book. She pursued this goal with the doggedness of a tax professor—that is, with the systematic and relentless focus of someone who can spend hours at a time poring over decades of tax data. She pitched *The New York Times* over a dozen times before succeeding. And she eventually did sell that book, *The Whiteness of Wealth*, to Crown, a division of Penguin Random House, and now has a second, *Getting to Reparations*, forthcoming from the same publisher. The publication of her work outside academic journals led her to be invited to testify before Congress three times and to privately brief multiple sitting congressional representatives.

If your end goal, like Dorothy's, is to eventually land an agent and publish a nonfiction book, the first piece of advice I always give is to **aggressively pursue publishing shorter work and to do so with as much upbeat imperviousness to rejection as your heart can muster.** It is much, much easier to land an agent, and a book deal, if you have had work previously published. Pitching a nonfiction book to an agent when you've never published a word of prose is a bit like buying a lottery ticket. There's no reason *not* to do it—buying lottery tickets is fun! And the ads are right when they say "You never know!" That said, while your odds of becoming a millionaire via the lotto are admittedly lower than landing an agent for a nonfiction book when you've *never* previously published anything, they're still, speaking frankly, not great. I always feel like the bearer of bad news when I share this fact, a much less fun part of my job than telling someone we have an offer on the table for their book, which never fails to give me chills. Publishing articles and essays will not only make you more appealing to agents once you start pitching them. Agents—particularly those of us who represent nonfiction—regularly read national newspapers, magazines and literary journals, and a whole range of media besides (often, in fact, when we should be reading books). If there is a golden ticket in nonfiction book publishing, it is writing an original piece and having an agent see it and reach out to *you*—which is, in fact, how I found many of my clients.

I'm opening this chapter with Dorothy Brown's story not only because it had a happy ending but because I think her thoughtful-step-by-thoughtful-step approach, and, above all, her attitude toward breaking into publishing, is a gift worth sharing. Unlike Brown, many writers would quit long before receiving that twelfth pass; how she thought about those passes enabled her to keep going forward. If an editor said no to a pitch, Brown didn't assume it was because the idea was terrible or that she was a terrible writer. Brown decided that when she heard "no," she was actually hearing "not yet" and intuited there could be a number of reasons an outlet passed on a piece that had nothing to do with the piece itself. (She also filed every rejected piece away in case it would someday be of use as part of a book chapter or another Op-Ed based on the ever-changing news cycle.) As Brown told me, and as I know to be true from years spent comforting understandably anxious clients, many writers can't help but assume editors' passes are due to "the substance and that's not always what the no means. The no could mean one of thirty-two million things: isn't a fit right now; we have something else on the topic; a former or current president just got indicted, and all of our focus is there."

Dorothy correctly intuited the black-box nature of a newsroom and how unsolicited pitches fit into it. There's a mistaken notion that editors (and by extension, agents) spend much of their time fielding pitches, but that is actually just a small part of what editors at media outlets do and how they think about what they publish. As Vann Newkirk, a senior editor at *The Atlantic* who works with many emerging writers, explained to me, being an editor is a "social job." The bulk of an editor's time is not spent sifting through over-the-transom pitches and giving deep thought as to which ones to take. Instead, the majority of his day is spent interacting with writers he is in the process of publishing: on Zooms, over coffee, on the phone, or improving their work on the page, and then working with the rest of his colleagues to figure out how the parts fit into the whole. Vanessa Mobley, an Opinion editor at *The New York Times* who oversees the guest essays team (that is, pieces by nonstaff writers), put this aspect of the job into context: Every week the Opinion section has a meeting where the editors talk about ideas for guest essays. Individual editors often lobby to push a writer or an idea into the "report," their term for the sum total of what the Opinion section of *The New York Times* publishes. Publication decisions are made not just by how much one editor likes a piece or an individual writer. Rather, any pass you receive is made in the context of a whole chain of decisions, calculations, and the ecosystem of other writers and pieces already commissioned that most likely have little to do with you or your talent. As Mobley's description of her job makes clear, editors themselves are engaged in their own version of pitching. Especially at major outlets with sizable staff, editors who work directly with writers must get a sign-off from their bosses to commission a piece. The mechanics are slightly different from publication to publication, but the overall process is largely the same. At *The New York Times Magazine,* for example, writers work with a story editor on their articles. As Jake Silverstein, the editor-in-chief of *The New York Times Magazine,* explains, "Story editors are ones who have their primary relationship with the writer. They're going to be the ones who developed the idea back and forth with the author." The story editor, in turn, "brings the pitch to one of the four 'top editors,' the editorial director, and myself, to advocate for it. That's the group that makes decisions to green-light or red-light a pitch." At *The New York Times Magazine,* much like at the Opinion section, story editors attend a weekly meeting, bringing in pitches from freelance and contributing writers with whom they have been in conversation or developed an idea, as well as from the contracted writers whom they are assigned to edit. To mangle David Mamet, editors, like writers, Always Be Pitching.

I believe this external context is why there's such a mismatch between how it feels to give a pass versus how it feels to get one. (It feels terrible! And personal, though in most cases, there's nothing personal about it at all.) In order to get published, you need to submit excellent materials and put a lot of time and effort into writing them. Far less time and effort go into reviewing the initial pitch, even for the most thoughtful editors, in large part because of the volume of submissions an editor receives and because any editor worthy of the title spends a good part of their day improving the pieces they do want to publish and advocating for them with their higher-ups. I share this reality not to make the process feel impossible (it's not—and the sample pitches at the end of this chapter will offer suggestions on how to improve and target your pitches so you have a higher success rate), but so that the weight of decisions rendered doesn't feel so very weighty. It's natural to think of editors as gods on high, the outlets that employ them as a kind of Olympus, but in many ways, editors are in a structural position much like your own—they too are fighting to get "their" pieces published. And just like you, it's in their best interest to do so—the more good work they manage to bring in, the more traffic or attention they bring to a website or magazine, the more they are valued by their employer. More encouragingly to know, writers who get published regularly in the same publication are usually published by the same editor again and again, a win-win for both parties. That editor, particularly if they "discovered" the writer, is in turn invested in the writer's work and career.

So I'd like to suggest the first of two ways to reframe how you think about the process of pitching articles and essays: **It is not (just) the quest to add the name of another media outlet to your list of clips. Imagine instead that you are seeking an editorial reader who will understand and advocate for your work, who will improve it and help bring it to a wider audience.** And when you get a no, it may just be a "not yet"—at least not with this person, at this moment.

The good news is that while it's intimidating to pitch articles and essays, it is easier to publish one than it is to land an agent. The bar to entry is lower for editors seeking regular content for their publications and thus the demand for material by media outlets is much higher than the publishing industry could keep up with for book-length projects. Digital outlets in particular have not just a weekly or even a daily demand for new content but an hourly one. (This volume issue is also why it takes so excruciatingly long to hear back from editors when you pitch articles.) The height of the bar for publication varies not just by format and outlet but also by section of the publication. Per Jake Silverstein of *The New York Times Magazine,* it's easier for a first-time freelancer or a new writer to break into the "front of the book" (FOB)—the beginning section of most print magazines where shorter pieces appear—than to get a commission to write a longer piece. This is in part a practical decision by the magazine, a bit like not planning a weekend trip with someone before you've gone on a first date. As Silverstein explains, "Sometimes we get pitches from freelancers who we haven't worked with before for features where we think the proposal is interesting, but it's a little too ambitious for us to assign to a first-time writer. Maybe it involves very expensive travel, or high-stakes investigative work. In those cases we probably won't assign, because we haven't worked with the writer before. We often encourage writers who are new to the magazine to pitch ideas that are a little easier to assign for their first features— profiles, domestic stories, that sort of thing." At *The New York Times Magazine,* "The Letter of Recommendation" in the front of the book is often a proving ground for new writers. Rachel Syme, now a staff writer at *The New Yorker* and an ambitious and assiduous student of magazines, charted her path to publication through learning about and then pitching the smaller, FOB sections. Her first piece published in *The New York Times* was, in fact, a "Letter of Recommendation" in the magazine. Getting it published helped her establish a relationship with the magazine, and more important, with an editor who appreciated her work and would continue to publish her. FOB sections vary by outlet and change all the time; becoming a student of them will help you understand where and what to pitch.

Your study of the publications in which you'd like to be published should not just include their content, individual sections, and tone, but also who works there. If you take one thing from this chapter—and this is my second reframing—it's that you are, or can become, the best pitcher of your shorter work and you can and *should be doing so directly*. There is a mistaken belief that you can't publish essays and articles without an agent, and your only path to having *any* of your work in print is to secure an agent to help you do so. I want to stress this is simply not true for nonfiction, and in many cases, pitching your articles and essays directly to media outlets is often much more effective than having an agent do it. Most media outlets, unlike book publishers, prefer to work hand in hand with writers, without an agent intermediary, for a number of reasons. As Vann Newkirk explained to me, he is more likely to *pass* on agented pitches because they tend to be "more PR-ish." Such pitches—the type this chapter will teach you to avoid—don't capture the voice and point of view of the author, an essential ingredient in good nonfiction. I hear this point again and again from magazine and newspaper editors, and it is especially true at smaller, more literary outlets. According to Mark Krotov, the publisher and coeditor of the literary magazine *n+1*, by far "the tiniest part of the pie chart" of material the magazine publishes comes from agents. The agent pitch letter, as Krotov sees it, "has a sort of necessary distance." It doesn't give Krotov a sense of the writer's voice, which is crucial to have in order to find good fits for a magazine that skews so literary. Additionally, smaller literary magazines have smaller budgets, minuscule (if nonexistent) contract staff, and a handful of editors running the entire operation. The go-between of an agent (and the chance that we'll ask for an exorbitant fee) can seem a little much, especially for an unknown writer, at least at the pitch stage. It's a bit like bringing a machete to spread the butter on your toast.

I didn't hear this sentiment only from editors at smaller publications. In her work as an editor of the guest essay section of *The New York Times,* Vanessa Mobley looks for a unique point of view above all, saying, "I'm interested in people from communities or with lived experience that haven't been shared, and that have something essential to bring to readers, because opinion is the one place where the world intersects with the newspaper. The world intersects with the newspaper all the time through the reporting, but it's mediated by these expert reporters, and in opinion, it's *unmediated.*" A pitch written by you, not an agent, can capture this unmediated quality. And by unmediated, I don't mean a pitch should be overlong, unedited, or stream of consciousness. Rather, the best media pitches reflect the voice of the person writing them and the voice that will appear in the eventual piece. This is what Vann Newkirk meant by not sounding "PR-ish," and why the majority of unsolicited pitches Mobley accepts are also unagented. Jeff Goldberg, the editor in chief at *The Atlantic,* concurred; even as someone at the top of the masthead, he values relationships with writers—and above all, with his own editors—more than those with agents. Unless it is one of the very small number of agents he knows well—he estimated they number only about five or six—a pitch from an unknown agent will get no more attention from him than a pitch from an unknown writer. This isn't true in book publishing or at top-tier literary magazines for nonfiction, where a key part of a book editor's job is to cultivate relationships with agents to have access to their submissions. The pipeline at media outlets, on the other hand, doesn't have agents at its center. Goldberg also said not to pitch *him* directly. Remember, at larger media outlets, section editors are pitching story ideas to the editor above them, or to the editor in chief. Those are the pitches Goldberg (and the editors in chief at major national magazines) are focusing on.

Also consider the role of the person on the receiving end of your pitch, and choose your targets accordingly. Goldberg sees the primary mistake of writers trying to break into *The Atlantic* or other major publications as starting too high (with him) or too low (emailing the anonymous general inbox, likely staffed by an assistant or an intern). Instead, aim for the middle and target the individual editors who work at an outlet, not the number one person in charge. (Be sure not to pitch multiple editors at the same publication with the same pitch at the same time. It just creates confusion on their end.) You might feel awkward at first, but do so knowing that the vast majority of articles you read online and in print were submitted, accepted, and sold without an agent. This chapter includes sample pitches for published articles, along with the stories behind how they came to be published; *none* of these pieces were pitched by agents and many were pitched at the very beginning of a writer's career, when the authors themselves were entirely unknown to the editor and publication they were approaching.

There is another long-game reason to contact editors directly—and have them get to know *you*—as part of growing your career as a writer. The "social" aspect Vann Newkirk emphasized in his job description will work in your favor once an editor does accept one of your pitches. Editors *want* to develop ongoing relationships with a roster of writers because their jobs become much easier if they have a Rolodex full of people they can publish again and again, often under short deadlines—another reason these relationships largely exist without the go-between of an agent. While Newkirk certainly accepts one-off pieces, the golden ticket he is always looking for is what he terms "rapport": responsiveness, professionalism, an interest in editorial back-and-forth with him and in the larger work of the magazine and the other articles it publishes. By removing the middle person in your pitching of shorter pieces, not only will your pitches best capture your own voice, but you will also be able to build rapport with key editors and publications.

•   •   •

So how do you find out which publications and editors to pitch? This is where I advise becoming a literary detective, a barely discussed but extremely useful skill set for all writers (and by extension, all agents and editors). All the sleuthing I'll advise you to do is based on techniques I've used myself in helping my writers place their own pieces and build their careers and in finding new clients for my own list. These are skills that, once developed, you will use again and again.

The first step is to make a list of ten to twenty currently active writers (no dead folks; Joan Didion can't help you here) you like. Concentrate on writers who work in roughly the same categories and subject area (say, personal essays or narrative nonfiction or book reviews or recovery memoirs). The list can be laser focused or more wide-ranging, though my advice would be to do a mix. If you want to write a book about disco, absolutely include some music writers. But also think about nonmusic writers whose work you like simply in terms of style or approach. Maybe you want to write about disco the way Robin Wall Kimmerer wrote about plants in *Braiding Sweetgrass*. (I would, for what it's worth, absolutely read a memoir about disco in the spirit of Robin Wall Kimmerer.) For this exercise, it's probably most productive to concentrate on early career writers, those who have published only one or two books. While you may aspire to write in the vein of Susan Orlean or Erik Larson—completely laudable goals—their careers were started long ago in a different-enough media landscape that using them as professional models won't necessarily be helpful. As models of writing itself, of course, it's a totally different story, and Didion away! If you can't think of any early career writers you like, I'm going to send you off to do more research. *The New York Times Book Review* always makes sure to include debuts every week. Many bookstores have a debut writers section and even an indie press section, where many writers make their debut. And if you are reading this from the upward side of thirty, don't assume that "early career writer" means under thirty-five or even forty-five. Yes, early career writers inevitably skew younger, but not always. (Though looking at the publication track of younger writers could be helpful, as they may know about, and thus are getting published in, periodicals that might not be on your radar—a good thing!) Finally, while I suggested ten to twenty writers as models to keep it manageable, if you find this exercise helpful and productive (and maybe even fun?), add more!

For mischief and fun, I also suggest adding the name of the writer (or writers—no judgment here) you most envy. I spend a lot of time with writers, and almost all of them can name another writer who just gets under their skin. Why did their dumb article on tarot cards go viral? Why did they win that fellowship you weren't even a finalist for? Why was *that* person's book so universally praised? (Trust me when I say surely someone else hated it too, and probably said so publicly. Add that dissenting critic or writer to the list of people to follow. The enemy of your enemy probably shares your literary sensi-

bility.) You're going to perform the literary version of the old and useful feminist adage: If you meet a woman who threatens you, befriend
her. Or at least, learn from your nemesis's success. (My guess is your
nemesis is probably really good at sharing those successes.)

Once you have your list, start with each writer's website. Authors'
websites often list articles they publish, and these lists will give you
some ideas for places you can pitch. You like a certain writer's work;
so does the *Oxford American*. This is an excellent reason to pitch an
essay to the *Oxford American*. You can also mention in your pitch
that you are approaching them because they publish Ben Fountain
or Imani Perry or Saeed Jones. You get bonus points if the writer
isn't super well-known and extra bonus points if you manage to track
down their specific editor—more on how to do that later.

While an author's website is a good first spot to try to figure out
where they've been published, bear in mind that often they are not
updated frequently and are rarely exhaustive. If the author has published a book, at the beginning, often on the copyright page, will be a
list of any parts of the book that previously appeared elsewhere. You'll
also want to look at the book's acknowledgments page. I can't stress
enough what a rich resource the acknowledgments page can be. It's
there that you can discover your favorite authors' agent and editor,
and it's the single best resource for ultimately making a shortlist of
agents. But the acknowledgments page also often gives shoutouts to
any magazine editors who have published and supported the writer.
However, the best, most up-to-date resource for figuring out where
writers you like publish, which media outlets are currently publishing
which kind of material, how different writers are connected to each
other, and, most usefully of all, who edits what and whom at newspapers and magazines, is social media.

Whenever I bring up social media to emerging writers, especially
those who weren't raised on social media or aren't already on it, I make
myself cringe. There is much about X, Instagram, Substack, Bluesky,
and TikTok that is unpleasant at best and harmful to our democracy
at worst, but I believe the particular turnoff for writers is that they
seem to demand relentless self-promotion and self-disclosure. If you
gain anything from this discussion, it's knowing you don't need to
use them for that, nor do you need to disclose anything personal on
social media in order to become a successful writer. You also don't

need to have a sizable social media following to publish a book—though I won't deny it helps. (I'll discuss this more in chapter 2.5, on platform.)

Instead of using social media to grow your platform, use it as a database to figure out where to publish your work and whom precisely to pitch it to. Start with that list of writers you admire, figure out what social media platform(s) they use most often, and follow them. More likely than not, when they publish a new piece, they will share their work on their social media accounts and you can see where they publish. Social media can also help you figure out who their individual editors are. One easy way to tell is that editors often repost and share the pieces they publish, and writers often follow the editors (and agents) they work with. If an author is already on staff at a magazine, they will always be published by the same editor. (And in general, once you start publishing with a particular periodical, the editor who "discovered" you often becomes your editor, the person you work with thereafter.) Following that editor can give you a sense of the range of what they like to publish. I can't overstate the value of pitching an individual editor over a generic inbox, as most editors themselves will tell you, and to make the pitch itself particular to the person and the publication. Starting a pitch with why you are approaching a particular editor or publication—even just to say you are a fan—gets you through the awkward salutation dance (don't we all struggle with how to open an important email?) and will likely be appreciated by its reader. Most editorial work goes unnoticed and, frankly, unpraised. As Mark Krotov at *n+1* explained to me, "It's really exciting to see engagement, so communicating with editors to say something is interesting or provocative has always felt completely intuitive." It's also, as Krotov said, "very, very, very, very rare" (yes, he used "very" four times) for someone to reach out to him directly to praise his editorial work or the magazine. If you love someone's work, it's certainly worth mentioning in a pitch. And while it can be a bit of a scavenger hunt to figure out which editor publishes which writers (or, as the ever-sanguine Jake Silverstein put it, "a worthwhile reporting challenge!"), many media mastheads list the beats of various editors and their bios often list their beats as well. An added bonus: The act of acknowledging an editor's involvement in a piece is an immediate indicator of your reportorial bona fides. Social media can be an excellent way to find exactly the people you are looking for.

Social media has another, less obvious research purpose. Trawling through a writer's social media is a way to do some excavation of their professional path. Even if a writer is now a staffer at *The New Yorker,* there's a good chance they moved around a lot before they landed a permanent gig, and quite likely started as a freelancer. Scrolling down their timeline is a helpful (if admittedly tedious) way to see where someone started as a writer and how they worked their way up. Through it, you can trace the web of connections that can help you build your own career.

I want to be clear here that you don't need to tweet, post, become a Booktokker or influencer or otherwise build your writing career on social media clout. *I* don't tweet, preferring to share my bon mots in texts to friends, who mostly ignore them. But I wouldn't be doing my job if I didn't share that social media, thanks to search engine optimization (SEO), is one of the most powerful tools a writer can use in getting eyeballs on their work. When someone googles your name, one of the first things that comes up will be your social media profile, if you have one.

I also want to distinguish between blogs and social media, how each operates at the moment, and how Substack and similar newsletter platforms occupy a helpful space in between. I'm frequently asked at writers' conferences if writers should (or need to!) "start a blog." If you'd asked me this question fifteen years ago, I'd probably answer "Why not?" When I first started in publishing, blogs were queen, each a world of their own where writers could write what they wanted to write on a platform they completely owned and controlled. Except for a handful of very prominent exceptions—those who started blogging in its golden age and have retained their readerships—starting a blog now is a bit like screaming into the void. Social media, by creating one-stop shopping for readers looking for things to click, minimized the prominence of the stand-alone blog as a tool for discovery and promotional purposes. Getting readers to find and follow your blog is a job in itself. However, the relatively limited audience of a blog can make it a safe space to practice as a writer and to create samples of your work that you can easily share with potential editors—*that* can be of great benefit. This is also the role that Substack and similar newsletter platforms have come to play, with the added benefit of having a social networking component, which allows you to connect with other writers and readers through the platform and make use of the platform's promotional tools and built-in audience.

Isaac Butler, author of the National Book Critics Circle Award–winning book *The Method: How the Twentieth Century Learned to Act,* began his writing career through blogging, albeit when blogging was still in its heyday. Looking back on it now, he sees "that a blog provided me with practice—all those reps in learning how to write and learning how to write effectively." Karen Han, freelance writer and Butler's cohost of the podcast *Working* (which has an excellent episode on the art of pitching), started a blog as a way to create clips—pieces of published writing authors use to show editors their range—when she was first starting out as a writer. When she began to pitch herself to outlets as a movie reviewer and cultural critic, the clips from her blog demonstrated she knew how to write a professional review, even though they hadn't actually been published by anyone but herself. Now her blog serves as a kind of author website, a place to gather in one place all the work she publishes elsewhere so any editor or outlet she pitches can see her range.

These days, a Substack or similar newsletter can serve the same purpose. Leigh Stein, a novelist and author of the publishing-themed Substack *Attention Economy,* explains how launching your own Substack can help you build clips, as you can say, "I've written on this topic; look at this one piece on Substack and look how well it did." It can also demonstrate proof of concept for your writing and your subject matter. Per Stein, Substack is where you can demonstrate that you have audience engagement: "When I speak at conferences or talk to emerging writers, something I hear a lot is 'I know there's an audience for my book.' The writer really believes, if someone would just publish my book, I'm certain there's an audience for this topic. And I would say to them, 'Prove it. Prove it on Substack.' You can actually prove to an agent—I know there's an audience for my book because I have this newsletter, and you can see in the comments section how engaged the audience is."

While a blog or a stand-alone author website faces the challenges of discovery, popular social media platforms are where folks already live and can serve many of the purposes that blogs—and even pitching—

do, and again, thanks to SEO, will probably be the first result when anyone googles you. So use the magical powers of your favorite tech oligarch's billions in your favor and make sure to put your author website, Substack, and relevant recent publications in any social media profiles you have. Doing this puts you in greater control of what the world finds out about you first, just as you are in control of what you do or don't tweet, or what you post on Instagram.

Social media can also act, in some instances, as a way to circumvent the torture of pitching articles. Clint Smith, now a number one *New York Times* bestseller, the winner of a National Book Critics Circle Award, and a staff writer at *The Atlantic,* began his entire, unlikely nonfiction writing career thanks to a tweet thread he posted in 2014 on James Baldwin and the Black Lives Matter movement. At the time, Clint was a graduate student in sociology and a poet. He used Twitter as a "mini blog," in his words, to work out ideas that didn't belong in term papers or poems. He had absolutely no connection to New York publishing or media, but Twitter let him meet other like-minded writers as well as introduce them to his work. His Baldwin thread led an editor at *The Guardian* to reach out to him to ask if he'd be interested in writing an essay expanding on it. With no small amount of trepidation—and a push from his wife to give it a try—Clint did. This first publication led to an ongoing relationship with *The Guardian,* and later Twitter threads led to other outlets reaching out, which in turn led to agents (myself included) and editors reading his work and reaching out as well. In Clint's case, it's precisely because he wasn't afraid to get nerdy and detailed in his social media posts that his work appealed to his editors. All the editors interviewed for this chapter mentioned using social media to find voices and experts just as Clint's initial *Guardian* editor did, particularly for specialized knowledge and unique points of view. For Clint, Twitter was a place to showcase his expertise in poetry, history, and politics and to bring those interests together in a public way. If you do have seemingly disparate interests that inform your writing, intentionally expressing them on social media (despite its Pandora's-box nature) can be a powerful way to explore them, to work out ideas, and to find readers. And while the social media platform of choice may have shifted again by the time you read this, the central principle remains the same.

The predominance of social media as a way for media outlets, writers, and editors to present their work doesn't mean you can't also pursue in-real-life opportunities. Panel talks are a great way to get to know editors, even if you never speak a word to the editor presenting. Organizations like PEN America, the Asian-American Writers Workshop, the National Book Critics Circle, and Aspen Words regularly have panel talks with writers and editors, as do local and regional writers' groups and conferences and even bookstores. Editors, along with the writers they publish, are often featured guests at annual events like the Atlantic Ideas Festival, the New Yorker Festival, and the Los Angeles Times Festival of Books, another venue to learn what an outlet publishes and who, exactly, publishes it. One of the few boons of COVID is that many of these talks are now held both in-person and online. If you get to talk with one of these editors at an event—great! (Though be aware there is often a scrum at the end of a panel and joining it might not be the best way to get to know an overwhelmed editor, who probably has to pee.) Seeing someone speak in person, even if you never engage with them directly, can give you a feel for how to pitch them. Are they formal or informal? Do they have a sense of humor or are they all business? Did they grow up in a place you write about? Do they mention they love dachshunds or '90s R&B or Virginia Woolf? After my own lunches with book editors, I try to take notes recording exactly these sorts of details, and thus if I end up representing a writer with a memoir about her dachshund or a history of the Rocky Mountains, I know exactly which editor to target with a personalized pitch.

As you think more about pitching your work to media outlets, the best lasting advice I can give you—and what I heard again and again from the editors with whom I spoke—is to be an engaged reader of those outlets. Just as you, as a writer, write to be read, no editor wants to publish into a void. Vann Newkirk has some advice, both as an editor and as a writer himself: "I can't say it enough. It's so cliché, but read us." This does not mean being a sycophant or a booster. In fact, the precise opposite can work in your favor, just as it once did in Newkirk's. As he explains, "I really appreciate people who come to me with reasoned and informed critiques of what we do. That is probably the most surefire way to get into the place, if you read a piece and you disagree with it, and you can put something down on why."

This was, in fact, Newkirk's own path to publication at *The Atlantic* and to ultimately being hired as a staff writer. In 2015, Vann started an independent online magazine called *Seven Scribes* with six friends. (I'll discuss this path, one used by a wide range of ultimately successful nonfiction writers as a way to get their work read without having to go through gatekeepers, in chapter 2.5.) Always a voracious reader of *The Atlantic*, Newkirk wrote and published a few pieces, largely critical ones, of *Atlantic* essays. His "reasoned and informed" critique resulted in an invitation to pitch pieces to the magazine.

•   •   •

Waiting for a response to a pitch is often as hard as writing the pitch itself. Unfortunately, there's no magic formula for how long an editor or publication will or should take, or how long you should wait to respond. In the spirit of being in charge of your own writerly destiny (or at the very least, writerly neurosis), I suggest setting up your own internal deadline for following up and for moving on. Thus, let's say you send a pitch on a Monday. Mark in your calendar that you'll follow up the following Monday (and give yourself the gift of not obsessing in the week between); you'll follow up again on Friday; and if you don't hear by, say, end of the day that next Monday, you'll try pitching the piece to your next target. Decide this schedule in advance of sending the pitch, and then once it leaves your inbox, make like Elsa and let it go.

It's also completely reasonable to email after not hearing back for a few weeks to signal you are moving on, another good means of taking back control. Here's some language for inspiration or theft: "Thank you so much for considering. I will now be pitching this piece to another outlet." Worst-case scenario, you get a belated response saying, "Hey, we love this, and we'd like to run it!" after you've committed it elsewhere. That will only make them want you all the more, and at the very least, you have been the one in charge of your own, evenly spaced-out calendar of worry. And in all cases, check the submission guidelines to see if an outlet accepts simultaneous submissions and be sure to indicate if yours is one.

If your pitch is particularly timely and tied to a pressing news hook, it's okay to speed up the clock and to indicate that you are doing so. Clear and collegial is always the way to go: "I'd love this piece to be published by *The New Yorker* online, and you will have it exclusively for the next forty-eight hours. If I don't hear from you by the end of business on Thursday, I will pitch it elsewhere. Thank you for your time." And a reminder: It never hurts to say *why* you are trying a particular outlet and why you'd be so eager to have them consider it exclusively. It's a particular type of person who is put off by a sincere compliment, and my guess is that they are not the type of person you'd want to do business with.

Once your pitch is accepted, remember the overall goal: to develop a mutually productive relationship with an editor in hopes you'll work together again and again. Veteran freelance writers and magazine editors often talk about the three qualities a successful writer should have: punctuality, collegiality, and brilliance. Here's how Rachel Syme breaks them down: "You can be on time and punctual, always filing before the deadline, completely nailing it, never giving anyone any doubt that you'll ever file on time. And you can either be incredibly lovely and wonderful to work with, an absolute delight, joy, easygoing, not a hard-ass, not precious about your edits. Or you can be a brilliant writer." In other words, *no one expects you to be all three,* so aim for two. And in my own words, try not to make a habit of assuming you are brilliant, so always try to be punctual and collegial. The last two are, at the very least, the qualities most under your control. They'll also make you appreciated by overworked and overwhelmed editors, people who by the nature of their jobs are always operating under multiple tight deadlines. Once an editor knows you are reliable, you also become someone who can save their ass. Syme explains further: "A lot of people get work because they're brilliant and they can back it up—but they're not easy to work with editorially. And then you have the people who are not brilliant writers, but they're always on time. And they're awesome to work with. And honestly, they're workhorses. And editors love those people because they're reliable."

I wrote this chapter a few weeks after a slew of high-profile mass layoffs at media outlets. I fear this statement will be perennially true and will apply to the media landscape into which this book will be published and continue to exist. Most newsrooms are understaffed, which means most editors are overworked. This also means you might not hear back on things as quickly as you'd like and you'll want to follow up and check in, but think about why you're following up and checking in. There are legitimate reasons to follow up with an editor. If your piece seems to be stuck in the editorial pipeline, Karen Han suggests sending a polite follow-up and framing it in terms of "Is there anything that I can do to help move the piece along? Or is there anything else you need from my end?" She also pinpointed the following-up/desperate-need-for-assurance feedback loop particularly well: "Part of me always wanted to get in touch with editors who I was working with on a piece because really, what I needed was to be told I was doing a good job. It was actually like an emotional neediness, an insecurity on my part that was totally normal, but was not really about the piece at hand. So ask yourself, are you reaching out for affirmation or because you need something done?" I share this as an anxious person who wishes she didn't need so many pats on the head, but also as someone who has learned other people's hands get tired, as I now pat a lot of heads on a daily basis. I have my own formulation of Han's question, which I often ask myself before I press send on anything: "Am I writing this email because I am nervous about something and want someone else to make me less nervous, or I am actually trying to get something done?" If it's the former, remember it's natural and human to reach out to folks—friends, your partner, and yes, your agent—for reassurance, but know that it's not the role of your editor to tell you that you're a good writer, so reconsider pressing send. As Isaac Butler advises, "Not every editor gives a ton of positive reinforcement. It's always welcome when they do but you can't control that. It's helpful to have a relationship or two in your personal life that you have cultivated, where you can just say, 'God, I'm feeling really insecure, I sent this thing off to *Slate*. I haven't heard back, what if, what if I've ruined my career with this terrible piece I wrote?' And you know, every now and then, your friend or your therapist or your partner, can say, that's not going to happen, you're just feeling very vulnerable right now. Just like take some deep breaths, it's going to be fine. So that you don't end up putting all of that energy into your communication with the editor." Comfort yourself with the knowledge that having your work published and the interest in you as a writer in general *is* assurance. Karen Han got over her need to send "Am I doing a good job?" check-ins by reminding herself that "if you are working with the editor, they wouldn't publish what you wrote if they didn't think it was good. The publication is the ice cream. Someone praising you or your work is the sprinkles on top—delightful, but even without them, you still got to eat some ice cream."

KEY TAKEAWAYS

- If you want to find an agent and publish a book, you should begin by publishing shorter work. It is easier to land an agent, and a book deal, if you are already published.
- You are, or can become, the best pitcher of your shorter work, and you can and should be doing so directly. There is no reason to find an agent before you begin pitching as much as possible.
- Don't take an editor's rejection as personal. They are managing a magazine, or a newspaper, a section, or a number of writers. No matter what happens, the only way to make sure you get published is to keep trying. Always Be Pitching.
- It is important to cultivate a relationship with editors. Do not think of this as adding more media outlet names to your list of clips; instead imagine seeking out an editorial reader who will understand and advocate for your work, improve it, and help bring it to a wider audience.
- Become a literary detective and read as much work by new and currently published writers as possible. Follow them and think of their careers as inspiration.
- Use social media as a database to figure out where to publish your work and precisely to whom to pitch it (never pitch to the general inboxes). In addition to what you can learn from others, you should build your own presence on social media for the many benefits it affords writers.
- Pitching and commissioning work can take a long time. Be patient, follow up, and do not take it personally.
- No writer can have all three of these qualities: punctuality, collegiality, and brilliance. Since brilliance is subjective, focus on punctuality and collegiality.

SAMPLE PITCHES
(AND THE STORIES BEHIND THEM)

Sample #1: A Reported Piece for a Literary Journal

Heather Radke wrote a widely read piece about a revolutionary jumpsuit, or more precisely, one that proposed to liberate women from the "irrationality of fashion." The piece is a delight to read—Heather forces herself to wear the same jumpsuit for three weeks straight and places the jumpsuit's life-changing claims in context of the long history of clothes that purported to help women live less cumbersome lives.

Heather found wearing the jumpsuit far less arduous than pitching and placing the piece. She can't remember how long she waited to hear back from editors, and whether it was longer than she spent in the jumpsuit, but it certainly felt so. She pitched it to four outlets before placing it in *The Paris Review*.

After it was published, it was included in the Longreads Top 5 (an excellent resource for finding publication) and anthologized in several books, including one called *How to Write About Anything*. Beyond the page views and the anthologizing, the piece brought Heather something more important and worth thinking about as you make goals for your own career: "The success of this piece for me was about being able to do a certain kind of work I wanted to do and find homes for other pieces. It's pretty important as a freelancer not only to think of success in terms of clicks and money and prestige, but also did you get to do something you were excited to do in the piece itself? A few editors wrote to me after this came out and offered that I pitch to them directly. That felt like another win."

Heather's Successful Cover Letter

Dear XYZ,

I wrote a piece for *The Paris Review* last summer for Caitlin Love and am hoping you are the right person to send a pitch to now that she's gone.* I've been reporting a story about Rational Dress

---

* As mentioned, Heather pitched four other outlets, though not simultaneously. She had been previously published in *The Paris Review,*

Society, an artist collective who use jumpsuits as a way to critique capitalism and the fashion industry.[*] They opened an exhibit about revolutionary fashion last week and will be doing counterfashion panel discussions and workshops during Fashion Week (I imagine the piece could run during Fashion Week).[†] As part of the reporting, I've been wearing the same jumpsuit every day for a few weeks to see what happens when I throw off what the artists call "the tyranny of choice."[‡] I'll paste the full pitch below. Thanks so much for your consideration.

Sincerely,

Heather Radke

Heather's Successful Pitch

How can we make America rational? Artists Maura Brewer and Abigail Glaum-Lathbury decided to do their part by collecting "gently used and emphatically discarded" Ivanka Trump label clothing to

---

but when she pitched this piece, her old editor had left. She opens by briefly mentioning this relationship and then moving on.

* While Heather's piece is about jumpsuits, she's pitching it to a very literary magazine, so she immediately makes clear that the context of the piece is cultural and political, which is their bailiwick.

† More situating in time here: She reminds the editor (subtly) that Fashion Week is coming up! I think the news hook is particularly smart in this context. The Style section of *The New York Times* likely gets dozens of Fashion Week pitches. A more literary magazine like *The Paris Review* probably less so, which makes Heather's pitch stand out while also seeming timely. (I can imagine the editor thinking, "Oh, right! Fashion Week! We need to do something about that!")

‡ Heather also makes clear that she is already at work on it—hence the present progressive use of "reporting"—and situates where we are in the story unfolding. At the time of her pitch, the artists she is profiling had just had an exhibition.

melt down into a polyester slurry that they will transform into mil-
lennial pink jumpsuits. The project, called "Make America Rational
Again" is cheeky, and it might be impossible—the artists have had
a hard time finding a company that will take their small amount of
fabric to recycle—but it is also a direct critique of both the Trumps
and the fashion industry, which is the second dirtiest industry after
oil and is notorious for terrible labor practices abroad.[*]

Make America Rational Again is only one part of Brewer and
Glaum-Lathbury's practice. They also wear handmade jumpsuits
every day and sell them in 248 gender-neutral sizes, host exhibitions,
and run workshops under the name "Rational Dress Society." The
artists are currently featured in MOMA's "Items: Is Fashion Modern"
exhibition and will open an exhibition in the garment district on
January 26 that will be both a survey of experiments in revolutionary
and utopian fashion and a laboratory for exploring alternatives to
the fashion system. The exhibition will culminate during New York's
Fashion Week, when Brewer and Glaum-Lathbury will host pan-
els and provide counterprogramming to traditional Fashion Week,
including a workshop on the subversive history of pockets, a sew-
your-own H&M garment workshop, and a discussion on the history
of clothing in revolutionary movements. The program isn't affiliated
with Fashion Week, but provides an opportunity to think about fashion as a revolutionary force. The artists in the exhibition and program
include Nick Cave, Frau Fiber, and Andrea Zittel.[†]

Brewer and Glaum-Lathbury began the Rational Dress Society when

---

[*] There's a lot going on here, and I often advise against starting with a
rhetorical question (so first-year English seminar), but Heather quickly
takes that dorm-room philosophizing and turns specific, gives names,
clarifies her focus, and ends the paragraph with a damning fact.

[†] During the early Trump years, I saw a lot of pitches about things that
had nothing to do with Trump shoehorning themselves into a Trump
theme. This often happens when an issue or a person dominates the
headlines. If you have to think really hard about how your piece connects to the most important person or issue in the news, they probably

they were students at the School of the Art Institute of Chicago. They wanted to create an art project that functioned as what they call counterfashion, which they say "isn't a rejection of fashion, it's dressing in a way that signals ideology." To that end, they looked to both the future and the past, borrowing their name from the Victorian reform movement that advocated for pants and other "rational dress" in an era of bustles and corsets, and choosing to promote a garment that is emblematic of science fiction. Part of the proceeds of all their work go toward the purchase of a full-page ad in *American Vogue,* and once they raise enough money for that endeavor, the project will end. For them, wearing the same handmade garment every day is a way to subvert the tyranny of choice that is the foundation of capitalism, and thwart the relentless pace of newness that makes the fashion industry thrive.[*]

I would like to write a profile of the Rational Dress Society over the next month as they prepare to open their exhibition. I attended a workshop they hosted at MOMA, which included both instruction on sewing and informational presentations about the history of political fashion; have talked to the artists they are working with in their exhibition; and am wearing a jumpsuit for several weeks in order to participate in their imagined utopia of "rational dress."[†] The piece will ask: can fashion ever be revolutionary? It will also look at the ways that an art project can and cannot provoke, change, or transcend a $3 trillion global industry.

---

don't belong in the pitch. Here, the connection isn't conjectural or associative but quite specific and literal and even surprising.

[*] This is the "show you know your stuff" part. Some outlets will consider only pieces that are already fully written or that the writer has a full sample to show. This piece was pitched without a sample, but Heather makes clear she has already done significant work and research.

[†] Here Heather reiterates how much research she has done on the subject. While she did not write the full piece on spec, she makes clear she has a relationship with her subjects, has already done research, and is ready to dive in.

My work has appeared or is forthcoming in *The New York Times Magazine, The Paris Review, The White Review,* and *The National.**

Sample #2: A Reported Piece for a General-Interest National Magazine

This pitch by Dan Kois is one of my favorites of all time: he persuaded *The New York Times Magazine* to send him to Iceland! This is a high level of difficulty in pitching conviction. Magazines aren't generally looking for reasons to fund expensive international trips, but Dan makes an excellent case for why they should.

Dan's Successful Pitch

Why are Icelanders some of the happiest people in the world, despite living in a cold, remote place where it's dark pretty much all winter?† There's been no shortage of investigations into the "happiest nation" phenomenon, from books like *The Year of Living Danishly* or *The Almost Nearly Perfect People* (both about Scandinavia) to a rash of Op-Eds making the case for why Costa Ricans are so happy. (No military! Environmental protection!) But Iceland's national contentment—rated second in the world in a recent baloney survey—is unique, I'd argue, because I think the factors that drive it can be distilled in the story of one civic feature shared by every Icelandic town: the public pool.‡

From Heimaey in the Vestmannaeyjar Islands to Raufarhöfn in the far north, every Icelandic town, no matter how teensy, has its own

---

* Heather puts her previous publications at the end. Easy to spot but doesn't clutter the top.

† Bad pitches often start out with Carrie Bradshaw-esque rhetorical questions. If you want to open your pitch with a question, make sure it's specific.

‡ And that your proposed answer is also specific and, ideally, surprising.

geothermally heated, outdoor, open-all-year pool. There are fancy city aquatic complexes with multilevel hot tubs and the awesomest water slides in the universe. There are ramshackle cement squares squatting under endless rain clouds in the middle of nowhere. All told there are about 130 geothermally heated outdoor pools in Iceland, a country with a population roughly the same as that of St. Louis. Born as an afterthought to one of the great public works projects of the twentieth century—the postwar heat taps that used the island's volcanic energy to drag the citizenry out of sod-roofed houses and into the modern era—the pools are popular year-round; in fact, they often see their heaviest visitor load in the cold and dark of winter, when there's nothing else to do.*

The pools of Iceland serve as village square in a climate too grim to sustain a proper plaza in the Italian or French style; they offer a place to rub elbows with one's neighbors in a country with little pub culture thanks to prohibition lasting until 1989. And, most relevantly to my interests,† the pools give Icelandic families a place to assemble, share leisure time, and incorporate multiple generations into their

---

* This paragraph, as well as the entire pitch, not only conveys surprising information but also Dan's voice best. I'm not sure "awesomest" is a word, but it's the kind of one Dan uses, and it feels appropriate for the whimsical, irreverent yet awe-inspired subject. In sum, it's okay—even ideal—for the pitch itself to show the voice you would use in the actual piece.

† Signposting—reminding the reader that the information you are giving relates back to the specific, larger thing you are trying to sell them—is awkward but essential in pitches, and as we'll discuss, in book proposals. Here Dan quickly transitions from the information he is giving to why it matters with a quick line of signposting. He doesn't hesitate to use the first person, signaling that this will be a reported piece with a point of view. Yes, he is interested in these crazy pools, but he is more personally invested in the far more compelling question of community cohesion and happiness. He connects the two here by quickly inserting himself and stating why he cares about these pools.

community. Unlike in America, there are no safety concerns or social taboos in Iceland about children sharing hot-tub space with adults. Teens, of course, find their way to the pools on their own—but often discover their only wintertime social outlet overlapping with their parents', everyone showering naked in the same locker rooms under the watchful eyes of the same hygiene cops. (Because the pools aren't chlorinated, all bathers must thoroughly soap up, nude, before they are allowed into the water.)

I'm proposing a feature for the magazine about the geothermal pools of Iceland and the dramatic effect they have on the content-ment of Icelanders. I'll travel to Iceland for a few winter weeks, accompanying a team of sociologists from the University of Iceland for fieldwork on the first comprehensive study of public bathing and Icelandic cultural identity. I'll interview Jón Karl Helgason, the direc-tor of a new documentary on the pools of Iceland. And most impor-tant, I'll don the traditional Speedo (Iceland is, apocryphally perhaps, the country that purchases the most Speedos per capita) and swim every day, braving the freezing outdoors to meet parents and grand-parents and teenagers and kids at pools in cosmopolitan Reykjavik and way out in the sheep-strewn boonies.[*]

Why me, and why this topic?[†] Like most parents I know, I strug-gle with a nearly overwhelming sense that for all our comforts and advantages and great schools and children's yoga classes, we are liv-ing as a family in fundamentally the wrong way. I work all the time (gassing on about "parenting") while going days without even talking to my wife or children; we replace conversation with exasperation

---

[*] And here is the nitty-gritty of what he sets out to do, naming places, interview subjects, and even costuming. (I did not intend to include two pitches with sartorial experiments. I promise this is the last.)

[†] All pitches (and book proposals) should answer this question in one form or another. In pitch letters, the answer usually comes at the end of the pitch and is often a list of previous publications or professional qualifications—a totally fine approach! Dan does something different here, which is to make the "why me" section much more personal. This, or a hybrid of the professional and personal, can work quite well too.

and introspection with a series of screens; my kids complain that our house, nicer than the residences of 99 percent of people on earth, is too small. I rarely feel at ease in my own life.

And so when I heard the Icelandic researcher Katrin Gudmundsdottir describe a certain indescribable emotional state to me, a native Icelander's sense of comfort from being in her local pool, I felt my spirit thrum like a perfect G major chord.* "It's not exactly like you're happy," she mused. "It's that you know how to be in the swimming pool. You know how you should enjoy it." I think many, many readers, like me, are still struggling with the question of how to be, and how to enjoy. A funny, well-researched, well-reported look at a culture that has figured out these basic existential questions, thanks in great part to the humble municipal pool, would make for a fascinating and memorable read.

Sample #3: An Op-Ed for a National Newspaper

As an academic, Dorothy Brown's Op-Eds and articles tend to be part of her ongoing, lifelong research on the racial wealth gap. She frequently pitches and places Op-Eds that are either part of longer works in progress or give readers a quick snapshot of her book. Her Op-Eds function as a proof of concept for her ideas and introduce potential readers (and importantly in her work, policymakers) to her work. Because she is getting her message to the audience that reads *The Washington Post* and *The New York Times,* the two primary places she publishes, they work as mini advertisements for Dorothy's books.

As you think about your own work-in-progress, think too about which parts of it may be adaptable to be pitched as stand-alone shorter works.

In her prescient column that follows, published in *The Washington Post* in 2021, Dorothy explores student debt forgiveness in the context of the racial wealth gap.

---

* And here is another good example of the pitch reflecting the voice of the author. The editor who receives this pitch knows what they are getting in terms of tone and approach.

Dorothy Brown's Successful Pitch

President Biden has made it clear that he is not interested in forgiving more than $10,000 in student loan debt. He believes that the government should not pay for debt forgiveness for people who went to "Harvard, Yale, and Penn," as his own children did.[*] He is not alone—he has Republican support. Former Education Secretary Betsy Devos called student debt relief "government gift-giving." While a recent poll showed that two-thirds support some form of broad student debt relief, the majority of Republicans do not.[†] By not factoring in racial differences, however, what they miss is how Black Americans experience college differently from their white peers.[‡] My book *The Whiteness of Wealth: How the Tax System Impoverishes Black Americans—and How We Can Fix It* demonstrates how Black and white Americans experience the same activities differently—including college.

One of the Atlanta college graduates interviewed for the book is Je'lon Alexander. He is a Morehouse Man who graduated in 2018, which means he was ineligible for the generous gift of Robert Smith that will pay off the student debt of the class of 2019. Je'lon is pursuing his master's degree at Georgia State with plans to get his PhD. He has roughly $55,000 in debt and his parents have advanced degrees with close to $400,000 of debt between them. Ten thousand dollars, while better than nothing—will have no discernable impact on Je'lon and his family's financial future.[§]

---

[*] Dorothy knows where President Biden stands (or stood) on debt forgiveness, but she doesn't assume the reader does, so she quickly summarizes the situation at the top.

[†] She then aligns the president's position with the opposition party and more to the point, a particular figure within it. She gives receipts, quickly.

[‡] And then Dorothy quickly signals (but doesn't spell out) what she feels the Democratic and Republican positions overlook.

[§] This is an Op-Ed on policy, but Dorothy grounds it in real people. Keep in mind what Vanessa Mobley said about what the Opinion section of

The opponents to debt relief have a point, however, as 30 percent of people with incomes over $114,000—a group that is predominantly white—carry student loan debt. For them loan forgiveness would largely benefit their ability to build wealth.* But they are wrong however when it comes to Black college students like Je'lon. Black student debt is a significant contributor to the Black-white wealth gap because Black students are more likely to not graduate yet have higher student debt balances. Even when they do graduate, Black Americans have financial burdens outside their debt repayment obligations that their white peers do not. College is not the same experience for Black students as it is for their white peers.

College graduation rates vary by race. The majority of white Americans (64 percent) who attend college graduate compared with the majority of Black college students (60 percent) who do not. Biden's children, like most white college students, graduated. For those Black Americans, they leave college saddled with debt and no prospects for a better-paying job based on the degree. For them, debt forgiveness seems the least we can do. Unfortunately what we actually do is give them a tax deduction for their student loan interest—capped at $2,500 a year. For the average Black debt load, that won't allow the borrower to deduct all the interest they pay in the early years of repayment. God forbid two Black college graduates get married†—their maximum deduction remains $2,500. When they were single they each could have deducted a maximum

---

the newspaper should do: provide insight into "people from communities or with lived experience that haven't been shared." Although this pitch contains facts, figures, and academic research, it also contains real people affected by the numbers.

* Here Dorothy clarifies the difference between how white and Black Americans experience loan debt and how it affects a seemingly unrelated but persistent problem: the racial wealth gap.

† Dorothy's colloquial language signals to the editor she's pitching to that she will handle this somewhat wonky material in an approachable way.

of $2,500, but now that they're married—their combined debt notwithstanding—they are still limited to $2,500. Tax policy, which is quite generous when it comes to mortgage debt (allowing interest to be deducted on two homes), is quite stingy when it comes to student debt.

Racial gaps in graduation rates also vary by type of institution. Which institutions have the smallest racial gap in graduation rates? Elite institutions like the ones President Biden mentioned.[*] For the University of Pennsylvania, the white graduation rate is 96 percent compared with 94 percent for Black students. For Harvard University, the white graduation rate is 98 percent and 96 percent for Black students. For Yale University, there is only a one-point differential: white 98 percent and Black 97 percent. Unfortunately very few Black college students attend those elite institutions. The percentage of Black students at the nation's top colleges is roughly the same today as it was thirty-five years ago. Take the other end of the spectrum, for-profit colleges that are disproportionately attended by Black students. The white graduation rate is 37 percent compared with 20 percent for Black students. If you are a Black prospective college student, then going to an elite institution pretty much guarantees you a degree. Given that 60 percent of Black college students do not graduate, those graduation rates are not to be ignored.

Now assume we are talking about the 40 percent of Blacks who are college graduates. They have on average higher debt loads than white college graduates. Black debt rises over time,[†] white debt diminishes. Research shows that even at the top end of the wealth spectrum, Black students have higher student loans than white college students and Black parents are more likely than white parents to take out greater

---

[*] A callback to the top and the mention of Ivy League grads who are also debtors. Callbacks are always good if you can build and expand on what has been previously said.

[†] Does your pitch need evidentiary support? It's more than fine to add relevant hyperlinks. Dorothy linked this phrase to a supporting article in her pitch.

loans to help pay for college—like Je'lon's parents. (Robert Smith's gift generously included paying off parental debt.)

But what about a Black graduate from an elite university—don't those elite degrees come with good-paying jobs? The argument there is that those graduates will have high incomes and will not spend the debt relief but increase their savings. Government subsidies should not be "wasted" on them. Yet, Black college graduates take their degrees into a racist labor market that requires more of them than it does from their white peers. Black elite graduates have a much harder time securing high-paying jobs and do not get equal pay commensurate with their qualifications.

A study showed that a Black Harvard graduate had to send out eight résumés before getting an interview offer while their white peers had to send out only six. But as the selectivity decreased, the disparity increased.* For example, with a University of Massachusetts Amherst degree, white graduates sent out nine résumés before getting an interview offer while Black graduates had to send out fifteen. Now we can compare how Black students from Harvard sent out eight résumés, while white students from UMass Amherst had to send out only nine. The research suggests that it is white students who can afford to go to less prestigious (and presumably less expensive) institutions and the labor market will continue to reward them. For Black students the opposite is true: the difference between sending out eight résumés and fifteen means Black students almost have to work twice as hard when they don't go the elite route. But it gets worse. That same study showed that the Black applicants who received responses from employers were asked to interview for lower-paying jobs than the ones they applied to—but not the white applicants. Black college graduates have higher student debt and may wind up in lower-paying jobs.

Finally, assume a Black student makes it through college and gets a good job, they are faced with higher financial burdens than their white peers. Research over a twenty-four-year period showed that

---

* Another callback to the Ivy League argument, again building on it as she tries to debunk it.

white college graduates are far more likely to receive money from their parents compared with Black college graduates who are far more likely to send money to their parents.*

All this debt results in an increased Black-white wealth gap. In 1989, college-educated white households had roughly five times greater wealth than their Black peers. That gap had tripled by 2013. Dr. Fenaba R. Addo and Dr. Jason Houle, researchers of racial disparities in student debt, suggest that student debt represents roughly 10 percent of the racial wealth gap when a college graduate is twenty-five years old, but by age thirty to thirty-five, it explains about 25 percent of the gap. Complete loan forgiveness is the least Black college students deserve. It represents the difference between a financial future of hope or one of despair. President Biden needs to pick hope and push for student loan forgiveness—if not for his children then for those of Black Americans.

---

* Throughout her pitch, Dorothy tries to give a 360-degree view of the lived experience of Black college grads and how it prevents them from building wealth. She anticipates counterarguments and debunks them.

CHAPTER 2

AN AUTHOR'S EDUCATION: ON STUDYING WRITING (IN SCHOOL, OR NOT)

I was a kid who wasn't allowed to watch *The Simpsons* because when it debuted, all the spiky-haired boys in my elementary school started wearing T-shirts that said UNDERACHIEVER AND PROUD OF IT (a Bartism, obviously), and my parents were afraid I might get ideas. I was in total agreement with my parents on this one; I hated all media that made fun of teachers, school, and the performance of being smart, a performance that was deeply tied to how I saw and valued myself. I assumed *The Simpsons* just wasn't for me. (School clearly hadn't yet taught me to be a good-enough close reader to recognize that *The Simpsons* was written for and by Lisas, and I am, in fact, a Lisa. Shout-out to the boyfriend, a former Bart who spent college chasing Lisas around, for spelling that one out to me.)

I entered a PhD program in English literature after college, not because I was excited about researching and writing about Jane Austen and Charles Dickens. Rather, the only version of an ideal life I was able to imagine would be spent reading books and then sitting around a large oaken table discussing them while my teachers, and eventually my students, beamed at me with admiration and delight at my brilliance. My own relationship with school has been passionate and affirming as well as misguided and fraught. If this describes you as well, know that, at the very least, you are in excellent literary and real-world company. While I wish my job involved more beaming admiration, I did manage to find a way to get paid to think about books, in a profession I never could have imagined or conceptualized when I was younger. Not unrelatedly, I now have a more expansive view of "education."

I write this chapter as someone who *loved* school, sought a graduate degree in a field I ultimately didn't pursue a career in, racked up a bunch of debt in the process, and dropped out of my doctoral program midway through to run around Italy for a year. Now, well over a decade after fleeing grad school, I see that I learned a lot of useful things there, though nearly none of them were emphasized at my program's orientation. Instead, the skills I acquired in graduate school that I now use most often were part of its much-maligned dirty work. Grading composition papers taught me how to give constructive criticism in the margins and locate and then sharpen other people's arguments, essential tools in guiding a writer through crafting a book proposal. Persuading college first-years to care about *Pride and Prejudice*—to trust me when I say, no, really, you must read this book, and not just because I'll fail you if you don't—requires the same confidence, credibility, and persuasive powers as persuading a book editor to put the submission you just sent them on the top of their to-be-read pile. The period of my life when I was furthest from any sort of institutionalized learning or validation—when I was living in Italy on an expired tourist visa and teaching English under the table (and not a fancy oak one)—did more to give me the courage of my convictions, an essential skill in agenting, than winning any arguments over Henry James. (No shade on Henry James; it's thanks to him that, as a directionless young woman, I got the bright idea to haul myself to Italy. Luckily, I had no fortune to steal, and Rome has eradicated malaria.)

In interviewing over two dozen successful writers, educators, and editors about their educational experience, I found that while their paths varied widely, so many of the essential things they learned in school were acquired, much like my own, in a sideways manner, only to reveal themselves years later. Some of the most useful resources and skills their programs gave them weren't those listed on the website. Others had to rebel against the institutional culture and assumptions of the programs they were in to achieve the careers they actually wanted. Still others were unable to or just not interested in pursuing any kind of formal education in writing and managed to get the experience and relationships with which to build a stable and fulfilling career by other means. Nearly every person I spoke with who went to a writing program would "do school" a bit differently if they had another shot at it—or perhaps not get a degree at all. My hope is that their advice will help you make the most of your educational choices and also help you avoid some mistakes. But no matter what you choose or how you approach your education as a writer, know that someday you'll look back on your choices and see mistakes were made, and most likely, you were the one who made them. Every single person I spoke with had a few of these regrets, and they are largely people whom *other* people look to and think they got it all right.

As this chapter will affirm, a credentialing degree is not necessary for a career as a writer. I won't be detailing the differences between individual MFA or journalism school departments, but I hope I will provide you with a framework to understand the differences between them and to clarify the opportunities and potential drawbacks of a few different paths. I'll also share advice and wisdom from folks who didn't finish college or attend any postgraduate programs, including one well-known writer who detested college, dropped out, and found he was more productive spending his day writing in the quiet of museums. He went on to win a MacArthur.

THE MASTER OF FINE ARTS IN CREATIVE WRITING: AN INVITATION TO GENEROSITY

Among the questions I get asked most often by emerging writers is whether or not they should get a master of fine arts (MFA) in creative writing, and more specifically, how seriously agents and publishers take the MFA credential. I'd put the first question into the category of inquiries like "Should I buy this house? Should I marry this man?" Answering it is too much responsibility for any outside party to take on, which is why God invented the Magic 8 Ball. As for the second—how seriously do the gatekeepers of publishing take the MFA credential?—there is a surprising amount of hesitancy among agents and editors to address this with absolute candor. I think this hesitancy is because of the painful math of writing as a way to make a living. Yes, an MFA can give you expedited access to editors, agents, and well-established writers, all of whom can help you tremendously in pursuing a career in such an insular and inaccessible industry. Yet the MFA is far from a guarantee of publication, much less publishing success. The whole system can feel a little pay-to-play, and any agent with a conscience (and I promise you all the best agents have one) would be reluctant to encourage such a costly investment with so uncertain a return. The possibility of making as much through your writing as you spent on your unfunded MFA is, frankly, slim. In a parallel to the dire academic job market, which I'll touch on later, there are far more MFA graduates than there are opportunities to publish books, especially as you'll be competing not just against your fellow MFA grads but also with everyone else who wants to publish a book—a reality that is easy to lose sight of in the hothouse of an MFA program. If you think of the slots for books in each publisher's catalog each season as seats in a concert hall, they simply don't have the capacity to offer one to every talented and hardworking writer, regardless of their MFA status. Of course, any MFA administrator would tell you what I tell writers all the time: If you're going into writing just for the money, you need to choose a different career. That said, the difference between trying to write and sell a book and entering an MFA program that doesn't provide funding is that, although living life while writing on your own isn't free, only one of these things actively charges tens (and sometimes hundreds) of thousands of dollars.

Yet it is precisely the difficulty of getting published that also makes MFA programs difficult for emerging writers to resist and impossible for agents to (completely) ignore. A lot of agents would be understandably reluctant to say anything *too* critical of a particular MFA program, or even of the MFA system, out of fear of offending the very programs through which many of us have found clients. Herein lies the rub: Agents are often invited to visit MFA programs and we often rep writers who teach in them, who will in turn refer students they particularly love (or at least have potential) to their own agents if they think it could be a good fit. The networks an MFA creates can help you circumvent the slush pile, and they help agents to skip it as well—and we dread slush as much as you do. As one fellow agent framed it to me, an MFA program is a sorting mechanism. The use of such a mechanism gets back to a theme I'll return to throughout this book, which is how agents and editors actually spend their days versus the misconception of it—and how you can use this knowledge to your benefit.

Because there are only so many hours in the week, institutions that make it easier and quicker for agents to find good clients are materially useful. We make campus or virtual visits to MFA programs for exactly this reason. As Heather Radke, who has an MFA in creative nonfiction from Columbia and authored *Butts: A Backstory* (Avid Reader/Simon & Schuster), explains, "I absolutely don't think you *need* an MFA—but an MFA helps you access power in a way that I just never could have without one. My teachers had access to editors and stuff that I just never had." While an MFA alone, even one from a very prestigious program, offers no guarantee of securing an agent or a book deal, it can offer you the opportunity to be in the room, often quite literally, with agents and editors.

MFA programs vary widely in how much they emphasize getting published and the practical skills and relationships necessary to do so. Though many offer networking opportunities and professionalizing skills, if you are considering one primarily for these reasons, be warned that this variance in terms of professionalizing was one of the greatest sources of discontent among the MFA graduates I interviewed. The recurring theme I found in talking to MFA grads was that those who had a good experience in their programs put themselves in charge of mining the resources of their programs to meet their goals. Looking back on her MFA experience, Radke wishes her program more directly addressed "what it means to be a professional writer" and helped students focus on reasonable, publishing-related benchmarks rather than the amorphous end goal of eventually publishing a book. In lieu of that, she set one for herself—to publish one long-form essay by the end of her degree. Now, as a teacher in the same MFA program she once attended, Radke has her students set shorter-term goals for themselves as part of her classes. While your program likely won't provide specific publishing objectives to achieve, nor do I think such an approach would work on a mass scale, Radke represents an instructive example of someone who set a tangible but relatively manageable goal for her time in her MFA program and, by the end of her course of study, achieved it. Steal this strategy and adapt it as you wish.

Harrison Hill, who was in the same creative nonfiction cohort as Radke and, as of this writing, has his first book under contract with Scribner, also wished for a bit more formalized instruction on professional skills. In time, he learned to seek out such information from his fellow students, and in retrospect thinks peers, rather than professors, may have been the more useful professional resource. The physical proximity to other emerging writers became a means to exchange information. As Hill explains, "The professors at Columbia are extraordinary. But they're also very established writers. And so the publishing issues that they're encountering are just not the same." His best tips about editors and publications to pitch were acquired while shooting the breeze with his fellow students in front of the MFA building.

By contrast, other graduates felt that an overemphasis on publishing and external markers of success in their programs limited their artistic growth during their MFA years and made it harder to experiment with style, subject, and genre. Leslie Jamison, now an influential essayist, was feeling "a bit workshopped out" in Iowa's legendary fiction program, as if she'd absorbed too many truisms about writing fiction and couldn't quite get free of them—a feeling that ultimately drove her to take her first nonfiction workshop. After so many fiction workshops and trying to follow her classes' dictates, "the form of the essay just felt gloriously lawless and without rules to me"—and this lawlessness was exactly what Jamison needed to do good work. For Radke, Hill, and Jamison, what they see as the "usefulness" of their MFA experiences was in direct proportion to their own ability to work outside the strictures of their programs, rather than in proportion to the degree of support provided by the school.

Whatever the pedagogy of a school, your choice of program should consider the (admittedly vast) question of what it is about being a writer that is enticing to you, and what your perspective is on a writer's life. Your MFA teachers will have different perspectives on this as well, and I encourage you to ask them about this. Wendy S. Walters, associate professor of writing in Columbia's MFA program and former director of its nonfiction concentration, who earned her MFA/PhD at Cornell, admittedly feels "mixed," in her words, about teaching her students about pitching their work to publications and publishing professionals. Before they do so, Walters asks her students to consider why they are looking to get their work published while they are still in grad school, stating that "there are students who are looking for affirmation in that pitching process or in selling something." For Walters, this is an extension of her understanding her desire to get an MFA—which she now sees that she did in part to be affirmed as a writer—and how she realized, after finishing hers, that this was an identity no degree could grant, and by extension, no publication. Finishing her MFA in a program she did not like wasn't affirming, because as soon as she finished the goalposts moved to publishing a book with an indie, and then to publishing a book at a major publisher. She counsels her students to be aware of that desire to chase the affirmation dragon and not to seek an MFA, or an agent, or publication, as part of it. Walters advises instead that "you can't control what other people are going to do with your work, all you can do is control what you put into your work." She counsels you to emphasize "your work in terms of commitment, in terms of aesthetics, in terms of values, in terms of what is art to *you*, putting all of that into your work, so that you can sleep at night." Of course, even the most self-assured writers need external affirmation from time to time. My advice is to Save Your Praise. Keep a record of all the good things people have said about your writing in a notebook or Google Doc so you have a well to return to when self-esteem inevitably runs dry. This may also help prevent you from seeking the dopamine hit of reassurance from more dubious sources.

Meredith Talusan, author of the memoir *Fairest*, learned this lesson in part through ignoring the prevailing culture of her MFA program. Talusan attended Cornell's tiny and highly selective MFA program, which admits only eight students a year. This selectivity ended up being a drawback for her; everyone around her seemed to be dead set on having a book published as soon after graduation as possible. Talusan felt pressure to produce work similar in style and subject to that which got her admitted (and which also felt like the most expedient approach to getting published), and to turn in pieces in a near-publishable state for critique. Talusan found this emphasis on publication and polish creatively stifling, and it was only after she learned to ignore such internalized pressure—and to use her MFA time as a period for risk and exploration—that she got more out of her experience.

Now, as a teacher in Sarah Lawrence's MFA program, her pedagogical method is decidedly "process driven" rather than publication focused, to allow for the experimentation and risk-taking she felt her alma mater dissuaded—which, not incidentally, she also feels well matches the dominant mode of Sarah Lawrence. Talusan notes that "the base expectations of the institution" shape the experiences and attitudes of the students. Because there is "a lot of incentive for you to be process driven and noncompetitive" in the program where she currently teaches, approaching the degree otherwise would "basically be swimming upstream." While acknowledging that students will undoubtedly be shaped by the culture of a given program—and should try to find out as much as possible about that culture before committing—Talusan suggests that they not take their department's mandates and prevailing mood too seriously. Meeting the requirements of an MFA degree and excelling by its metrics has almost nothing to do with becoming a successful writer, much less a fulfilled one. Talusan notes, "The person who gets all A's in their MFA program is not the same person who becomes a published author." She advises that students always keep in mind "the ways I will benefit from the program in order to further my [own] artistic goals," not just fitting into the program's mold of a successful writer.

All the folks I talked to, both recent graduates and current teachers (most of whom were MFA students once themselves), emphasized that prospective students should talk to as many people as possible in any program they are considering, while acknowledging that such question-asking can be intimidating when you also feel like a supplicant. I'll put this bluntly: Get over it. Getting over rogophobia (the fear of asking questions) as well as the fear of asking follow-up questions (I couldn't find a word for that) will serve you incredibly well as a writer—in fact, it's a key part of a writer's education. (Learning to talk to strangers and ask difficult questions of people in power is one of the foundational skills taught in journalism school, as every journalism professor I spoke with emphasized, and as I'll discuss in the next section of this chapter.) It will also serve you well in finding the best educational match for you. This chapter would be so much easier to write if the complaints about MFA programs were universal and actionable, but the only universal theme I heard was something along the lines of "I wish I had known my MFA emphasized X instead of Y," or alternatively, "I wish I had known I could ask about Z." Before signing on any dotted lines, ask, ask, ask. And trust me when I say the website won't offer any illumination.

Know, too, you can be as specific as you like in your questions; if asking about how much a program focuses on or deemphasizes publication seems too amorphous to yield helpful answers, ask instead about pedagogy. Meghan O'Rourke, a poet, memoirist, critic, and teacher who is as painstaking with her work in the classroom as she is on the page, urges prospective students to find out, as she puts it, "What will we actually be learning?" This question stems from what she found the most satisfying about pursuing her own MFA at Warren Wilson College and what she feels is sometimes missing in graduate-level creative writing classes. O'Rourke states, "I always want my students to leave at the end of the semester knowing a lot more than they came in with. One thing I sometimes saw while visiting MFA programs was that the content could be a little light. Some of the workshops felt overly subjective; at times classes lacked the intellectual, theoretical, historical, or structural frameworks that might help a student learn quickly or that help clearly break things down in ways that could be replicated and used at home." With this in mind, O'Rourke offers some questions to (kindly and respectfully) ask instructors, which could also apply if you are already in school and are thinking of working with a particular teacher: "How do you run your workshops? What are your goals for class? How do you read work that isn't to your tastes? How do you approach the task of trying to actually leave people with actionable knowledge?"

MFA pedagogy is in a moment of enormous flux as well as lively debate, which makes your asking questions about pedagogy both understandable and not unexpected. For years, the dominant structure of the writing workshop was the one crystallized by Iowa: an appointed student submits work each week, which her peers then critique, and during the crit, the student is not allowed to respond. The "cone of silence" approach was subject to rigorous criticism by the writer and teacher Matthew Salesses in his book *Craft in the Real World;* the influence of his book has changed not just classroom dynamics but the expectations of total acquiescence by students to the dominant culture of a program. While many instructors still follow the cone of silence method—and feel that its efficacy is in mimicking how readers will encounter writing in the wild, which is without any authorial framing—instructors like Talusan and O'Rourke ask students whose work is being critiqued what they would like to focus on and what they want to get out of the workshop. You're allowed to ask how your professors run their classes and what voice, if any, students have in critique sessions. You can also ask what direction a department is going in. Because faculty is often composed of many visiting practitioners rather than tenured, long-time professors, the faculty page isn't the only indication of who will be on campus while you are there.

But what if you don't know what kind of workshop methods or pedagogical approaches you prefer? Isn't an MFA program the place to figure that out? While I think you should enter your studies in the spirit of openness, confidence, and curiosity, I'd also say you might not want the first week of your MFA program to also be the first time you take a writing workshop. This isn't because I think you need extensive workshop experience to make the most of an MFA, but I do think it'd be a good idea to know if you actually *like* taking writing workshops. Look into local writers' groups, continuing education classes, writers' conferences, and online courses to get your feet wet. You may also find these experiences scratch your MFA itch.

.   .   .

All the MFA alums I spoke with sought graduate degrees to improve their work, though for some, that was primarily achieved through the opportunity to carve out dedicated time to write, and for others, it was through access to the feedback from the writing faculty. If the former drives you—or if finding time to write is a struggle for you— I'd suggest not only closely considering how the program is structured, but how and where you write and work best as you make your decision about which programs to target. The material conditions of their MFA programs—funding, time, location, location, location— were topics that came up repeatedly in my discussions with MFA grads. These were also often the ones they wish they'd considered before making the leap, though not necessarily the subjects MFA programs tended to emphasize in the way they pitch themselves. The primary choice you'll make is deciding between two general setups: full time or low residency. With the latter, you work remotely and then meet in person a few times a year for more intensive work. For many people, especially those comfortably postcollege, low residency is the only route if you don't have the option to peace out on your own life for two to three years, which is how long MFA programs typically run. They can also be an excellent choice if they suit your actual, rather than fantasy, work habits.

To help you think about this, I'm going to steal from a questionnaire Sanyu Dillon, president of the Random House Publishing Group, developed for herself, her colleagues, and questing friends, called "Best Day Ever." In it, Dillon asks respondents to "describe the last time you feel like you had a terrific workday. What was it that made it so good?" Her questions get quite granular—"How many things on your calendar had you planned vs others planning for you? What did you do for breaks that day, if any? What time did you take for yourself? What did you wear to work that day? Was there something about your appearance, makeup, hair, jewelry that made you feel great?"—and I think it's this particularity that makes the exercise so generative. Your physical, emotional, and intellectual environment will shape your experience of a program as much as if not more than its prestige and name recognition. Ask yourself, what were the conditions during which you produced the piece of writing you are proudest of? Do you work best in short, dedicated sprints (the low-residency experience) or with long stretches of relatively unstructured and uninterrupted time (the full-time approach)? The latter is everyone's dream (or at least mine), but how do you actually best get stuff *done*? Thinking about how you can re-create the conditions of "Your Best (Writing) Day Ever," whether or not you end up formally studying writing, will help you throughout your career.

Think not just about time but about place, and how place will determine your experience. New York City and its suburbs have several excellent MFA programs, including Columbia, New York University, Sarah Lawrence, and Brooklyn College. It also remains the center of America's publishing industry, for better or for worse, so it's a city swarming with writers, editors, and agents, and, if this is your focus, opportunities to meet them. Of course, you needn't be in an MFA program to do so, nor am I implying as much. But by sheer dint of these schools' locations, it's quite easy for agents and magazine and book editors to visit open houses and pitch sessions and, conversely, for students to meet such people at panel discussions and author events. In other words, if you do go to an MFA program in New York, you may have opportunities to jump more quickly into professionalizing and all the excitement as well as the pressure and anxiety that entails.

Regardless of where you do your MFA, think hard about the question of whether you will want and need to do paid work outside your program and how much. Some writers I spoke with saw their rent jobs as anchoring while others wished they hadn't worked during their MFA years so they could take complete advantage of what would likely be the one season in their life when they could fully concentrate on their writing. Heather Radke always had side hustles during her MFA and saw those as inextricable from the lessons her MFA was teaching her on how to be a "working writer." She saw working other jobs while finishing her thesis as a lesson in "what it's like to be a writer," and her MFA was training her in how to do both. Radke sees her rent jobs as "making her creative life more possible," not just practically but emotionally. She "likes the feeling of sort of cheating on one with the other." "Cheating" can also be a productive way to experiment in new genres. Leslie Jamison initially thought of nonfiction writing as her "mistress genre"; a sense of creative adultery freed her up—the inherent appeal of any mistress worthy of the title.

But even if your program doesn't emphasize professionalizing—and even if that is not your primary concern during your MFA years—know that your teachers are there as a resource, not just in terms of craft but also as examples of how to build a writer's life. One of Heather Radke's bits of advice is, once in school, talk to your teachers about how they do it, "it" being crafting a life as a writer. (It's worth noting that Radke's adulterous, magpie approach mirrors that of Jamison's, her former teacher and mentor.) Jamison, in her own words, "can't write when she is working a 9–5 job." After completing her MFA and before she published *The Empathy Exams,* Jamison found she did better work as a writer having two part-time jobs and carving out writing time in between. Now Jamison's work as a teacher helps her refuel her writing. As she states, "I'm sort of afraid of the version of my life in which my main focus, or my sole professional focus, is my own writing, and the dissemination of that work in the world. I am afraid of the person that I would become if it was just that kind of monoculture." Her classes as a teacher "end up refracting back onto my own work or making me think about my work in new ways." To her, the classroom is a place of exchange between student and teacher rather than a well where students extract the teacher's experience, knowledge, and contacts. The notion of exchange can be extended beyond the student-teacher relationship in generative ways. My favorite framing of the MFA experience came from Wendy Walters, who asks students to ask themselves, "Do you want to give your time and attention to other people's work? Do you want to become a much better reader by engaging with other people's work that is newly made, kind of freshly killed? It's an invitation to generosity in some ways, and, you know, not everybody is up for that."

As you think about the kind of community you want to be part of during your degree, you might also want to think about the ratio of writers to nonwriters you want in your daily life and how intimate and intensive you want those relationships to be. Unless you are a more evolved person than every other writer I've met, you *will* be competitive with other writers in your field of vision. Do you want to be in a campus environment surrounded by a small group of other people focused on the same thing, what I think of as the spin class approach? Or do you do better where you are one of many, all with different paths, ambitions, interests, levels of success, and deep indifference? I learned through time and experience—-and fleeing a bucolic but claustrophobic college in Upstate New York for school in New York City—that for me, it's the latter. I find the evidence of big stakes around me energizing, while anonymity makes me feel cozy. I related deeply to the experiences of Wendy Walters, for whom the small size and isolation of her program was one of its drawbacks. For some, such an intimate program can be nurturing; for Walters, there wasn't "room to grow or change." She found herself heading to New York City for the weekend. For others, such an environment will always be distracting and overwhelming. If that's you, that's okay! I'll offer suggestions on how to access the resources of the publishing and media worlds without ever setting foot here.

The final bit of advice I heard is the most materially valuable and one you should keep in mind throughout your writerly career, as it will be useful at many stages. If you are in a program that is unfunded or only partially funded, *ask for more.* Heather Radke was initially hesitant to do so, until she found out another student in her cohort received more fellowship money. The two ended up conspiring, playing their offers against each other to get respective improvements. Radke was honest about the initial discomfort in this ask, a discomfort that is all too familiar to me as a former scholarship kid at an elite institution. I think the degree to which we feel uncomfortable asking for greater financial support is directly proportional to the wealth and status of the environment we are in. There's something about being surrounded by people who don't need money—who also tend to be the people who avoid talking about it—that makes one all the more reluctant to admit that you do. Whether you are pursuing an MFA at an institution as wealthy and powerful as Columbia or at a smaller or publicly funded program, try to internalize the mantra of "Don't ask, don't get." There will be plenty of times as a writer when you are going to have to ask for a better rate, and I promise you that honest conversations about needing more money get easier with practice.

As someone who now asks for more money on the regular, I'd also encourage you to do so in as immediate a way as possible. If an email is all you can muster, write that email, being frank about your needs. That said, if you could instead schedule a phone call with your school's dean to discuss your financial package, even better. An in-person meeting is best of all. I know it sounds excruciating to sit across from someone in power and express vulnerability and need, especially given all the cultural shame we have around money, but it's much easier to say no to an email. It's harder to say no to a fully embodied person. This is why whenever I ask for an improvement of a book advance, I pick up the phone. The cultural anxiety around talking about money, once you overcome it, can become a tool you use to your advantage. The sooner you learn to wield it, the better off you will be.

J-SCHOOL: TALKING TO STRANGERS

While "professionalization" can be a fraught topic among MFA faculty and students, journalism school's particular purpose *is* professionalization. Every journalism professor I spoke with repeated the maxim "journalism is a trade" and emphasized that journalism school, at its best, works to acculturate you into it. Linda Villarosa, a *New York Times Magazine* staff writer and a journalism professor at the City College of New York, distills the work of a journalist into three key interactions: "reporting and research, interviewing people, and then creating a narrative."

J-school breaks down each of those steps and helps students become good at them. You'll work on your writing, but above all, you'll work on a set of skills—how to investigate and conduct research, how to interview, how to file Freedom of Information Act requests, how to write in a range of forms, from news writing to features. You also learn storytelling across various forms of media—print, video, audio, and digital, in order (ideally, at least) to gain entry into the profession.

This chapter covers creative nonfiction MFA programs and journalism schools in tandem despite the different aims of the programs, because the resulting books (and long-form articles) often look quite a bit similar. Many works of "creative nonfiction" include extensive reporting, while narrative-driven long-form articles and narrative nonfiction books are regularly produced by journalism school graduates. The class read for Columbia Journalism School's 2024 cohort was *Strangers to Ourselves,* a deeply reported study of how people with mental illness understand their own diagnoses, by creative nonfiction MFA grad Rachel Aviv. The winner of the 2022 Pulitzer Prize for General Nonfiction was awarded to journalism school graduate Andrea Elliott for her book *Invisible Child,* a narratively immersive and intricately structured story of a young girl raised in poverty in New York City, praised by the prize committee for its "literary" approach. Per Keith Gessen, now a professor of journalism at Columbia (and a graduate of Syracuse's MFA program—in fiction, no less), you can get an MS in journalism or an MFA in creative writing and "end up in the same place." You can engineer your MFA degree to give you some reportorial experience, particularly by choosing a school with faculty whose books have included reportage. Every journalism professor I spoke with emphasized that while their classes teach technical skills, they also always spend time with their students analyzing what makes successful stories work—just as one does in a writing workshop. Jelani Cobb, the dean of Columbia's Journalism School, *New Yorker* staff writer, and PhD in American history (I hope you are sensing a theme here), calls this approach "reverse engineering," wherein "you take the finished product, and then disassemble it, as if someone gave you a delicious meal, and then you sorted out

each of the spices. You're going backward into, not only why did
they quote this person, but they quote *this* person in *this* paragraph.
How do they lead you into the story?" This process of learning craft
through disassemblage is precisely why most graduate-level creative
writing courses include extensive reading as well as writing.

Journalism school's primary goal, however, is to teach you how to
report, and reporting, more than polishing your line-by-line craft as
a writer, is what you'll spend the bulk of your time doing. You will
learn the specialized skills of your trade, professional protocols and
standards, and above all, you'll be forced to get over any hesitancy to
"talk to strangers," another phrase I heard again and again in talking
to journalism school instructors.

To learn these skills within a professional structure, journalism
school classrooms often replicate the newsroom, with journalism
professors playing the role of editors. Instructors may assign stories
for you to cover, or you may be tasked with pitching stories to them,
which they can reject or accept, reshape and tweak, as they guide you
toward producing a finished product (if not a fully finished article,
one with enough meat on its bones that you can then pitch it). You'll
learn how the pipeline works from pitching an idea, to having it
assigned, to reporting it out through finding sources, to writing it to
fit the demands of a particular genre. Through these exercises, you'll
also accrue sample clips.

Until recently, aspiring journalists could get much of this training,
and the portfolio that comes with it, on the job. Opportunities for
paid on-the-job training through an apprenticeship model, in journalism and in many other professions, have become fewer in number
and far more competitive. Rather than offering that experience to
an interested but as-yet-untrained aspirant, internships often require
previous experience. In this environment of scarcity, journalism
schools see themselves as providing an increasingly valuable resource
to those who wish to enter the profession, providing the training that
can no longer be found on the job, as entry-level jobs no longer come
with the same level of support. Jelani Cobb explains, "One of the
unfortunate side effects of the industry contraction is that it's actually
harder to learn the craft by doing, because there are fewer of those
seasoned reporters. When we think about how to report, who to call,
how to do a Freedom of Information Act request, how to cover the

courts, or whatever, that is traditionally taught through mentorship. When you come into a publication and you're green, you don't know anything, they pair you with someone more experienced, who has been covering the city for fifty years. You learn by doing. The value of journalism school is that we accelerate that process."

Journalism school can fill in the gaps in the absence of on-the-job training. It gives you a chance to "do journalism"—to interview, to report, to write and even to pitch—in the laboratory of the classroom.

Through repetition, you learn not just the mechanics of "doing journalism," but what a story *is,* and which publication format best suits the particular story you want to tell. As another professor detailed for me, working with his students on developing stories for his classes often involved steering them between being too micro and being too macro. Time and time again, I find myself having a similar conversation with writers thinking about their first book: Is this subject big enough to sustain book-length attention? Is it so big that I won't be able to get my arms around it? As you begin to learn "story sizing," be it at journalism school or in an MFA program or out in the wild, you'll learn what it feels like to get the size right. Make doing so, rather than the length of the story itself, one of the measures of your success. Every time you get to yes, you are learning a bit more about *how* to get to yes.

Part of getting to yes, in publishing a piece or in getting a staff job, is knowing whom to ask and not being afraid to do so. You are not making the most of journalism school if you are not making the most of its networking benefits. This means not just getting to know your professors—or better still, making sure they know you—but also building relationships with your peers. Your professors may write you the crucial recommendation letter that gets you a fellowship or a job, but it is just as likely that someone in your data reporting class will be the editor you end up pitching someday. Dean Cobb urges students to think about school networking not just hierarchically but also laterally. In journalism school, Cobb explains, "You have a cohort of people, professional friends, who you come out with, who can make connections for you. Most of us have gotten jobs, or at least leads for a job, from our friends. Here's a set of friends that you start with." The connections you can make aren't just within the campus gates. Nikole Hannah-Jones recommends journalism students take advantage of the resources beyond the classroom by writing for your school's newspaper or small community papers, which can help solve the problem of needing an internship to get an internship and accumulating those all-important sample clips.

No matter where you go to journalism school, you'll be made to ask strangers questions, so acclimate yourself to this even before you matriculate. As you look into applying to journalism schools, investigating a school's expertise will make for a better fit. Presumably, if you are reading this book, you want to be a writer. Some schools, geared more toward aspiring journalism instructors, emphasize journalism as a concept rather than as a practice. Look at your school's course requirements to see how much writing is emphasized and what kinds of writing you'll be tasked with doing. If you want to do feature writing, make sure your school offers it and has faculty with experience feature writing. Investigate the school's relationship with the industry. Find out which institutions come to campus to recruit and which ones have hired recent grads. While MFAs often offer access to the publishing industry, they can have a culture of being cagey about this. Journalism school's wholehearted embrace of being a professional program means you can—and should—push hard to find out if your degree-granting program can give you access to networks of people you'd want to hire you or publish you.

ACADEMIA AND POST-ACADEMIA

A few years back, I was invited to visit Stanford's Public Humanities Initiative to address a group of academics interested in writing for nonacademic audiences, a situation I increasingly find myself in. I gave a talk outlining the basics of nonfiction trade publishing, e.g., books written for a general readership and "available wherever books are sold," and then met with each of them individually to discuss their respective projects, ranging from books on Greek drama and the birth of democracy to the pre-1619 Caribbean to a memoir on learning to surf in late midlife after decades spent in the archives. I loved every minute of it, in large part because it recalled my favorite part of grad school (talking to academics) and none of the unpleasant responsibilities (writing papers). That visit was the germ of inspiration for this book. No small part of my pleasure was being treated as someone with a body of specialized knowledge by people who carried around very impressive bodies of specialized knowledge themselves. The continual switching back and forth between novice/expert (or student/teacher) infects all author/agent relationships, but I find it is particularly acute in ones between academics and those of us, loosely speaking, who bring your work to a wider audience. You are insecure about navigating the marketplace and engaging with a vaguely defined "public"; we are insecure about our dilettantish and mercantile ways. I'm acknowledging our respective tote bags of insecurities in hopes of helping you, at least for a few moments, put yours down.

This section will differ from the previous ones just a bit as I know I am not speaking to a general audience of academics, if such a thing exists. I won't cover what to expect in a doctoral program, as most people who find themselves in doctoral programs aren't there in hopes of publishing a trade book. But thanks to the "crisis in the humanities" and the state of the academic job market (no scare quotes needed), I meet with increasing numbers of academics interested in writing outside academia. Here, I'll share some helpful ways to think about "public" writing and publishing if you are, or have been, on an academic track, based on my own experience working with academics writing crossover books and from interviewing trade book and media outlet editors who regularly publish academics.

Scholarly expertise is respected and valued by publishers; look at the long list of nominees from the last ten years for the National Book Award for Nonfiction or the finalists for the Pulitzer Prize in History, chock-full of practicing academics or those with academic training, to understand why. No matter where you are in your academic career or in academia's brutally delineated hierarchies, your training and depth of knowledge are likely reason enough for someone to consider a pitch from you on topics within your field. I'm stating this up front because more than any other subcategory of writers I know, academics seem to be the least confident in reaching out beyond their own institutions without some sort of connection. You don't need an agent to pitch articles and essays, and, as my chapter on pitching details, it's often preferable *not* to use an agent when doing so. While a referral always helps grease the wheels in getting an agent to read your query, it's certainly not necessary, especially if you are targeting agents who rep other academic clients. (As for finding agents who rep academics, as I detail in chapter 4, start by looking in the acknowledgments section of your favorite trade books written by academics. If you don't have any favorite books in this category, it might mean you don't want to go this route, and that's okay too.)

Editors at trade houses, particularly those who regularly publish academics, even reach out to and will sometimes directly negotiate with scholars. While I don't recommend negotiating a deal with a trade publisher without an agent, take this as proof of trade publishing's interest. Dan Gerstle, the editor in chief of W. W. Norton, often finds academic authors in nonacademic spaces such as *The Atlantic, The New York Times,* and even on social media, and solicits submissions from them directly. Molly Turpin, a senior editor at Random House, first encountered historian Tiya Miles's work at the American Historical Association conference, where she went to scout for authors. Turpin eventually acquired Miles's book, *All That She Carried: The Journey of Ashley's Sack, a Black Family Keepsake,* which went on to be a *New York Times* bestseller and to win the National Book Award for Nonfiction. In these cases, the authors benefited from being at the right soda fountain at the right time. Precisely because of your demonstrable expertise, if you are at where you are discoverable (published by a national media outlet or even just appearing in an agent's or editor's inbox), you are more likely to get noticed. (As for whether or not you should work with an agent, I'll quote Gerstle here as he is a less interested party than I: "I do suggest to every author in that position that they at least consider getting an agent. A good agent is invaluable. Even if it means we pay more, a good agent is valuable to us too.")

When I speak with academics interested in writing for the trade, they often approach the endeavor as one of translation or conversion, but I think a better way to view it is as one of reorientation. As an academic, you are already addressing a variety of audiences. You give lectures to undergraduates and present papers to your peers; you approach writing a monograph differently than a review. You will be making the same sorts of decisions about subject and register as you think about writing for the trade.

Anne Helen Petersen, who left academia after earning a doctorate in media studies and used her cultural studies training to launch a very successful career as a freelance writer, says making academic work more accessible "doesn't necessarily mean dumbing down, it just means taking the most exciting parts and making them primary." Often when I receive first drafts of book proposals and manuscripts from academics looking to write for the trade, they foreground the arguments within their field, no doubt due to academia's requirement that you show mastery of the current state of your discipline. The subjects that appeal beyond academia aren't rooted in intramural debates (and you can always show you did the reading in your endnotes). As you imagine a different audience, think less of your department peers and more about readers in different disciplines or even your favorite students. Your own teaching experiences are a good frame of reference and source of inspiration. Petersen continues, "If you're committed to being a good teacher, you are trying to make both fundamental and niche components of your discipline interesting to your students." A good exercise is thinking about which subjects have interested your students most. Which approaches have proven most engaging?

In terms of language, don't think simply in terms of making it more colloquial—first drafts by someone talking down to their audience too often fall into "but I'm a cool mom" silliness—but rather how and where you define terms. Merve Emre, literary critic at *The New Yorker* and Shapiro Silverberg Professor of Creative Writing and Criticism at Wesleyan, describes developing her voice as a literary critic as distinct from her academic one: "I wanted to take ideas seriously but to present them stripped of any kind of technical vocabulary that would have been a barrier to understanding." You can also make explaining technical vocabulary part of the work of a piece itself, especially if doing so furthers your argument or enriches it for your reader. Here's an example from Emre, who was guided in how to do so by her *New Yorker* editor, Leo Carey. (You're getting two-for-one advice here, so I will quote at length):

My tendency as an academic has always been to complicate and then clarify. In a technical sense, I had to change the way I thought about the syntax and the structure of my sentences and paragraphs. This is vocabulary that I have taken from Leo: academic writing tends to enshrine what he calls indirection, which is introducing a concept before you illustrate it. In scholarship, you assume that you can give your reader a complicated term or phrase and that they will simply accept it or patiently wait for you to unpack that word or that phrase. The writing at *The New Yorker* operates according to the opposite principle; you always illustrate the complicated concept first and then name it. To give a very simple example, when I was writing the piece on John Guillory's book, *Professing Criticism,* I had a paragraph that started with, "Guillory's previous book, *Cultural Capital,* was a sociology of judgment." Leo said, "No, no—you can only call it a 'sociology of judgment' at the end of the paragraph, after you show us what it means for something to be a sociology of judgment." There were all of these little rules that I had to learn to uncomplicate my prose.

Knowing if you are using technical vocabulary is a challenge if you are deeply immersed in your field, as I am reminded again and again in writing this book. The question I ask myself when I'm stuck is, "How would I explain this to a newly arrived intern?" You might want to ask yourself, "Would my best undergraduate students understand this term? Do they need to know it?"

Note that Emre explains her style in terms of *The New Yorker*. Media outlets have house styles, not passed along in a handbook but picked up through reading and writing for them yourself. The approach of a *New Yorker* review is different from those for the more scholarly *New York Review of Books* or of the more polemical *Harper's*. As an academic, you are already addressing a variety of publics. You give lectures to undergraduates and to colleagues; you write for journals and academic presses. You learned these different registers through practice, exposure, and apprenticeship, and it's not dissimilar in writing for the trade. Language and style are particularly osmotic, as anyone who spends time with both first-year students and seniors will tell you. Read writers in your field who appear outside academic publications and nonacademic writers who write on your subject. Above all, read the outlets you'd want to publish you. The skills you already have as a researcher will help you understand how these writers construct their arguments and even their sentences. The apprenticeship relationship comes into play if you eventually start working with an editor or an agent. As you saw in the earlier quote, Emre's editor schools her as much as she schools him.

There are different types of crossover work, and your approach will change depending on which one you are pursuing. If you are a cultural anthropologist who specializes in medical anthropology, you likely have a lot to say about COVID, but you also bring the tools of participant observation to nearly any setting. Always remember that you are considered an expert in your wider field to the general public, even though you're seen as a specialist within it. General readers may question your argument, but rarely your expertise. The presentation of the argument or analysis is as important to its accessibility as is the line-by-line language. Your conclusions shouldn't be hard to find and might not even need to appear at the conclusion. See what happens when you start with your conclusion rather than end with it and work backward from there.

Academics are more connected to trade publishing than they realize. In terms of my own list, and those of other agents and editors who work with academics, most of our authors come through referrals. Simply put, if you are at all interested in writing trade work, tell your colleagues, especially those who already do so. Don't just share your work with them; articulate how you want your work to be shared. Don't be shy about sharing links to your writing on social media or asking others in your field who have big social media followings to do so. How Dan Gerstle, the Norton editor in chief, uses Twitter (now X) is helpful here, so I'll quote at length:

> When I "find" writers on Twitter it's not through their own tweeting, necessarily, but because others are talking about and sharing their work. (I don't want to be seen as encouraging writers to get on Twitter. Because I don't think it's necessary to do so, whether to get noticed or, later on, to promote one's book.)
>
> Reading Twitter is a means of surfing the discourse; it's central to my media diet; it offers frames of reference for what's going on in the world. Of course it's not Real Life, as everyone says. But, for instance, I don't have to actually read academic journals front to back—I can rely on people in the field to express their excitement or admiration for a particular article, and then I can read that article and think about reaching out to its author.

By the time this book is published, X may no longer exist; it may once again be Twitter. I share Gerstle's quote because I think its logic applies to the usefulness of sharing your work with any social network, virtual or otherwise.

TWO WRITERS, TWO PATHS

And finally, I can't in good conscience conclude this chapter on education without some counterexamples, as the message I least want to give you is that you need a writing-related degree to be a writer. I offer the experiences of two writers who are at the far end of the bell curve in terms of stamina, conviction, and success, and for those reasons, not easily replicable, but I share them so you can cherry-pick some wisdom (and tactics) from two singular careers.

Hanif Abdurraqib and Isaac Fitzgerald have established themselves as beloved and acclaimed multihyphenate writers; neither took a traditional educational or institutional path to their success. They're both known in literary circles not just for their talent but also for their remarkable generosity and commitment to community. There are other meaningful parallels in their careers. Both were deeply involved in their local punk scenes and bring punk's DIY spirit and its emphasis on creating and sustaining communal spaces. They are both writers deeply tied to and appreciative of place, albeit loosely defined. Abdurraqib is devoted to his hometown of Columbus and Fitzgerald, more of a nomad, quickly became involved in the literary scene of San Francisco when he moved there in his early twenties and did the same when he moved to New York years later. Fitzgerald also came to the literary world by being deeply online (he's a bit less so these days), participating in an early part of what has been called "the literary internet," meeting and then supporting the work of other writers through relationships built initially via social media. Abdurraqib has a similarly generative and generous relationship with social media. A self-admitted introvert who isn't much for parties and formal gatherings, he spends much of his time in his lovingly maintained East Columbus home with his records, his sneakers, and his dog, Wendy. He shares glimpses of this life on Instagram, along with candid meditations on friendship, loneliness, lost loved ones, and writing. While

Abdurraqib and Fitzgerald both have many IRL friends, they are also thought of as a friend by countless people they've never met. Both are omnivorous readers. In sum, they managed to acquire many of the benefits of a degree program—peers and mentors, a deep knowledge of literature, a network of readers—on their own terms, with the tools and resources at hand and the ones they successfully sought out.

Fitzgerald grew up in a working-class family in Worcester County, Massachusetts, spending his early years in a shelter for the unhoused, later in a series of low-income apartments, and eventually in a rural and isolated farmhouse. Much about his childhood was precarious, but one consistency he could count on was a familial love of books. He was raised by parents for whom books were "holy relics," and he read in a passionate but nonprogrammatic way. Fitzgerald explains, "At the time, as a child, I felt very lucky for that informal education from my parents. They made books very important to me. I did not have any grasp of any current literary situation. I had no idea what genre was or even fiction versus nonfiction." Fitzgerald's love of books led him to avoid any formal study of literature, feeling that "I loved books so much that to bring school into it, which I did not love very much, felt like an affront. It felt like an insult. There's something about reading for pleasure that I wanted to separate from school." Because of this love, Fitzgerald, as a young man who, having made his way to San Francisco, became involved there in 826 Valencia, a nonprofit creative writing foundation dedicated to "supporting underresourced students." It was there, after seeing marked-up manuscript pages from published books tacked to the wall, that Fitzgerald realized books are something people who walk among us make. While this initially got Fitzgerald interested in the editorial side of publishing, it also motivated him to share this discovery with others:

> Maybe it's from a friend or family member, or an editor or teacher, but we want to show kids that, while writing is this very lonely art form, that through community, whether it be your friends, family, teachers, other students, they will give you feedback on your work, and it can make your work better. You don't always have to take all the edits, but they can give you edits that will help make your story stronger. And I at the age

of twenty-three, in that moment I realized, we definitely gotta teach eight-year-olds that, but never in my life had that thought crossed my mind before. In a way, I was learning right along with the kids.

While working with kids at 826 Valencia, Fitzgerald realized that he could create for himself what he was giving to children. Working at the foundation, "what really clicked in [his] head was, surround yourself with people who are better at this than you. And I all of a sudden realized, there is a modern literary community out there. I just need to go find them and be a part of it. And the second thing that it really taught me was this idea that writing was not a gift from God." Fitzgerald next became involved with online independent literary magazine *The Rumpus*, first in organizing events and then as a managing editor. He was not initially paid for this work and supported himself by working at what he describes as "the San Francisco equivalent of the Olive Garden." *The Rumpus* was his passion, and through it, he met—and eventually edited—talented and influential writers such as Cheryl Strayed and Roxane Gay early in their careers. These relationships were central to Fitzgerald's education. As he put it, "And then truly, the story of the next 10 to 15 to 20 years of my life is spent trying to learn from [other writers]." Years later, he is the author of *The New York Times* bestselling and New England Book Award–winning memoir *Dirtbag, Massachusetts*.

Hanif Abdurraqib also began his literary career in a highly local and DIY manner through writing reviews of punk shows and albums for Midwestern zines, which he largely did, in his words, "to stay out of trouble." Over time, his reviews grew "too poetic and meandering" for his zine editors, so Abdurraqib decided to start writing poems. He then schooled himself in poetry, taking advice from poets he'd met in the Columbus scene and working his way back from contemporary poets to Gwendolyn Brooks to Mary Oliver to Sylvia Plath. Abdurraqib studied poetry with rigor, drawing from his early training as an elite high school soccer player, stating, "I would go out, maybe go to a poetry reading and read or go to a show, and then get home and then read some more poems before sleeping a few hours, and then doing it again. . . . I still think like an athlete, in a lot of ways.

I played sports my whole life. I was treating it like I was training for something." As in athletics, training led to performance. Abdurraqib first performed his poems before punk shows, which taught him how to engage with an audience.

> If you're reading to open a house punk show, you have to cap-
> tivate the people who are not there to see you. You have to be
> engaging in a way that is unique enough to captivate an audi-
> ence who came to see a punk show. I learned that really quickly.
> I also learned how to read language out loud. There's also just
> an ethos that comes with connecting with people on that level
> because there's no real barrier. What I loved about coming up in
> the punk scene was that there was never a real barrier between
> the artist and the audience. I think it impacts my work because
> I want to give readings that feel intimate. I also want to interact
> with the people who come to see the reading.

Building on skills developed from his adolescence in athletics and punk, Abdurraqib developed into a kinetic performer, one whom even non-poetry lovers sought out to see live. At these shows, he made a point of spending time talking with everyone who wanted a book signed, no matter how long it took, always standing up while doing so instead of behind the usual signing table so he could con-nect more directly with his readers.

Unsurprisingly, Abdurraqib's big break as a writer came through friendship and DIY publishing. He'd met the poet Eve Ewing online via Twitter. Ewing eventually cofounded the now-defunct internet magazine *Seven Scribes* with a group of friends. After chatting with Abdurraqib about his thoughts on the then-blockbuster song "Trap Queen," Ewing offered to publish it. That piece "In Defense of 'Trap Queen' As Our Generation's Greatest Love Song" went mini-viral. Its popularity led to an offer to write for Pitchfork and then MTV.com, admittedly with modest pay, and eventually to an equally modest book deal with Columbus-based independent publisher Two Dollar Radio. He held on to his marketing job throughout these years, and it took convincing by a mentor for him to commit to writing another book. Abdurraqib remembers, "I was so afraid of losing stability. I came from a background where I didn't have stability. I was unhoused for a bit, and I grew up really poor." Even now, after winning a MacArthur "Genius Grant," hitting *The New York Times* bestseller list, and being a finalist for the National Book Award, Abdurraqib still applies the "idea that everything I'm writing has the opportunity to be my last thing. So make it your best thing." He not only doesn't take publication for granted. He is grateful simply to write.

Like Fitzgerald, Abdurraqib has made the teaching of others part of his work and his ongoing education as a writer. Each year, Abdurraqib reaches out to Columbus City Schools teachers to ask if they have any students who are interested in poetry and want to do group critiques of poems. A handful of students always answer the call and reliably meet one Sunday a month. How Abdurraqib runs his classroom mirrors the open, nonhierarchical way he approaches other aspects of his creative work. He explains:

My main teaching practice is, broadly, the same shit as my reading practice, where we all have a responsibility to each other in this room to make each other better writers. That includes you all with me. There's no real hierarchy here, because I'm not an authority figure to you. I'm not your teacher. I'm not your parent. I am a writer. You are writers, and so we have to really make each other better. So they workshop my poems too. And I hold them to a standard. Obviously, they know that I'm a writer, and they see my name and stuff like that, but they're not impressed by that. We workshop each other's work. I treat them the same way. I workshop their poems the same way I workshopped Eve Ewing's poems, and it's tense. Sometimes they hear stuff they don't want to hear.

That's the exchange, and I always tell them, listen, if I can take this critique well, then we all have a responsibility to. And by the end of the year, it's incredible. We form real relationships. I play basketball with some of them at the end of the year. A lot of them will not become professional writers. But they are looking for an avenue to write and express themselves in, and they don't really have that at the high school level. So it just provides that for them.

Abdurraqib's teaching method reflects the spirit of punk rock, but also reminded me of Wendy Walters's view of the MFA as an "invitation to generosity." One doesn't need to be accepted into a prestigious graduate program to accept the invitation to be generous, nor is one needed to find literary friends, peers, and mentors. I can say, though, that those who are generous with others often have more fulfilling and sustaining literary careers, as we'll see again in chapter 6, on the publication process.

I initially approached writing this chapter determined to spell out "how to get the most" of one's education, and the answers in large part are the same as in other parts of this book: by asking questions, by deeply researching, by doing the hard work of determining what you really want, and by allowing yourself to be vulnerable enough to ask for it. I hope you will do all these things again and again in your literary career, but I also hope you'll approach any education you step into not in the spirit of extraction of resources but of exchange, and that you will think as much about what you give as about what you receive.

Interview with Chloé Cooper Jones

Chloé Cooper Jones is the author of the memoir *Easy Beauty,* which was a finalist for the Pulitzer Prize and looked at her relationship to beauty and her body as a person with a visible disability. Jones was also a Pulitzer finalist in feature writing for her profile of Ramsey Orta, the man who filmed the killing of Eric Garner. I conclude this chapter on education with Jones not only because she has taken on more formal education than almost anyone I've ever met, but because I admire the voracity with which Jones pursued not just education but knowledge, as well as the holistic way she thought about becoming a writer. While Jones did a lot of school, hers wasn't a direct path, nor was it rushed.

So many writers fear being behind where they imagine they should be. Getting a glimpse of Jones's wild but unhurried ambition was an unexpected gift to receive while in the midst of writing my first book. The wisdom she has about the publication process is another, and I don't think it's unconnected to the time she took in getting there.

Given that you're trained as an academic, and built a career as a journalist, and are now a very successful memoirist, I am interested in talking to you about how you managed to do this. Can you walk me through your graduate school journey?

It was crucial for me to feel like I had generated the foundation of thought that I really wanted. I don't think there's been a day in my life that I wanted to be a writer for academia. I think there's amazing academic writing out there, but I've wanted to be a writer for a general audience since I was a kid. I went into the MFA thinking that I wanted to spend a lot of time with craft. I've been writing nonstop since childhood and generated a ton of material in my degrees, but I wanted to get this foundation of knowledge before I wrote seriously.

Take us back to the beginning. When you were doing the MFA, clearly there was always the desire to write for audiences outside academia. So then how did it transition to writing for academia? What was the process?

When I was in my MFA, I got exposed to literary theory, and that opened this window into the way that literary traditions had been thought, talked, and written about. I did a PhD in literary theory because I thought the more that I can study, the deeper I can go into my craft. I thought that, inevitably, would help me write better books. Every year a lot of books get written, published, and are successful, and yet we will never hear about them ever again. I wanted to write books that would stay on bookshelves and feel like they were adding something valuable to a conversation that people would want to desperately return to. If I'm going to have that high and lofty a goal, I better do the work to figure out how certain books—from Plato's *Symposium* to the writing of Toni Morrison—have stayed so relevant across time. I felt like it was important to study that huge range of work.

I felt the same way about philosophy. Especially as I was transitioning into doing a lot more journalism and nonfiction, I thought it was really important for me to have some baseline understanding of intellectual history. The history of Western thought, the history of the biggest questions that people are asking, and how various brilliant people have dissected questions that I also want to write about. For example, what is love and beauty and friendship and justice and the self and knowledge and reality? Those are the subjects of artists, and the philosophers have a lot to teach us about them. All these degrees were done in service to this larger goal that I had, and still have, which is to write something for any person in the world. To write things that are very serious and complex on one hand, but profoundly accessible on the other. I don't want to exclude a single reader. I want to invite everybody in, as much as I can. They were all in service to trying to do that in a way that would be worth other people's time and a place on their shelf.

I felt that when I've read you. It's such a rare quality, the quality of not just the thoughtfulness of the writing, but that it was years of rigorous and difficult thinking to get us to that writing and then to have it appear effortless. I try not to keep anything as a physical book that doesn't have weight for me, but there are certainly books on the shelf that were good books, but don't have that quality. I think you wrote one of the rare works of nonfiction, where that thoughtfulness is there, and it's also a thoughtfulness, as you so beautifully framed it, that is very generous toward the reader. I don't know if you could have done it without those years of work. It speaks to their importance—it's not wasted time.

I really appreciate that. That's the dream response—somebody reading the book and saying, "This feels like it's for me, it feels like it's challenging me, and I want to keep it around. I need to keep a copy of this book"—because I have my own versions of books that are as beloved to me as many of my friends. I just had a very good instinct as I was writing. If I have one actual skill or talent as a writer, it's an instinct about whether or not I've gotten deep enough into something yet. That's the one thing where I feel really proud of myself. I was writing all the time, and there were books I wrote that, luckily, I put on a shelf and didn't show anyone. There were stories that I wrote that I knew—I had this instinct—that I needed to think a little more about. Like, I need to read a little more, I need to work, I need to be in constant relation to my craft, but I'm not there yet. It's not deep enough yet. I don't think any of those years of studying were wasted.

I think there are a lot of other ways to go about those years of study or serious contemplation. I don't necessarily recommend doing all this academic work.

What was it like being within an academic program when everyone around you had a goal to become a professor? What were you doing? How are you interacting with your peers? And how did you express that to your adviser?

It's tricky because academic environments can be very competitive. There are a lot of egos, a lot of people are competing for extremely limited resources, and the job market is always terrible. There is also a culture of, if you're not giving every single ounce of your time and energy and intellect to this one teeny tiny question that will maybe be published in a journal that six people will read, you're a failure. There was some skepticism, especially in my PhD program, of me wanting to be a journalist, or because I was working at literary magazines, or I was going to literary events, or I was reading novels alongside reading Aristotle. You are not rewarded for having a wide range of interests, or having interests that are outside the narrow focus of academia. I survived because my deep curiosity is what I always lead with, and my curiosity is very genuine. There was never a class or a situation, or an assignment, or a reading, that I was dismissive of. I was always really open. I was like, "I'll read this, maybe I'll get an idea and it will make me a better writer." Or it would certainly make me a better thinker, and I was really willing to dive in. I think that people were sort of responsive to my positivity.

From having interviewed other folks on this, I think it's changing, but it hasn't changed fully.

It's funny. Now that the book has had some success or done well, all my old professors are like, "We knew you would do great!" And I'm like, "No, you thought I was weird, but that's okay." I thought about all my graduate degrees in terms of resources. I got fellowships, I got to teach through graduate teaching, so I got the experience that I wouldn't have gotten teaching in classrooms otherwise. I got health insurance, but I also got access to killer libraries, databases, and really brilliant people. I also took a lot of courses in other departments. I would pop over to the anthropology department and audit a class. I audited more classes in the literature department. I would meet professors of other disciplines and just get as much free knowledge acquisition as possible. I went to public universities. I was broke, but not going into debt. People can tell me I'm doing this wrong all they want. Go ahead! I'm just here to soak up all this knowledge, all these resources, and make my goals come into focus. I think that is one way to approach academia, especially if it's financially and logistically viable. You don't have to get a PhD and go be a professor, you can just get a PhD and be smarter, and have more time for yourself and then transition to some other greater things.

I know from reading your book that writing material that was so personal, and so self-revelatory, wasn't what you were interested in doing. During those long years of studying and thinking, you wanted to be a writer, you wanted to be a writer for a general audience. But what kind of writer were you thinking of being? What did you think those books would be?

At first, it was definitely just novels. Then I started doing culture writing and I thought that was fun because I had this background in the humanities. How I conceived of myself as a writer was: novelist, then critic, then art critic, then cultural critic. I ended up doing this piece about Ramsey Orta, who filmed the death of Eric Garner, and I wanted to use my research skills, because I had just acquired some to do investigative journalism. And I thought, Well, that's a nice third "orb" of work. None of this was, All right, I am going to write a deeply personal, revealing thing about my life and my body. But I think in those "orbs" of my literary conception of myself, all were leaning very heavily on what I saw as my intellectual strengths, which have been a source of great agency and gotten me very far in terms of my goals as a thinker and a writer. But that is also a space that rejects my body and the reality of my body in the world—it is a disembodied space. I had this sense that I wasn't being as truthful, that I wasn't going to the most dangerous places. I was staying in a safe zone. Doing the memoir writing was digging into more violent, uncomfortable, vulnerable spaces. I was avoiding it and knew that there was something more rich and urgent.

Now that you've gone to the rich, urgent place, and written this memoir that is personal and revelatory, how has that changed what you'd write next? Has that colored how you are going to do other pieces if at all, or other books?

I sold two more books, and I'm pretty deep into the second book. The second book has to go into a new, dangerous, urgent, uncomfortable space, and I think that it will. That's the new bar that has to be met on big projects. I'll take smaller projects that are easier—I'll do book reviews and journalism, things that don't make me feel like I'm ripping my guts out. The experience of writing *Easy Beauty* was one of trying to get into the darker or cloaked aspects of myself. We, as very complex human beings, have a lot of dark corners— and I don't mean dark as in bad, I just mean unexamined. This isn't easy, but sometimes the greatest moments of my happiness, I was distanced from and unexamined. With *Easy Beauty*—well, any good book has to narrow its focus—so I'm looking only at one little aspect of the self or the way that I'm processing a problem in the world. The other books have to also meet and clear that bar. They also have to clear the bar of: If I do this searching work, will it be relevant to anybody else? Because, at the end of the day, who cares about my unexamined areas? I care about that, and maybe my son cares, but nobody else really cares. Does this searching have something in it that feels like it's in a conversation with something universal, because the ick—I'll claim the ick that I feel—around memoir is that they're so profoundly inward looking, and they're not very outward looking. The inward looking and the outward looking have to be in direct relationship with each other so that I'm not wasting people's time with self-obsession or something like that.

I know you wrote books that never saw the light of day. Now that you have written a book that was successful, how do you determine if an idea is worthy of being a book? Now that you've done it, how do you carry that standard forward?

In any art form, there is a sense of discernment that tells us that what we are on to is worth cultivating. Artists should always be looking for what sharpens that discernment. I think the easiest place to start is to read as voraciously and widely as possible and do so with a deeply critical eye about what books have really stuck with you, challenged you, got in your guts. Then study those for no other reason than to sharpen discernment. That is the controllable thing that everybody who's writing can do. And reading very widely, with no snobbery—reading genres that you don't always read, reading criticism, reading from every time period. I have a Scrivener file where I write down everything I'm reading, with a list of notes about what I like about it, what I don't like, whose agent represented it, and getting a 360-degree view of what makes literature a part of the landscape.

The less discernible thing is that I have been good about being patient and waiting for questions or experiences that just won't go away. With the book that I'm writing now, it began with a painting that I saw in 2013. I had a very strong reaction to it and I read everything I could about the artist and the painting. I just had this instinct from a decade ago that I would write something about the painting, but I didn't know what it was. As a writer, essayist, and journalist, you might encounter twenty things a week that would make an essay, that could work, or could be cool, or you think that you should write about. But they go away and maybe you get it done, or maybe you don't. There is always a certain question that won't go away; that lives inside me, that is constantly screaming at me.

What you're describing is exactly what I've seen. Really successful, artistically successful, creatively fulfilling books come from a place of genuine curiosity and obsession. Often it's like, "Oh, my God, fuck! I don't want to write about this thing," or it feels like I can't handle it, or like, it'll ruin my life, but you can't look away from it. That's different from the authors who come at me with "These are ten book ideas, and they're all totally different." They just want to write a book for the sake of writing a book, which is never a reason to write a book.

That is why it was important to have an understanding of the publishing industry—the landscape, what people were interested in, what sold well, and didn't sell well. That was helpful knowledge, so I could enter this as a professional. That self—my professional self—I try to keep separate from this hungry animal writer-self. You absolutely can't write because you want some external thing, that you're chasing some trend, or you're chasing a publisher's interest, or you're chasing sales. You can't chase any externals. It's like, what is the animal thing in me that is just clawing at me and I can't look away? If I don't want to quit a minimum of ten times while doing a project that I'm working on, I know it's not good. I have to want to quit it. When I was writing *Easy Beauty,* I must have cried every other day while working on it. I would wonder, "Why am I doing this? I don't want to do this. This sucks. This is horrible. Can I get out of my contract?" I would work every day on it, but it felt deeply challenging. It also felt really essential that I stay in that uncomfortable, urgent, searching place and not worry about anything other than telling the best truth that I could tell; the most crucial truth that I could tell.

WHAT IS A PLATFORM AND HOW DO I DEFINE MINE?

If you haven't yet been introduced to the idea of "platform" in your book-world conversations, don't worry, you will. Much as I would like to, it's a word I can't escape. "Platform" is one of the things I get asked about most consistently when I give a talk or appear on a panel. It's usually in the form of the question, "How important is it to have one?" I suspect the hope behind the question is, "Please tell me it's not very important at all."

While I wish I could tell you, "No worries! Next chapter!" I'd be doing you a disservice. Platform *is* important, but I believe the reason it freaks out so many writers is that its meaning is often misconstrued. If you have been introduced to the word "platform," you may very well think it means a gigantic number of social media followers. This is a common misconception as well as something that seems impossible for the noncelebrities among us to achieve, not to mention irrelevant to the work of being a writer. Don't worry, I'm here to help you think more expansively. This miniguide is where I break down what platform does and doesn't mean, and how a platform—when considered creatively and holistically—is more obtainable than you might think.

By my own definition, **platform is publishing's vague and somewhat Orwellian term for an author's already-established means of (1) reaching their potential audience, and (2) persuading them to buy books.** At every stage of the publishing process, having an effective platform—and explaining it well—will make you more appealing to the professionals deciding whether or not they want to work with you. Your platform first comes into play when you begin querying agents—you'll be giving details about it in your book proposal. (Chapter 3 offers advice on how to do so.) Publishers will take your platform into consideration when they decide whether or not to make an offer on your book and, if they do, the size of the offer. It is fuel for your publicist's efforts in getting your book attention—a hard job in any scenario, but one that becomes a little easier if you already have an audience you're able to access and/or a widely recognized expertise. All this, in turn, translates into more readers for your book.

When aspiring book authors learn this, they are often filled with disappointment and dread: *I* have to bring readers to a *book publisher*? And it's true, publishing's interest in an author's platform can seem a little like David helping Goliath. The publisher has, presumably, millions of dollars' worth of resources. You, not so much. You might be wondering, "Why can't a publisher build my platform for me?"

The simple answer is that it is very, very hard to get attention for books. While publishers *do* have resources and will market and publicize you and your book in advance of its publication, there are practical and structural limitations to their abilities. (I'd also argue that you have resources they don't by nature of being an individual with talent and expertise, who is not a faceless corporation.) Some of these are shaped by the profound shifts we've seen in the media landscape over the past two decades. The rise of social media, the decline of book review sections and other book-focused media coverage, and the increasingly diffuse nature of traditional media (remember watching *60 Minutes* every Sunday night and eagerly awaiting *People*'s "50 Most Beautiful People" issue? If you are under thirty, probably not!) make it challenging even for major book publishers to get lots of eyeballs on all their many titles. It can also be challenging to get traditional media—book reviews, public radio, television, magazines—to pay attention to a book if the author is either entirely unknown or has no proven expertise on their subject. Meanwhile, the influence of social media means many people prefer to hear directly from authors rather than from an anonymous, monolithic corporation. (If you are on social media yourself, think about how many corporations you follow by choice and if you pay any mind to what they post. Would you really buy a book because Penguin Random House recommended it?)

There are also limits on what a book publication can do for

an unknown author in the short window of time a publisher has to devote to it. The work of a publisher's publicity and marketing departments for your book will start in earnest about six months to a year before your book comes out. (For more on this process and its timeline, see chapter 6.) But building a platform is a long game, and six to twelve months doesn't give publishers a lot of time to build recognition from scratch for each of their authors. In an ideal scenario, Goliath does help David, but David comes armed, ready, and with targets in mind. That's what makes him David.

I purposely left out any mention of social media when introducing the idea of "platform." Too many discussions of platform overemphasize it and end up being reductive and inaccurate as a result. While social media can play a role in establishing or defining a writer's platform, it is by no means the best measure of an author's potential audience or worth. Publishers know that. Jynne Dilling Martin, deputy publisher at Riverhead and former publicist, says, "Being good on social media is really not that important. To a point, maybe. Depending on what the book is, or if your presence is so compelling on it, that could be interesting information and additive, but it's not subtractive. [At Riverhead], we would never think, 'You're not on social media so we're not interested in your book.'" Riverhead is not alone in this. Nearly every editor and publicist I spoke with about platform defined it by saying it's *not* all about raw social media numbers. These definitions-via-negation show how widespread (and frustrating) the assumption that it's all about numbers can be, though it doesn't necessarily get us closer to understanding what platform *is*. That is in large part because the word contains so many different meanings.

Additionally, platform is not the be-all and end-all of how *every* book is marketed and promoted. Its importance varies greatly depending on the book's category and intended audience, so what makes for a good one varies too. Writing a lyrical literary memoir? Your voice and style will be key; any platform, if you have one, is just the cherry on top. Is your book journalistic? It helps if you are a journalist, even better if you're one at a well-known media outlet. Working in the lifestyle space—food, design, wellness? Platform, particularly social media, is central to your book's promotion as the audience for these topics follows social media quite closely. A celebrity memoir? I hope you are famous, the more so, the better. It will help you get on the *Today* show. A how-to book? With any book involving giving advice, having a strong platform as a nationally recognized expert is key. These are also instances where social media numbers are integral to the case an editor makes for acquisition and the kind of money they might be able to offer.

Thus, how publishing professionals think about platform often depends on their own areas of specialization. An agent who works on books about politics, activism, and public affairs told me, "When we talk about 'platform,' we are actually talking about community (or network, a word I like less well), i.e., who can you reach? The 'platform' piece of it is the how." (Note that she makes no mention of social media.) Another agent who works with a lot of TikTokkers, YouTubers, and influencers places more emphasis on social media in his definition, albeit in a nuanced way: "Platform is an author's ability to reach an engaged and enthusiastic audience, oftentimes an audience that *chooses* to consume the author's product. Huge Instagram numbers matter, but *engaged* Instagram numbers matter more. Patreon and newsletters have the highest engagement and subsequent sales returns." A fellow agent who specializes in memoir and creative nonfiction has a more fluid and personal understanding of it: "Platform is a combination of an author's existing audience, social media presence, publication history, and/or any relevant lived experience that makes them uniquely positioned to tell their story." So, when you think about publishing's understanding of platform, and how to build your own, look to your own category first. How did you first find out about the books and authors you love who write in the same genre as you? Other than in their books, where can you find their work? Are they on social media? If so, what is their social media like? How do they engage with their audience?

All this talk of public recognition, social media, and cultivating an audience gives authors (not unfairly) another reason to dread conversations about platform; it seems to have nothing to do with *you* and *your* ideas, with your talent and the quality of your work. "Can't I just write a great book?" you may ask. Yes, you can, and please do. And as any good agent, editor, or publicist will tell you, if a book isn't very good, being famous or having a ton of social media followers is no guarantee of a book's success. We all know plenty of cases of popular podcasters or influencers or even movie stars who got huge advances only to write mediocre books that no one bought because word quickly got around that the book was a boring cash grab. Sometimes the key plank of your platform *is* your amazing story or voice.

The expansiveness of platform as understood by publishers presents its challenges but also some opportunities. There are as many ways to build your platform—and to explain it to publishers—as there are ways to reach potential readers. Good book publicists know and embrace this. Michael Goldsmith, senior publicity director at Doubleday, says, "When I think about platform, it's a way of asking, what does the author bring to the table beyond the words on the page? And that might be a big social media following. That might be a broad professional network of people who are going to be helpful in supporting the book. That might be an interesting backstory or lived experience that is going to be helpful for a publicist in terms of crafting a narrative about why the book exists. I think that every author has a platform, whether they realize it or not. It's often up to a publisher to help them articulate what that platform is and the way that it's going to help them succeed."

•   •   •

Unfortunately both for you as someone looking for answers and for me as your guide, platform can't be reduced to "Do these three things to build a platform! Amass 100K Instagram followers in sixty days! Become a YouTube star!" As it turns out, something that seems like a calculation—the polar opposite of the magic of creative work—isn't so easy to pin down or capture in a one-size-fits-all guidebook. To make matters worse, given the ever-changing nature of both social and traditional media, platform is also ever changing. When I sold this book in fall 2022, X was still Twitter and navigating it to your advantage provided a good chunk of the material for my sample chapter on pitching articles and essays. While I was writing it, author newsletters, particularly Substack, rose in importance and at least a dozen media outlets shut down. Surely, in the year or so between the moment I deliver this book to my editor for publication and when it is available for sale, the media ground will once again shift in ways we never could have predicted.

Therefore, my approach here isn't to reveal the secrets to gain-ing social media followers (there are none, or at least I don't know them), but instead something more evergreen. I'll offer advice and examples from experienced hands—publicists, authors, editors, and agents—on ways to think about platform. I'll prompt you to look for and use the tools close at hand, to think about your abilities and inclinations, resources and relationships. Teach a writer to fish, and all that—though I'd give you the fish too, if I could. (Don't hoard your fish!) Part of the challenge of platform is delineating it—you'll have to explain yours in any book proposal you write and you may be called on to discuss it when meeting literary agents and editors. Instead of panicking at the thought, I am here to help you think through what you already have, and ideally, to build on it.

TEN WAYS TO THINK ABOUT PLATFORM

Your Professional and Personal Experiences Are the Foundation of Your Platform

Think about what a platform literally is: a place from which you speak. Sometimes that place is a physical or institutional designation—say, the university where you research or teach, the hospital where you practice medicine, the business you founded or developed, the newspaper or magazine for which you write, the agency from which you agent, the pulpit from which you preach (literally or metaphorically). Sometimes it is simply your job: You are a current or former veteran writing about your combat experience or a teacher writing about education or a sommelier writing about wine. Sometimes it is your education: your MFA, your journalism training, your doctoral work. All this experience forms your expertise and your authority, which is one component of your platform. You'll want to find ways to succinctly address it in your book proposal, as well as in any other pitches you make where it is relevant.

There may be institutional resources available for spreading the word about your work. Can your former or current place of work offer any support for your writing career and in building out your reach? For instance, does it have a newsletter or mailing list? Social media accounts? A lecture or reading series or opportunities for public speaking? Could it host a book event or panel? Or allow you to invite speakers in to visit, thus creating opportunities for you to network in your field? Can it cover your participation in professional conferences or workshops?

The same questions apply to any organizational relationships you may have outside work, from your alma mater, to your place of worship, to community groups. Any network you are already a part of can be put to good use supporting you, especially if you are offering something—a talk, a workshop, an event series, attention, and glory—in return. Institutions don't always publicize such resources, so you might need to shake some trees to get those peaches, but institutional or communal support is often easier than building something from scratch.

Show and Share Your Work

John Maas, editorial director at the literary agency Park & Fine, specializes in helping "experts"—largely health professionals and academics—develop their book proposals for sale to publishers. These are books that give advice, or what the publishing industry calls "prescriptive," a category that prioritizes platform. An author's platform is how Maas's agency finds many of their clients—they often directly solicit the people they end up repping rather than finding them through the slush pile. In order to do so, those authors need to be discoverable. Make yourself so. Maas advises, "For an academic, the writing that they're doing on their own isn't that important for how they're going to get their book in the marketplace. It is the other work they're doing. If they are researchers, is their research being published? If they are online, what are they saying on social media? Are they doing [traditional] media?" Publicizing your work might also mean sharing it with colleagues and friends who have a strong social media following, especially if you don't yourself.

Maas offers another important reason to share your work: "The more you get to know other people who are also trying to write books, regardless of category, the better it gets, because the publishing world is small. They are going to meet someone with an agent eventually, and that is important."

This advice applies to writers of all stripes. Don't be shy about telling people in your professional and personal networks about what you are working on and what you would like to publish, and, where appropriate, asking them to share it. This can be one of the best ways to spread the word about your writing and your work.

Pitch *Yourself* to Media

As I outlined in chapter 1, you can and should be pitching your own articles and essays directly to media outlets. You don't need an agent to do so. You also don't need an agent to pitch you to the media as an expert. (In fact, pitching you to the media is mostly not an agent's bailiwick.) If you are an expert in a given field, especially if it's a subject in the current news cycle, you can pitch yourself to the media directly to speak about it.

Your local public radio and public affairs shows are a great place to start, as are your local papers. Think about media outlets and formats that have a constant need for fresh content. Newspaper opinion columnists, both local and national, are under constant pressure to come up with fresh things to say about familiar topics. Same goes for hosts of popular podcasts and writers of popular newsletters.

So are more established writers who cover subjects you are interested in. Get to know the work of those who write about what you write about, and try to track down their contact information. Let them know about your own writing, research, or expertise. Let folks interested in similar topics know about you and your work, even if it's just through introducing yourself as a fan. The worst that could happen is you'll be ignored; at best, you'll make a new connection or even a friend.

If your workplace has a communications department, they may also be able to help you with pitching yourself; the same goes for many media outlets, which usually have a public relations department.

Anyone who worked with you on a piece of writing may also help you to publicize it. If you publish a piece that you think might interest public radio programs or podcasts, ask your editor if the publication has means to pitch you and plans to do so. If not, pitch yourself.

Specialization Can Be a Strength

Elyse Cheney, an agent who focuses on serious nonfiction, offers this advice: "Writers should try to establish authority in an area. It is not to say you can't be sort of catholic in your tastes, but it does really help if you have some specialty or zone that you're really, really familiar with. Once you become the authority on something, then as an agent I can say, 'Well, this person is *the* expert.' This doesn't mean you can't pursue your own intellectual or artistic interests; in fact, those interests can become the basis of your reputation and your work. It also needn't be an area of research like protozoa or the Balkans." Paraphrasing Johnny Cash, who famously claimed all his songs were about either love, God, or murder, Hanif Abdurraqib, whose work strikes most readers and reviewers as being remarkably wide-ranging, says it always comes back to his three recurring obsessions: grief, place, and devotion. I've never met a writer who thinks less about "platform" than Abdurraqib, despite having built such a loyal following, but this approach has clearly worked, both in terms of his productivity and in establishing the terms by which his work is understood. What might your Johnny Cash Three be?

Your Network Is Your Platform, So Build It

Lots of my clients are referrals, and the same holds true for many nonfiction agents. These referrals happen because a current client knows a prospective client's work and thinks I may like it. Sometimes these relationships happen because two writers were in the same graduate program or worked at the same magazine, but just as often it's because Person A reached out to Person B to say they like their work.

Platform includes the people you know, the ones who can refer you to agents and editors, who can blurb you or do an event with you. Knowing other writers is also a great way to learn about writing opportunities: fellowships and writers' residencies, which editors at which magazines are great to work with, newer agents looking to grow their clients list. Remember what Harrison Hill, the Columbia MFA grad introduced in chapter 1, said about his MFA experience:

He learned so much about pitching—how to do it and whom to pitch—while hanging out in front of the writing building talking to other students before class.

And don't be shy about introducing yourself to writers you admire, either online or at an IRL event. Then pay it forward for any writers who may introduce themselves to you.

Start Your Own Club

You can also solidify your connections with other writers through a writing group or some other more semiofficial means of staying in touch and offering mutual support. A group of (now quite successful) writers I know are in constant contact through their fantasy basketball league. They met before they became well established as writers, which makes it all the better. Their bonds grew over time and were strengthened over a shared love of poetry (and imaginary basketball teams). They continue to attend one another's events, read one another's work, promote one another's publications online, blurb one another's books, officiate one another's weddings. Their respective platforms couldn't be reduced to each one's individual social media following or reputation as they are constantly helping one another out and multiplying one another's efforts. A grad school friend of mine joined an informal writers' group while we were both avoiding writing our doctoral dissertations. His writers' group was a crucial means of emotional and professional support as he tried to make the difficult transition out of academia and into a full-time writing career. Reader, he succeeded, though perhaps the *most* successful member of his group was a woman named "Nora," better known now as N. K. Jemisin.

Don't Be Afraid to Strategically Self-Publish

Pitching and placing your work is a great means to build name recognition (which is another form of platform), but you can also take charge of the means of your own production. Per John Maas, aspiring authors "shouldn't be afraid of self-publishing. In the world of prescriptive nonfiction, there's no stigma. It is such a valuable tool, because if you self-publish, you're going to learn a lot. It's also going to give you a reason to get in touch with people. If you are self-publishing a book, even if you are just promoting it through your network, you're doing it through the work you already do, you're going to go to conferences, you're going to speak, you're going to meet the other authors who are speaking, you're going to solicit endorsements, you can reach out to people that you otherwise would have no reason to reach out to."

Self-publishing is a particularly good option if there is a topic you want to address that doesn't lend itself to the full-length book treatment. This is especially true in the prescriptive/how-to space; think handbook or pamphlet, not chapters and chapters. As Maas explains, "If you have something really niche that you know needs to be out there, that's a great thing to self-publish. For a personal development person, it may be a very specific journal. For a health person, a very specific condition that they want to share their knowledge about." Doing so can help you establish your expertise and gain you an audience for a longer project.

Starting your own newsletter is another form of self-publishing and can be a great way to become known for your expertise. Leigh Stein, the novelist who also works as a career coach for writers, launched her Substack to promote and expand upon her career-coaching business. She describes the newsletter as "the place where creative writers can find honest advice about making a career on the internet" and suggests that "you think about your content strategy and your one-liner description of what you're doing on the internet as 'where *blank* can find blank.'" Social media can feel less intimidating when you think of it as a means of self-publishing rather than just a tool for self-promotion.

Several of the writers profiled in this book published their work via literary journals they started with friends (Keith Gessen with *n+1;* Vann Newkirk with *Seven Scribes,* which was also the outlet where Hanif Abdurraqib first published his work via an online friendship with another cofounder). You don't need the green light of traditional media or publishing to successfully publish your work or to gain an audience for it.

Work Locally

Seek out the writing communities, resources, and elders close to home. (In the previous chapter, the story of Hanif Abdurraqib's and Isaac Fitzgerald's early careers gives some good examples on how to do so.) Go to your local readings, take a local class, or perhaps set up a writing group or reading series of your own. Meet writers who live in your area or come to town on a book tour. Research to see if there are literary journals or independent publishers in your area.

Unlike the Big Five publishers we'll discuss in chapter 5, many indie book publishers are based outside New York and seek to publish writers from their own geographic region. Some also consider unagented submissions. The Community of Literary Magazines and Presses (CLMP) maintains an extensive directory of independent book publishers and their submission guidelines.

Effective Social Media Isn't Built Around Self-Promotion

While social media can be an excellent tool for promoting your own work, if you use it only to share your own work and accomplishments, no one will want to follow you. This doesn't mean you need to "tweet about what you had for lunch," a phrase I hear every time someone wants you to know they are too high-minded to spend time on social media. (If they actually did, they'd know social media is low on lunch pics and full of folks providing interior monologues for their pets, and I thank them for it.) Effective social media is like any good writing: It's entertaining or smart or even moving on its own terms and within its own format. As Leigh Stein explains in her newsletter, "I think what I'm getting better at all the time, through running experiments, is creating content that is meaningful, and entertaining, to the readers who will buy my books—my backlist, like *Self Care,* and my novels in the future—so that I can continue working as a novelist." Stein saw her social media engagement improve, and her book sales increase, when she started to create content that was fun in and of itself. Of course, it helps that she's funny (and not incidentally, she writes satirical novels), which means parody videos play to her strengths as a writer.

If you want to try building an audience on social media, I'd advise you to think about your own strengths and interests as a writer and what you can offer via its formats. You can push yourself to try new things, and push yourself to stick with it for a bit, but you don't need to become the lunch-posting, oversharing, wannabe influencer you're not. That will make you miserable, and also won't lead to any real engagement or fans. A better example is pop-science writer Cody Cassidy, author of books like *How to Survive History* and *Who Ate the First Oyster?* His books are mock instructionals drawing from the history of science, as entertaining as they are informative. At his publisher's suggestion, Cassidy started making humorous science tutorials on TikTok on subjects like "How to Run from Pompeii" and "How the Polynesians Discovered Hawaii." Much to his surprise (and his publisher's delight), he soon raked up hundreds of thousands of views, which in turn increased book sales.

Great Writing Makes for a Great Platform

Nobody goes into publishing because it was their life's dream to talk about platform all day, and no reader's passion is ignited by an author's fame. Platform is simply a means to get attention and build an audience, and in the best-case scenario, great writing is as well. One final word from Michael Goldsmith:

> I'm working with a debut memoirist. She doesn't really have a lot of professional writing experience in a media or journalism sense. This is her first book. She hasn't published very much journalism. And I am getting more enthusiasm and excitement in my pitches for her than almost any other nonfiction book on my list right now because I think the book is wonderful. And it is such an awesome embodiment of her real, lived experience. In a way, she's bringing a platform of a rich personal life, that sort of thing made with honesty and with vulnerability. It's just so rare. I think that falls very much within the sort of parameters of a platform, right? Someone who is able to translate their own life into an empathetic reading experience, and someone who's willing to share that publicly, that, to me is as valuable, if not

more valuable of a platform, than the author who is a journalist, who's reporting on other people's lives, who has a lot of professional credentials or a really robust professional network. Those two platforms look very different. But they're both incredibly valuable in different ways.

I love the book and it's lining up to have one of those fantastic campaigns. We're going to have the profile and the personal essay and the national broadcast media. I think her platform is her honesty, her courage, her willingness to be vulnerable. And those are huge, huge assets.

The book, *More,* by Molly Roden Winter, went on to be a *New York Times* bestseller.

CHAPTER 3

THE BOOK PROPOSAL, OR DON'T BE BORING

Poor little book proposals. They are so unloved. Some writers like writing; some writers like having written; no writers like writing book proposals. I have two pieces of comfort to offer. First, in feeling overwhelmed and frustrated by the prospect of writing a book proposal, you're in excellent company. I'd happily take a bet that the writer of your all-time favorite nonfiction book hated writing theirs too, complained to spouses and friends, lamented the quirks of the genre and the requirement to write one to get a book published. Second, by understanding how book proposals are actually read, circulated, and considered by agents and publishers, the process becomes far less intimidating and much more manageable. The proposal itself is a kind of map of what your book will be, with the absurd quirk that you are drawing this map for others without having taken the trip yourself. The good news is that the path to writing a book proposal is well trodden; knowing its topography, on which I'll be your guide, will help you figure how to traverse it yourself.

A book proposal has an aim that makes it different from almost anything else you write—which is to sell that very writing. You are conveying information about yourself and your book, ideally in a compelling manner, while also creating a selling document. Most books or long-form articles don't also contain a pitch for said book or article. There is a self-aware quality to book proposals that isn't a feature in other nonfiction: Proposals give you the story, but also signpost why the story matters, and why the person (you) writing it is uniquely qualified to tell it. Balancing the "selling" apparatus of the book proposal—the pitching, the positioning of the book, and the market, and of your own bona fides—with the actual content of the book would be a challenge for any writer. First drafts of book proposals almost invariably get this balance wrong.

But first, the answer to one of the top ten questions I get asked: Do I *have* to write a book proposal? Unless you're Beyoncé—and if so, thank you for reading my book, and also for *Lemonade,* which got me through my divorce—the answer is yes. **The majority of nonfiction books, particularly those that require any research and reporting, are sold to publishers on proposals, often, but not always, with a sample chapter.** This is the polar opposite of fiction, where you almost always need a full manuscript to sell your book to a publisher. If your follow-up question is why *can't* you just go ahead and write the damn book, my answer is that I'm not going to stop you—but you'd be going well beyond the requirements and the preferences of agents and publishers if you choose to do so. If there's good news in this, it's that you don't need to write a full manuscript to sell a book or to get an agent. In fact, a full manuscript is neither expected nor even desirable for most nonfiction.

Knowing how the book proposal fits into the publishing pipeline will make it easier to tackle. If you are reading this and are ready to write a nonfiction book but don't yet have an agent or any connections to one, your first step in getting one is to write a book proposal and use it to query them. Of course, you'll want to check each agency's respective submission guidelines first: Some don't want to see unsolicited materials and prefer you send just a pitch. Others ask that you pitch with a proposal and a sample chapter included. In any case, once an agent is interested, they will want to see your proposal and, most likely, a sample chapter. If you are already a well-established writer with lots of clips, you can sometimes get away with a short synopsis instead of a full proposal. In most cases, though, you'll want to have that proposal ready to submit.

Once you start working with an agent, the process of finalizing a proposal is often—even ideally—quite collaborative. To steal (with permission) a handy analogy from Elyse Cheney, a literary agent working on nonfiction is both "architect and broker." The brokering is what you see on television—all imperious telephone calls and statement jewelry—but helping to craft the foundations of a book is an equally important feature of the job. Proposal writing lends itself to exactly this sort of collaboration, so be prepared for and open to it. You might be offended (or think, "Haven't I done *enough*?") but know that an agent gives these suggestions because they *want* to be editorially involved, and doing so shows their intellectual engagement with your work. They may also be providing these suggestions to make the book more marketable to publishers, and understanding that sort of positioning is part of an agent's job. Rest assured that you certainly don't have to take all or even any suggested changes. These conversations, though, are almost never not worth having, so if an agent expresses interest but "wants to chat about some editorial suggestions," take that call! If you are lucky enough to choose between agents, hearing their different takes on your proposal will help you figure out if you have a shared vision of what your book could be and if you are on the same page editorially. The more fleshed out your proposal, the better you will understand your own project, and the richer and more substantive those editorial conversations will be.

When you and your agent are both satisfied with your draft of the proposal, it will then go on submission to publishers, that is, sending it to editors at publishing houses to consider (for more granular detail on this, head over to chapter 5, on the submission process). The submission of your proposal by your agent to editors will result in even more editorial conversations, especially if you have more than one publisher interested in your work. In each of these instances, you might get radically different takes on the book you are proposing. This is in part the beauty, and the risk, of our current system of selling nonfiction books in this way. Because a book proposal is essentially just a blueprint for a book, anyone who reads it can then think of different ways to put on an addition, or to knock out a wing, or sometimes, to make a ranch into a colonial. In this way, the creation of a nonfiction book is unusually collaborative. The germ of an idea will go through multiple readers, all of whom give feedback, as it develops into a finished book. Sometimes the editorial feedback involves a full overhaul. To extend Cheney's architectural metaphor, sometimes you think you have the blueprint for a bungalow, but someone (an editor, an agent, or both) says that while it's currently just a pool house, if we do this, this, and this to it, you might just end up with Fallingwater. That kind of editorial magic is the best sort of lightning strike, and its possibility speaks to what a proposal can do: find you great editorial and publishing partners to help you figure out the best version of your book.

Before we get into the actual structure of the proposal, I want to zoom out and address the questions it's supposed to answer. These questions are there to help you figure out what should go into a proposal, but I also include them because the actual form of a proposal isn't set in stone. All agents direct their authors to write them a little bit differently. I'll include advice from multiple agents and editors in this chapter, though the formats and methods I suggest are my preferred ones. But if you successfully answer these questions, regardless of the precise format, your proposal will fulfill its aims:

- First, what, precisely, is the book? (the "Publisher's Paragraphs," term my own)
- Why should we care? (the Publisher's Paragraphs)
- How will the subject sustain itself over the course of 70,000–100,000 words? (the Publisher's Paragraphs; the chapter summaries)
- Are you qualified to write it, and if so, why? (the About the Author section)
- Who are the potential readers of the book? (the Dreaded Marketing Section)
- How will the book unfold? (the chapter summaries)
- And throughout every section, you'll be answering the question on every reader's mind: What is your writing like? (the whole damn thing)

Let's start with a means of answering that final question, which will also help you kick off the proposal.

WHAT IS YOUR WRITING LIKE?

The most common way that most first-time book-proposal writers fall short is by falling flat, usually by focusing solely on the expository requirements of a book proposal and then creating a document that just isn't interesting to read. I call this method "Death by Power-

Point," and I blame Google. If you search sample book proposals on the internet, you'll find a lot of formulaic advice along with dry sample proposals with even drier "marketing" or "platform" sections, often involving bullet points and statistics. Despite what the internet tells you, this is not the most successful approach to getting an agent's, and eventually an editor's, attention. A book proposal is a selling device, but it's not an ad campaign for homeowner's insurance. Always keep in mind that the thing you are trying to sell is a piece of writing, and thus **the proposal can and should be as interesting and engaging as the book itself.** This is something I hear from editors again and again. Per Denise Oswald, editorial director of Pantheon (and my editor), "Buying on proposal is a leap of faith for the editor and everyone above and around that editor and needs to be rallied to the cause to green-light an offer. If the proposal is not compellingly written, it's then hard to believe the final book will be, or that the author will be able to find a way through any aspects of the proposal that are not currently working." Per Andrew Miller, publisher of Holt (though we chatted while he was still in his role as an executive editor at Knopf and editorial director of nonfiction), "The best proposals are ones that feel like pieces of writing themselves." From Yaniv Soha, an executive editor at Atria who specializes in nonfiction, "If it's not well written, I can't really get anywhere with it." From Tom Mayer, executive editor at Norton, "A proposal as a business pitch deck is not appealing to me." And from Chris Jackson, the publisher of One World and its editor in chief, some characteristically candid advice: "Don't be boring."

Like so much of the proposal-writing process, this might seem counterintuitive. Because submitting a proposal feels a bit like sending in a CV, you may feel you need to be as formulaic as possible. That approach feels safe and perhaps appropriate—you are, in a sense, "applying" for the job of being a writer. But a proposal is a job application in the same way that an audition is. You're showing you're qualified for the job by doing a distilled version of it and giving a taste of the finished product—the actual book—in the process. This chapter will guide you through how to make every section of your proposal interesting—even the Dreaded Marketing Section, even the awkward author bio—and will liberate you from the PowerPoint approach to nonfiction proposal writing.

HOW TO OPEN THE PROPOSAL

Option #1: A Mini Sample

I'll be giving advice and sharing examples of how to use the proposal to showcase your own voice, even while drafting its drier bits on audience and bona fides, but you can be juiciest and most voice driven at the top. I often advise writers to open their proposals not with a description or synopsis of the book, which is the format you usually see when you google "book proposal," but with a mini-scene or sample from the book itself. This suggestion elicits the most surprise and then relief when I share it at writers' conferences: **You don't need to open your book proposal with a summary of your book. You can open it with a short sample scene instead**—a "teaser" of your writing style, as Elyse Cheney calls it.

Surprise and relief, but also disbelief. I get to do that? Isn't that cheating? You can, it's not, and, in fact, it can be both generative to you and very effective in selling your book. The proof? It's the method I use that has produced the most quantifiable success, eliciting competitive offers again and again. To see how this is done, here are the opening paragraphs from a book proposal by my client Caitlin Dickerson, a staff writer at *The Atlantic* and winner of the Pulitzer Prize, working on a book about deportation. The 850-word opening sample scene is not a description of the book itself—she does that later in the proposal—but it does foreshadow many of the proposed book's themes while also showcasing Dickerson's writing style:

Two hours southeast of Atlanta, near the border with Alabama, surrounded by acres of pine trees that sprawl across the hilly landscape in every direction, lies the town of Lumpkin, Georgia. It has only a couple of restaurants, no hotels, and importantly, no lawyers. Lumpkin is home to little more than a factory that churns day and night, but it is not the kind that produces garments or canned goods. Instead, the factory processes people born outside the United States. Thousands of men are detained here at any given time, sent from all over the country to be deported, leaving bereft spouses, children, and grandchildren in their wake.

Once the men arrive in Lumpkin, they are rushed through a legal process that has been so thoroughly stripped of the rights and protections afforded to criminal defendants under the American Constitution that it can hardly be called legal at all. In the beige, windowless courtroom attached to the immigration detention center, few defendants are represented by lawyers and the statistical likelihood of winning out against a government prosecutor is next to nil. Judges dole out deportation orders in the monotone drawl of someone who may not have bothered to review the evidence before them. As soon as a detainee's fate is decided, he is led in shackles onto a bus and then flown far away. He is replaced within hours by a newcomer who will clutch the same filthy pay phone and pay two dollars a minute to say goodbye to loved ones whom he may never see again—and if he does, whose lives will have been irrevocably harmed by his prolonged absence.

The fact that this process often plays out in rural facilities that are hundreds of miles from public view makes it easy to ignore. And though one might like to blame heartless or hawkish politicians for its existence, in reality, the process is part of a system to which all Americans contribute and from which we reap benefits. Detention facilities like the one in Lumpkin are full of people who have spent years, if not decades, picking, processing, and delivering essential goods to American households both Democrat and Republican, while also supporting their own families. And though their labor, often unseen, supports our economy by keeping the prices of goods and services low, they are banished to places like Lumpkin under policies that are written to appeal to voters rather than to acknowledge reality, or to actually work. Despite what our laws claim, our insatiable and unacknowledged appetite for cheap labor can be satisfied only by a population that is willing to work for illegally low wages, and to endure abuses in silence because of the ever-present fear of deportation. These individuals, 98 percent of whom are nonwhite, are often employed within days of their arrival in the United States, if not recruited for their positions before leaving home. Some will inevitably be deported, ensuring that the cycle continues.

Good, right? Let's break down *why* it's good.

Starting with this sample scene grabs a reader's attention more readily than a book summary would; the narrative approach does a lot of work in a short space. Dickerson opens the proposal in rural Georgia. This setting supports the arguments she'll make further down: that deportation affects all America, not just urban centers; that undocumented workers can be found in every corner of our country; and that both their labor and their treatment are often kept out of sight. It also allows her to quickly show she can write descriptively of place, which will be essential in a book that features a range of distinct communities across the country. The obscure nature of the facility highlights one of Dickerson's strengths—her dogged pursuit of stories that are difficult to crack. Dickerson then uses metaphorical language to hint at her argument:

> Lumpkin is home to little more than a factory that churns day and night, but it is not the kind that produces garments or canned goods. Instead, the factory processes people born outside the United States. Thousands of men are detained here at any given time, sent from all over the country to be deported, leaving bereft spouses, children, and grandchildren in their wake.

Comparing the detention and the deportation center to a factory not only recalls the setting where many immigrants work, it also allows Dickerson to hint at the dehumanizing approach to deportation proceedings without editorializing.

The second paragraph is largely explanatory. Dickerson wants to show how the system that undergirds much of American life but remains out of view actually works. She also wants to convince her initial readers—in this case, publishers she hopes will bid on her book—that she can relay bureaucratic detail and educate readers on its salient features without getting bogged down. The quick courtroom scene accomplishes this, while also underscoring the point that deportation happens with brutal speed—one paragraph, out of the country.

In the third paragraph, Dickerson lays her cards on the table, previewing the argument of her book while also making clear that it is the sort of book that will advance a case. In the paragraphs that follow, Dickerson introduces a father who was detained in Lumpkin and faces deportation and gives a brief sketch of his backstory. While the eventual book will be making a clear argument—that our deportation system is pervasive, inefficient, and unjust, and all American lives are touched by it—her approach, like this sample, will do so both through argument *and* characters. In other words, in just four paragraphs, Dickerson shows, rather than tells, how her book will work: It'll be descriptive and character driven, though in service of advancing an argument and explaining how an underreported and widely misunderstood part of American society actually works.

The opening teaser approach needn't include all these elements; its primary purpose is to be an engaging piece of writing and representative of your book's themes and approach. The opening of John Donvan and Caren Zucker's proposal for their book *In a Different Key: A History of Autism* is almost entirely narrative. In the original proposal, it was over two thousand words, which is relatively long. In it, they presented two different scenes, each one of the earliest diagnosed cases of autism. Here is a short snippet from the very first paragraphs:

> She only knew he was blind. That's what the ad in the back of the newspaper had said. "Blind Child Slow Learner." The word "autism" wasn't mentioned. Not that it would have meant anything to Alice Gibson, who also had no notion at all of adopting a child when she'd picked up the paper that morning to keep some brief company with her coffee. But then she'd reached the back pages, and the boy's photo caught her eye, as it was meant to.
>
> It was 1970, an era when adoption agencies still routinely bought ad space, much as animal shelters still do today, to hook some soul sympathetic enough to take in those big eyes and read that sad story and then upend their lives by taking an unknown into their homes. "Blind Child Slow Learner." It parsed like a traffic sign. But on Alice, it worked like an incantation. "What do you think?" she asked her husband, George, who immediately raised an eyebrow. Then he saw she was serious.
>
> Maybe it was the utterly fluky fact that Alice knew Braille.

In the late 1960s, purely for the novelty of it, she'd set out to become a fluent reader of Braille. She took classes, acquired a Braille-imprinting machine, and joined a group of volunteers who translated schoolbooks into those ingenious readable bumps on a page. Though her skills were still only rudimentary, she could suddenly see herself teaching this young boy to read, opening his life to books and much more. She liked the picture that made—she'd be Anne Sullivan teaching Helen Keller in *The Miracle Worker*.

"So how much of a slow learner is this little boy?" Alice asked the agency woman in that first phone call. There was a pause, a silence sounding wrapped in reluctance. "Actually," the woman finally puffed out, as though expecting the conversation would be winding up shortly, "he's kind of retarded." Actually, he wasn't. But very likely she didn't know that herself. Indeed six-year-old Frankie, parentless in Santa Maria, some sixty miles away from their home in Santa Barbara, was attending a class with other "slow learners." Officially, he was labeled "TMR." Trainable Mentally Retarded.

But Alice hadn't hung up yet, and the social services woman took that as a cue to push. "Just come up and meet him," she urged, "and then we can talk about it."

Donvan and Zucker's book, which went on to be a *New York Times* bestseller and a finalist for the Pulitzer Prize in General Nonfiction, is a narrative history of autism. Both were journalists for ABC News, and as its reviewers noted, the book's storytelling reflects their training and cinematic sensibilities. It's dramatic and accessible, alternating between intimate close-ups of the book's main characters and zooming out to give historical and social context. Many of the stories and cases the book covers are presented, like the one here, as medical mysteries waiting to be solved. The opening scene of the proposal, with its compassionate portrayal of an adoptive mother and the mysterious child in need at its center, demonstrates Donvan and Zucker's approach. While the material is often serious, and at times heartbreaking, they lead the reader through it by presenting sympathetic characters and using suspense wherever possible.

In picking an opening scene, I often suggest my writers imagine pushing off the wall of a pool to swim a lap. The scene is that wall: choose material that will give you momentum to power the rest of your proposal, that demonstrates your strengths as a writer, and that sets up your book's thematic concerns. As for the oft-voiced fear of giving too much away, if there is ever a time to hide your light under a bushel, this is not it. Keep in mind why you tasked yourself with writing a book proposal in the first place: You want to sell a book, and in order to do so, you need to interest buyers. In the early stages of book writing, which is likely when you'll be crafting the proposal, great scenes might feel scarce, a little pearl pried from an oyster shell, in need of careful guarding. You're just at the beginning, though, and need to trust in yourself that there will be more pearls to come as you write and research your book. For the time being, do what you need to do to make sure your submission includes the best material you can pull together given what you know now. This will put you in the strongest position to find a great agent and a great editor.

(For more on how much sample material to include in a submission, regardless of where you might place it, skip ahead to "On Sample Material" on page 129.)

Option #2: Start with the Pitch

A sample scene is my go-to way to start a proposal, but it's not the only one, nor is it always the best fit. You can eschew the above and simply start with the pitch for the book. This is the most common method for prescriptive books—that is, books like this one that give you advice, tell you how to do something, or help you to identify and address a problem—and especially books on health, business, and self-help. (Not sure if your book falls into this category? Take a look at *The New York Times*' bestseller list and see how it divides nonfiction books into three camps: "Nonfiction," which is the first list you'll see; "Advice, How-to, Miscellaneous"; and "Business." On which of these three lists would your book be most at home?) This is also the approach you most often see when you google "how to write a book proposal," particularly because those online sample proposals tend to skew prescriptive.

This approach cuts more quickly to the chase but works best if it has a few "teaser" lines as well, setting the reader up to hear what,

precisely, the book is about. A good example of this are the two opening paragraphs from the proposal for *The Postpartum Human* by Ruth
E. Macy and Courtney Naliboff, a guidebook for the postpartum
period, sold by my colleague Anna Worrall at auction, and ultimately
titled *Your Postpartum Body:*

What should you expect when you're *done* expecting? Pregnant
people have access to abundant information about their bodies. They know what fruit to compare their growing fetus to,
the importance of prenatal vitamins, how their internal organs
are moving around to make room for an expanding uterus, and
how to write a birth plan. But once they are no longer pregnant,
the focus shifts abruptly to the baby. Books abound with information about infant growth and development, baby sleep, baby
eating, baby swaddling, and baby language. But what about the
birth parent's body and postpartum healing needs? Currently,
there is no book on the market that offers practical physical
steps you can use to heal your postpartum body from a medical,
evidence-based approach.

Postpartum people are often resigned to the fact that they pee
when they sneeze, their abdomens bulge, and their backs ache.
They may not know that they have a pelvic floor, let alone that
it may be injured or have dysfunction, and what to do about it.
They may not know which postpartum changes will heal without intervention, and which won't. They may be blindsided by
the physical and hormonal changes caused by lactation or wean-
ing, feel unable to return to intercourse with their partner, or
not understand their mental health needs. A lack of information and access to informed healthcare has led society to accept
these and other dysfunctions as the price paid for pregnancy.
The Postpartum Human gives readers the tools they need to
access information and techniques to fully heal and find func-
tional fitness in their postpartum bodies. Centralized access to
a book that covers a full spectrum of postpartum healing needs,
regardless of the method of delivery or cessation of pregnancy, is
absolutely necessary in a country where the average American is
not provided with free healthcare and cannot access affordable
healthcare. Nearly 40 percent of Americans are unable to afford

a four-hundred-dollar emergency, the equivalent of one to three pelvic floor physical therapy visits. This book can bridge a post-partum healing accessibility and equity gap for many people.

Like all good pitches, these opening paragraphs give a clear sense of what the book is about while also making clear why it's important. From the very first line, which references the most famous and best-selling pregnancy guide on the market, they suggest what sets this book apart and, without getting too into the weeds, give an overview of what the book will cover. They're also not without style—note, for example, the rhythmic repetition of the word "baby" in the first paragraph. They communicate, too, a sense of mission, always a per-suasive thing to see in a book proposal and particularly important in pitching a prescriptive project or one that aims to teach something. As Niki Papadopoulos, editor in chief of Portfolio, an imprint of Pen-guin Random House that focuses on business titles and prescriptive nonfiction, says, "I wish more potential authors thought about what they were doing as a service to others, and thought about the value that they are creating for others, and focused on that. Having that is the best compass you can have as a nonfiction author." It's also an excellent one for a publisher, and hearing yours can be galvanizing for anyone considering your book.

No matter your book's category—prescriptive, narrative, polemi-cal, all of the above—your proposal will need to include your pitch for it early on in its pages. While proposals are adaptable recipes—and my aim here is to teach you the basics so you can riff if you like—your pitch for the book is the key ingredient you can't leave out. Let's get into more detail on how to write a good one.

PERHAPS YOU SHOULDN'T WRITE YOUR OWN BOOK PROPOSAL (OR YOUR OWN BOOK)

Not all authors are writers, especially in the nonfiction category. How could this be so? The broad category of nonfiction includes many books authored by experts in their fields—academics, medical professionals, mental health experts, and personal finance and business gurus, among innumerable others. Top-selling (and beloved) memoirs are often authored by nonwriters who happened to have lived through something extraordinary. In short, these are books by people whose primary (or secondary or even tertiary) goal isn't becoming a "writer" and whose primary (or secondary—you get the point) passion or interest isn't "putting words on a page in a meaningful way" and then doing that again and again over the course of many pages and many years.

Or let's say you are not professionalized as a writer—no problem, this book is for you!—but you also have no interest in becoming one. You *do* want to share important information or a meaningful personal story, but you have otherwise never been someone who wanted to write or felt any interest in doing so, even (or especially) if you are not being paid for it. If this description applies to you, that does not mean you don't have an amazing book in you or something valuable to share. You are clearly motivated enough to have gotten this far in your research. It might mean, however, that you need some help of the professional variety beyond what this publishing guide can offer you.

When someone has a great book idea—say, a remarkable personal story or impressive expertise—it can be awkward, at least from my end, to tell them they aren't, in fact, "qualified" to write it. I suspect this awkwardness comes from a number of things: A lot of people are simultaneously insecure about their own writing while being convinced if given the time, they could, in fact, write a book. I mean, we *all* write, often several times a day— emails, texts, tweets, holiday cards. This doesn't mean, however, that someone who can write a zinger of a Yelp review is the person best suited to be the writer of their own book.

I hate when I have to give this advice. My natural tendency is to tell people they *can* do it (whatever "it" happens to be) and to make the world of books more inclusive. But I have also seen many people with fabulous books in them crash on the shoals of writing a book proposal because, despite their bookworthy story or idea or expertise, they are not, in fact, a professional writer. To help you avoid this problem, I turn to Karen Rinaldi, founder and former publisher at Harper Wave, an imprint focused on health, wellness, and lifestyle books and also an author herself. The authors of the books Rinaldi publishes are often not the primary *writers* of those books, but they are typically experts in their fields. Fittingly, Rinaldi frames the decision of whether or not to hire a cowriter in terms of expertise: "I've published a lot in the space of neuroscience. I know where the different parts of the brain are—the prefrontal cortex, the amygdala, the pituitary gland, etc. I've read and edited a lot of books on the subject, so . . . I think I'd like to do some brain surgery. And I don't see why someone shouldn't let me do that! Why can't I just walk into a hospital operating theater and be given a scalpel? Because even though I know something about neuroscience and the brain, there's no expectation that I would be able to do brain surgery. It's the same thing with writing a book. There is no expectation that you can and should be able to write a book, even if you are a prolific reader and a person who occasionally writes. You shouldn't take it as an insult."

If you think you'd like to work with a collaborator, bringing one in at the proposal stage is a good time to do so. You will have a stronger proposal for it, thus a better shot at getting an agent's attention and, eventually, getting a publisher's. Hiring someone to work on the proposal can also be a trial run for the possibility of extending that relationship further to working on your eventual book together. You don't necessarily have to retain the same writer for both jobs, especially if your initial collaboration is less than ideal. You do need to pay for this service, regardless of whether or not your book sells. As of this writing, the fees for writing a proposal can range from mid four to low five figures. Paying for a collaborator for a full book will cost significantly more. Per the most recent coverage in Publishers Marketplace, fees start at around $40,000 for a full manuscript to $300,000 if you are hiring an elite cowriter who has written multiple high-profile bestsellers. In looking for a collaborator, target writers who have experience in your category and are willing to provide references.

WHAT, PRECISELY, IS THE BOOK?

Take the suggestion that you begin your proposal with a narrative scene in the spirit of "why not?" While it can help you to find the voice and spirit of the book and, if done well, increase the interest of publishers, it's certainly not an essential component of a proposal nor the only way to do one. Try it, and if it doesn't work, you didn't waste your time. File away the material for your sample chapter or the book itself.

What *is* essential are the one to three paragraphs I suggest you include right after that narrative opening, or if you are skipping the narrative opening, right at the top. If you have opted to begin your proposal with Option #2, you have essentially already written this part. Read on to make these paragraphs as effective as possible. No matter how you construct or order it, no matter what you include or leave out, any publishing professional who reads your proposal will eventually ask the same question: *What, precisely, is the book?* The paragraph or paragraphs where you answer this are the most important ones in your proposal.

Let me break down this crucial part of the proposal. When you're writing the Publisher's Paragraphs, think of the journey your proposal will go on after it leaves your desk. Stop 1 is the agent. Stop 2 is the individual editor interested in acquiring it, who will in turn share it with colleagues to read and evaluate. This group is Stop 3 and might include the heads of marketing and publicity, and the editorial director or editor in chief of the imprint. They'll read it as publishing generalists, not category or subject-matter experts. Andrew Miller describes these two forms of reading: "When it's not for yourself, you can read a submission on its own terms a little bit more, because you don't feel like you have to make a decision at the end. You don't feel like you have to make that decision on every paragraph. And there's a clarity that comes with that." As you work on your proposal, keep in mind these two layers of readers: the initial one evaluating it closely from the front row and the others reading it subsequently (and likely much more quickly) from the cheap seats. Your proposal needs to land with both.

Among these secondary readers at the publishing house, one looms above all the rest: the publisher, i.e., Stop 4. The publisher is where the buck literally stops, because she is, among other duties, in charge of the money. Her many burdens include walking around with a confusing job title. The word "publisher" indicates both the business entity that publishes books (e.g., Penguin Random House, as well as the imprints that operate as distinct lines within Penguin Random House, such as Riverhead, Crown, and Knopf) and *also* the person in charge of each respective imprint. So, we use the word "publisher" to designate both the business entity that produces books and the person who runs that entity. A kind of job-as-metonym, the person *is* the business they are tasked with running.

For purposes of the proposal, put yourself in the shoes of that person. Their purview is quite wide: oversight of all the books published on a particular list, management of the people who work on them, big-picture publicity, marketing and sales, and above all, profitability. This keeps them busy. They spend much of the day in meetings, and while they likely got into publishing because they love books (I've yet to meet someone who did it for the money or the job security), they are also in charge of, and responsible for, the business side of the industry. There are a lot of demands competing for their attention and voices competing in their heads. There is a decent chance they are reading your proposal on the train or on their phone.

I coined the term "Publisher's Paragraphs" to describe these one to three paragraphs of your proposal because I want you to keep this sort of reader in mind. While she might be skimming (no one ever gets to be in charge of anything in publishing unless they are very good at skimming), she is not a superficial or lazy reader. More likely, she is a sophisticated and experienced one, forever wishing she had more time to read for pleasure, forever rushed. Above all, she is *dying* to read something good. A publisher loves books! So much so that she wound up in a job that requires a lot of spreadsheets and email in support of them.

Maybe what catches her eye will be your amazing sample chapter or beautiful narrative opening! Do a fabulous job on those in the hope that it does. If you made the publisher miss her subway stop while reading your submission, I look forward to being invited to your future beach house. But more likely, she's reading swiftly, getting a feel for who you are and how you write while also skipping ahead to zero in on the key paragraphs. She'd love to take her time, but she needs to get to the essential bits. This is why those paragraphs can't be diffuse or hard to find. Write them knowing that some readers, especially those not making a decision after every paragraph, will fast-forward to get to the money shot, so to speak, and will want a clear view.

While the publisher might be your most impatient reader, having a few strong paragraphs early on in your proposal that clearly explain your book will only help your case with everyone else who encounters it along the way. While good agents often have significant editorial suggestions about your book's approach and content, the clearer and more compelling your vision of the book is in your first drafts, the more readily an agent will understand it, and the more interested they will be in representing you. No matter how closely they read the sample material, your bio and bona fides, the chapter summaries, and any information about your platform, the acquiring editor will also want to know, in no uncertain terms, what the book actually *is*. If an editor decides to pursue a submission, he'll need to present it to colleagues, first through getting reads, and then in an acquisitions meeting, which is exactly what it sounds like. In that meeting, the editor will describe the book and explain why they want to acquire it. Your own framing shapes theirs and helps them make their case.

I use the same three words again and again when I guide my authors through writing the Publisher's Paragraphs: clear, concise, compelling. Publisher's Paragraphs that fall short do so because they don't hit these marks. Those that aren't clear write around their actual subject while never simply stating it, assuming too much of the reader while also risking boring them. Too often, they're diffuse. Just when you think they're going to say What the Hell the Book Is, they change tack and delve into a different, important, but not essential theme or subject the book will tackle. This frequently happens with early drafts of proposals for very ambitious books, or for books that want to seem ambitious. In attempting to describe the key to all mythologies, the Publisher's Paragraphs end up being too much at once and risk being a whole lot of nothing. This is also how you lose concision in the part of a proposal that should get to the point. If it takes you five pages to write a clear, concise and compelling description of your book, odds are likely you're not being clear, concise, or compelling.

And speaking of concision, within those Publisher's Paragraphs you'll want to have one to two sentences that *really* distill the book to its essence. You may have heard these sentences called the "elevator pitch," the idea being that if you are lucky enough to find yourself in an elevator with someone who could publish your book, you could explain it to them in the time span of your ride together. This puts a certain amount of pressure on you, but it reflects a similar pressure on us: agents, editors, and publicists are constantly in situations where they have the fleeting interest of someone who can help with one of their books, so they must convey why that book is worthy of attention quickly and impactfully. This is certainly the case when an editor brings a submission to her colleagues for consideration for acquisition, and later, when they have to position it in-house for their sales force and publicity and marketing teams. As Denise Oswald explains: "Editors are always having to come up with a compelling one-liner to pitch books in-house and out, and if a proposal is well crafted, it's either right there on the page or comes together very quickly. Making sure it's in there is both another useful self-check for the author and an aid for the editor in selling their colleagues on a project. If the author has a clear vision in this way, it helps build confidence with all the different people who need to thumbs-up an acquisition."

I've pulled some sentences from Publisher's Paragraphs that hit the target of clarity and concision. (We'll go over longer excerpts in greater detail later.) This, from my client Linda Villarosa's Publisher's Paragraphs: **_Under the Skin_ will be the first book to tell the full story of race and health in America and to show the costs of racism on the well-being of the world's wealthiest and most powerful nation.**" If it helps you in describing your book, go ahead and steal the formula of Villarosa's sentence: title of the book, a phrase on what it aims to do, and then a second phrase stating why that aim matters. While Villarosa's case for her book emphasizes its argument, your book description needn't have an argument to convey urgency and importance. Take a look at two sample sentences from the proposal for my client Clint Smith's first nonfiction book, which went on to become a number one _New York Times_ bestseller: "_How the Word Is Passed_ tells the intergenerational story of Black America through a tour of places—those that are honest about their past and those that are not—that have been central in shaping our collective history. . . . _How the Word Is Passed_ will show how some of our country's most essential stories are hidden in places right in front of us—

spots we drive by on our way to work, on the names of buildings and streets." Smith's book is less argument driven than Villarosa's and focuses on storytelling and observation. In describing it, he clearly states the subject—"the intergenerational story of Black America"—but then quickly moves on to *how* he'll tell this story—"through a tour of places." In Smith's book, the approach, an oral history-cum-travelogue, is its most central and distinguishing feature; this approach gets primacy in his Publisher's Paragraph.

The import of books about medical inequity or the historiography of race may seem self-evident, so let's look at a description of a book that isn't so life or death. Here is a line lifted from the proposal for my client Merve Emre's book on the development of the Myers-Briggs personality test: "*The Personality Brokers* is a cultural history of personality testing that takes the story of the Myers-Briggs Type Indicator as its narrative backbone." Of all the sentences I shared thus far, Emre's is the most straightforward: It's just the subject and then an explanation of how that subject will propel and shape the structure of the book. This straightforward explanation works as a useful counterbalance to the rest of her proposal, which is almost entirely presented as an allusive and playful narrative. (In this way, the proposal accomplishes in miniature exactly what the sentence from her Publisher's Paragraph says her eventual book will do.) Precisely for this reason, it was especially important that she have a few lines that make the subject and structure of her book as clear as a bell. I hoped—and I was right—that an acquiring editor would fall in love with her arch, knowing style and get swept along by her skilled narration. But we also made sure the proposal had a few sentences for the rushed reader who wanted to quickly get a sense of the book's subject and Emre's approach.

•   •   •

When I share sample work with new clients, I always underscore for them what I will now underline with you: <u>These samples didn't spring from their writers' heads like Athena, brilliant and fully formed.</u> Distilling a book to a few paragraphs always takes ample time, edits, and focus, and it's the part of the proposal I urge my clients to give the most rigorous attention to. Here's a little exercise for how to do so: Write your one to three paragraphs explaining your book in a separate document. See how they read on their own. Perhaps even share them with a trusted friend who doesn't know much about your project. How do they work without the larger context of the rest of the proposal? If someone read them in the absence of everything else, would they know what your book is about—and would they want to read it?

This last part is essential. Remember, your proposal is a *selling document*. While keeping in mind the requirement to be clear and concise, writers sometimes lose sight of the equally important requirement to be compelling. In early drafts of proposals, I see lots of sentences that, in an attempt to be straightforward, end up being bland, vague, or too tentative. "I intend to write a book about XYZ subject and show how it is important to American history." "My book tells the story of XYZ figure and why she is important to understanding American history." (Sorry, American history, for making you my whipping post here.) In the case of memoir, I often see distinctive personal stories described in vague terms: "My memoir deals with trauma, memory, and healing." Sometimes the writer errs too heavily on the side of the conditional, in an admirable but ultimately undermining attempt at humility: "I'd like to write a book about trauma and memory." That's nice, but what will make a reader want to read it and spend money to do so?

I know I'm giving you a lot of boxes to check. Expressing the breadth and depth of your book in two or three paragraphs, and making those paragraphs interesting, is no easy task. Who could possibly pull this off? I'm giving you examples from proposals that sold, but you don't need access to my desktop to find inspiration. Go to your bookshelf and pull out five of your favorite semirecent books (no *Moby-Dick*) and make a study of the jacket copy. Good jacket copy does exactly what I am suggesting your Publisher's Paragraphs do: It sells a book through clueing you in, as engagingly as possible, to what you are buying. A bookstore excursion can also be instructive. Browse the section of the store where you think your book would be sold and pick up titles that catch your eye. Read the flap copy and see what hooks you. Put down whatever bores you or turns you off and note why it does. Note the titles whose jacket copy managed to intrigue you. If you don't buy the actual books, that same copy is easily accessible to you on the publishers' website as well as other retailer sites. Study it as inspiration for your own proposal.

Or use a couple by three of my favorite clients. Both of these excerpts are taken from books that received ample publisher interest and multiple offers; both went on to be *New York Times* bestsellers. The paragraphs are theirs, annotations my own. This by Judy Batalion, for the book that was ultimately entitled *The Light of Days:*

> There has been no book in the English language that tells the incredible and integral story of Jewish female resistance fighters.[*] *Daughters of the Resistance*[†] will be that book and will introduce these formidable women in a sweeping, propulsive narrative nonfiction tale.[‡] In order to narrate a group biography,[§] I will

---

[*] As mentioned above, Batalion opens by declaratively stating what makes her book distinctive. This was particularly important as the field of books on World War II and the Holocaust is so crowded. If your book is in a similarly crowded field, or if when you tell people what your book is, they respond, "I can't believe there isn't already a book on that!" you'll want to establish what makes your book unique early on in your proposal.

[†] Batalion's book was ultimately titled *The Light of Days*. Should you try to come up with an amazing title for your book when it's on submission? Yes. Should you be prepared for that title to change? Also yes!

[‡] Positive adjectives describing your own work are tricky and this is one point where book jacket copy has slightly different rules than anything you write about yourself. Calling your own prose "luminous" is not as believable as someone else saying it (and even then, perhaps we can retire "luminous" for a decade or two?). Batalion sets a high bar for herself saying the narrative is sweeping and propulsive, but I think she gets away with it, first, because it's depersonalized (it's the narrative, not her writing or her own story she's describing), and second, because she is anticipating a possible hesitation about the subject matter, which is "how will she get the reader through such sad and heavy material."

[§] Batalion is telling more about the book's category and methodology here. Go ahead and steal the term "group biography" if it applies. I did not invent it, so you are not stealing from me.

focus on one character as a lead:[*] Renieh Kukelcohn (from the above excerpt) whose harrowing, eyewitness accounts of violent uprisings, of scurrying by foot and train across the country, of the limitations of friendship, are the most substantial ones in *Freuen*. This focus will enable my book to be grounded in personal, dramatic storytelling, as it relays Renieh's journey from building underground bunkers, to her fact-finding and weapon-smuggling missions across Poland, through to her migration to Israel.[†] Using my original translation of *Freuen*—the first in English—as well as archival Hebrew and Yiddish texts, scholarly literature, and interviews with these late women's families in the U.S., Israel, and Poland, the book will draw out characters and personal narratives, focusing on the passions and personalities of these heroes who have been left out of the history books.[‡] Since *Freuen* focused on Poland, I will also make this country the center of my study, looking particularly at Renieh's group of female fighters from the town of Bedzin, but I also will incorporate female fighters from other cities and countries.

Daughters of the Resistance opens in 1943, the height of the underground's revolt against Hitler. We follow Renieh smuggling across borders and fleeing through forests, under constant

---

* Here Batalion anticipates another possible reservation about her book. It's largely about women forgotten to history. How will we keep track of them all? What will hold this group biography together?

† This sentence does a lot economically: Batalion explains her storytelling method and its reasons and also gives a taste of the story's inherent drama. Strong Publisher's Paragraphs, like book jacket copy, give phrasal teasers of the best material in the book.

‡ These lines establish Batalion's bona fides, which show she has unique access to material through her fluency in several relevant languages. She also has personal access to the descendants of the women she will be writing about. These different means of access will allow her to disclose what likely hasn't been included in previous books written in English.

threat of death, as she encounters the complex bonds of female friendships and the power of her own agency. She learns how her small actions can have great ramifications. We also meet Renieh's allies, other women fighters—from the coy and flirtatious Rivka to the wise and maternal Fruma to the unforgettable Chana, exuberant and relentlessly optimistic. We follow the women as they fight back in an astonishing number of ways, from cunning negotiation to violent combat to sly and unexpected bursts of humor. *Daughters* will also explore how these women's formative years before the war—spent in remarkably egalitarian Jewish youth groups—shaped their senses of confidence and courage, transforming not only our assumptions about gender roles in the early twentieth century, but our notions about the possibilities for women's education going forward. This tale of extraordinary female bravery and agency against all odds reminds us of the importance of recognizing the control we have over our own lives. The ghetto girls took responsibility and action—even in the face of a seemingly impossible goal.*

There is a continued widespread fascination with World War II as well as in recovered histories of heroic women past. Recent bestsellers like the beautifully poetic *The Zookeeper's Wife,* a nonfiction tale of resistance focused on the Warsaw zoo-keeper's wife, who maintained a household of hidden Jews, and the dramatic novel *Lilac Girls,* about three different women, including a Pole who had a minor role as a messenger, show that there is popular interest in resistance tales. *A Train in Winter,* about the friendships between women fighters in the French resistance after being imprisoned at a Nazi death camp, was a powerful, popular success, as was *The Lady in Gold,* a riveting story of art, the Holocaust, and a female Jewish muse. *Hidden Figures,* a remarkable group biography of African American

---

* For the second paragraph in the Publisher's Paragraphs section, I often suggest writers give a bird's-eye view of the narrative arc. Batalion does so while also weaving in the book's themes. Batalion makes the central, and quite dramatic, conflicts in the book clear without getting too lost in narrative detail.

women who worked for NASA (and were key in the American World War II and Cold War efforts), and *Radium Girls,* about poisoned radium factory workers who fought to change employment legislation, are both works of narrative nonfiction that chronicle and recover the stories of heroic women lost to history. The newly published *Code Girls,* which unveils the story of women who helped break codes in World War II, is already a national bestseller. Scholarly works, like the foundational *Women in the Holocaust,* address the female experience in war, but do not focus on female fighters; more recent releases, like *Saving One's Own,* elaborate on different types of Jewish rescuers, but not specifically on women's roles or gender in war.[*] The story of Jewish resistance is rarely told; we almost never read about female combatants. The tale of Jewish women who fought the Nazis is virtually unknown. Now is the perfect time to reveal it.[†]

Let's zoom out to take a look at the structure Batalion employs here. In the first paragraph, she gives a description of the book. In the second, she gives a bird's-eye view of how its story will unfold. In the third, she explains both its audience and its methodology through its comps, which in this case also worked as the entirety of her marketing section. (No bullet points, no enumeration of TikTok followers, just a gloss of thoughtfully selected recent publications that help position her own book in relation to them.)

While I suggest you draft your Publisher's Paragraphs in isolation from the rest of the proposal to sharpen the precision, the level of detail in them can be balanced by the rest of the proposal. Batalion's

---

[*] We'll get deeper into comparative titles when we discuss the Dreaded Marketing Section, but quick spoiler here: Lots of great proposals don't have one. Batalion didn't, and instead just included a paragraph making a case for the book's audience through comparative titles ("comps").

[†] To avoid ending this paragraph with the focus on other people's books, Batalion brings it back to her own and underlines again what sets her book apart.

proposal was relatively short, about seven thousand words. Clint Smith's was longer (over ten thousand), and much more detailed in terms of its individual chapters. Smith, who is also a poet, is a lyrical, voice-driven writer. With his book description, it was important to get to the point:

> *How the Word Is Passed* tells the intergenerational story[*] of Black America through a tour of places[†]—those that are honest about their past and those that are not[‡]—that have been central in shaping our collective history. It is a story of the Monticello plantation in Virginia, the estate where Thomas Jefferson wrote letters espousing the urgent need for liberty while enslaving over six hundred people. It is a story of the slave ports in Charleston, South Carolina, the first destination for over half of all enslaved Africans brought to the United States, a veritable Ellis Island for Black families. It is a story of Angola Prison in Louisiana, a former plantation named for the country from which most of its slaves arrived that has since become one of the most gruesome maximum security prisons in the world. These are places that have indisputable relationships to the history of Black America,

---

[*] First things first, Smith explains the book's subject and method.

[†] While Smith's book was sold as the "story of Black America," the finished book ended up focusing exclusively on slavery. This is a good example of the unpredictability of the process of moving from selling to the proposal to writing the actual book—and that's not a bad thing! The process of writing a book is always one of discovery. While you want to avoid a bait and switch, you do want the material to feel like the ideas have progressed and matured across the course of research and writing.

[‡] While Smith's book isn't argument driven, it does have an overarching mission, which is to honestly reckon with American history and to give the lie to places and institutions that don't. This is the book's conflict, so to speak—the tension between truthfulness and mythologizing in how we tell our own history.

yet those relationships are largely unknown to the general public. Some places, like the Monticello plantation and the Whitney Plantation in Louisiana, have actively attempted to reckon with and confront their own dark histories. Others, like Charleston, seen by some as a "Disneyland for the Confederacy," have actively eluded reckoning with their past in a public way.* *How the Word Is Passed* will show how some of our country's most essential stories are hidden in places right in front of us—spots we drive by on our way to work, on the names of buildings and street signs we speak of every day, and on the dollar bills we use to buy our coffee each morning.† They are in the museums that chronicle our past, the memorials that document our predecessors, the statues that illuminate both this nation's noble truths and villainous lies. This book will unearth these stories in order to paint a richer and more holistic picture of this country's relationship to Black people, and in doing so will more fully reveal the parts of our history that we have suppressed, pushed aside, or blatantly refused to call by its proper name.

The structure of Smith's paragraph would work well for a wide range of book projects. In the first sentence, he states the book's subject and aim. In the sentences that follow, he gives more details about the subject and more thumbnail descriptions, with each individual sentence summing up a proposed chapter. He ends on a high note, making a full-throated case for why his book matters. Note that this

---

* These few sentences operate a bit similarly to Batalion's second paragraph. They give us a sense of how the book will be structured and also preview its actual content. Like Batalion, Smith gives only a sentence per each subject, each of which corresponds to a proposed chapter. This shows he has the material in his proposed book well sketched out, but he saves further detail for the chapter summaries.

† Here is where Smith makes his case for why this material matters. Even for subject matter where that answer seems self-evident—in this case, the Holocaust and American slavery—you still want to spell this out.

paragraph was written when Smith had completed only a few chapters of the book, which in time went on to be heavily revised, yet he presents the book as a fait accompli, in the tone and register (and with the confidence!) you'd see on a book jacket.

You can take the same approach with more personal pieces of writing as well. As discussed at greater length in my interview with literary agent Brettne Bloom, memoirs are sometimes sold with a full manuscript, but they are just as often sold with a few sample chapters and a detailed proposal outlining the rest of the book. The proposal should hit all the same beats mentioned in this chapter, including the Publisher's Paragraphs. If writing a memoir involves putting one's own life under a microscope, describing that memoir takes some telescoping out. Here is how my client Jenisha Watts described her forthcoming memoir in the proposal we used to sell it:

> My memoir *Nisha from Kentucky* tells the story of my childhood in Lexington, growing up in a family and a community ravaged by drugs and violence, and what happened when I tried to leave that life behind to pursue my dream: entering the literary world of New York City. Amid the chaos of my youth, I chiseled out a place for myself where words and stories gave me a route to a better life. My journey wasn't always a "crystal staircase"— I faced constant humiliation from friends and the adults who were supposed to guide me. America is always trying to sell us on how beautiful life is on the way up, but that wasn't ever my story. I'm writing this memoir in part because it is important to tell stories, particularly ones about poverty and "making it," that don't have a neat Cinderella ending. Still, I was determined not to be a statistic like my crack-addicted mother. I clawed my way through my education, working hard to earn a bachelor's degree and eventually a master's at Columbia University. The end of the book—my current life—will show how you never truly run away from your past, but rather learn to deal with the residue of a bruised childhood: the imposter syndrome that is unshakable, the burden of financially providing for the ones who are left behind, the risk in telling my story because so many relationships have been tested. Doing so revealed a deeper unresolved brokenness in my family while also redefining some rela-

tionships for the better. I will write about the invisible strings attached by some of the well-to-do people in my life who have helped me but wanted me to be their puppet. I will expand on the revelatory moment when I transitioned from always needing someone to being capable of standing on my own solid ground. I will address how I've mourned friend and family relationships I've lost in leaving the world of my childhood behind and what my life looked like when I finally decided to break away from people who had more control over me, and set my own rules of engagement. I will show how I tried to unlearn pleasing people at the expense of what I want, and what this lesson did for my psyche.

Watts begins with the book's overarching story, plainly stating where it starts and where it will take us. At a superficial glance, the story is somewhat familiar: a bright young person begins their life in poverty and moves to the big city to follow their dreams. Watts anticipates and then counters the assumption that her story will be like all the others, explaining, "My journey wasn't always a 'crystal staircase'—I faced constant humiliation from friends and the adults who were supposed to guide me. America is always trying to sell us on how beautiful life is on the way up, but that wasn't ever my story. I'm writing this memoir in part because it is important to tell stories, particularly ones about poverty and 'making it,' that don't have a neat Cinderella ending." By saying what her story is, and what it isn't, she also indicates its themes and what purpose she hopes the book will serve in the world. While the language is straightforward, especially her first sentence, she makes judicious use of imagery with the phrases "crystal staircase" and "invisible strings." The prose style is direct, but not colorless.

Watts's Publisher's Paragraphs detail what she learned over the course of the period she writes about. Later in her proposal, she says what she hopes readers will take from it. Referring to an essay about her childhood she published in *The Atlantic,* she writes, "In my essay I explained why I do what I do: I write things down to make people feel things. Here is what I hope my book makes you feel: restored, tolerant, encouraged, amused, wretched, distressed, moved, and hopeful. Life doesn't always have to have clean lines and happy endings to be beautiful." While working on her proposal together, I asked her what she wanted people to feel while reading her book. This was meant initially as a brainstorming exercise to figure out the tone of the proposal, but I loved her answer so much, we used it as the proposal's concluding note. Thinking about your own book, what do you hope it makes its future readers feel? And as you work on your proposal and your Publisher's Paragraphs, think about how you can evoke those feelings when you describe it.

THE AUTHOR BIO

The most common way to do an author bio in a book proposal is to write it as a kind of extended version of what you'd find on a book jacket: your name, your credentials, perhaps a cheeky personal detail or two, all in the third person. You can definitely approach it this way if it's appealing to you—no agent or editor reading your proposal would be at all put off or surprised by this method—but I have an alternative suggestion on how to best use your proposal's limited real estate. Use the About the Author section as an opportunity to relay to an agent, editor, or publisher what Google couldn't: to put flesh on the bones of your bona fides. **Instead of the corporate bio approach, tell the story of how you came to your book's subject and what makes you uniquely qualified to tackle it.**

To get the tone right, ditch the third person and try writing it in the first. The switch to first will immediately create more intimacy between you and your audience, an audience you are trying to persuade to work closely with you, to come to share your passions and to pass them along. This approach will also help us help you. All your readers who are publishing professionals will want to know the story behind the story, as that is the stuff of NPR interviews and magazine profiles and interesting panel discussions. If you have ever imagined yourself talking to Terry Gross, this is your moment. Tom Mayer, the executive editor at Norton, explains, "I prefer when somebody's bio says 'Here's the story I'm going to tell about why I matter to the world.'" This in turn helps Mayer with *his* job, which is "to craft a narrative of why the reader should trust the author on whatever the subject, and to explain why the reader should invest time and have confidence in the artist."

Think back to what sparked your own interest in the book you are proposing. If it's a good story, all the better; even more so if it reveals your specialized expertise, qualifications, or personal connection to the material. Judy Batalion hits all these marks in the author bio from her proposal for *The Light of Days*:

> Ten years ago, I was at the British Library doing research for a performance piece about Hanna Senesh, one of the few female Jewish paratroopers not lost to history, when I came across the incredible book *Freuen in di Ghettos—Women in the Ghettos*. Written in Yiddish, and published in New York in 1946 though now long out of print, it contained the accounts of dozens of young Jewish women from the Polish ghettos who fought in the resistance against the Nazis.
>
> Through my own family history, my Hebrew and Yiddish education, my scholarly background in women's studies, and my many Jewish-themed journalistic endeavors, I was familiar with Hanna Senesh and knew the battle song of the Partisans by heart. But I had no idea how many women—Jewish women— were involved in the resistance effort nor to what degree. No one I mentioned this to, including friends from the Holocaust survivor community I grew up in, had ever heard these stories.

Through telling the story of her first contact with her subject, we learn Batalion's academic background, that she knows both Hebrew and Yiddish, and that, as someone with both scholarly and personal expertise in the Holocaust, she can say with some authority that what she uncovered hasn't been written about in English before.

Personal doesn't have to mean "confessional." You don't need to have familial connection to your subject or relate your book to the death of your Pop Pop, but letting readers know how a subject took hold in your mind helps them to know you. In the author bio section for her book on the actress Anna May Wong, Katie Salisbury describes the moment she first became aware of Wong through a visit to the Chinese American Museum in Los Angeles:

One photo in particular caught my eye. In it, a glamorous Chinese woman sat smiling from the backseat of a convertible, the confidence of youth in her eyes, as she waved to spectators at a parade.

I lingered there for a moment longer, mouth slightly agape with wonder at discovering such a strange flower. "Who was she?" I asked the curator. What I was really thinking was: *I must know who this woman is.* I'd never seen anyone who looks like her on TV or in history books. She was Chinese and American, beautiful, chic, modern.

Thus began Salisbury's decade-long obsession with Wong, which eventually led to her book. Your author bio is also a place where you can convey your passion for your project in personal terms, and this passion can be persuasive, sometimes more so than professional laurels. Per Niki Papadopoulos, the Portfolio editor in chief, "I find obsession a huge turn-on. If someone is wholeheartedly obsessed with the topic and lit on fire about it, and they're just curious about exploring all of the corners of their expertise, it kind of doesn't matter what degree they have, or what credential they have. Because if they are going to be good authors, they're also going to be good teachers of those concepts." That said, you *will* want to detail your professional qualifications, and this isn't the place to be modest. You will absolutely want to list publications, awards, professional associations, and recognitions as well. But you can also think of the About the Author section as a mini intellectual biography or a snapshot of your mind. This can help make the details of career moves and pivots richer and more compelling.

THE DREADED MARKETING SECTION

The marketing section might be the most dreaded part of the dreadful act of writing a book proposal. I know there is some terrifying advice out there telling you to "think like a marketer" and "know your brand" and "platform is more important than ever in publishing." The result of this advice is authors drafting long-winded, misguided marketing sections for their proposals, none of which bear any resemblance to how books are actually marketed. If you are in the stage of querying agents and writing a proposal for that purpose, you can use the guidance here to help you position your book, but your agent, once you sign with one, will likely work closely with you on this section or even draft it themselves. My advice, in any case, is more about what *not* to include. Why? Because many first-time authors clog their proposals with marketing points that are entirely irrelevant.

This isn't because the publishing industry doesn't care about marketing. The hard truth is more nuanced than that: Many agents, editors, and publishers simply skip over reading that belabored marketing section you spent so much time writing because it's so irrelevant to how we think about books, especially books that aren't prescriptive or platform driven. If your book project is centered around your professional expertise and prominence, and you are using those attributes to sell it, your proposal should make that expertise and your means of sharing it central to your proposal. But if you are not, say, a celebrated dermatologist writing a skin-care how-to or TikTok astrologer pitching a tarot guide (all valid ideas and books I would read), your marketing plans and platform are of secondary importance to the proposed book itself.

Don't *just* take it from me. Per Chris Jackson, the publisher of One World, "One of the hallmarks of something I'll decline is the **first** thing that you tell me is about the audience for the book. You don't need to tell me that football is watched by 140 million people every week, or whatever. Then I know it's not going to be for me." Per Yaniv Soha, "I've worked at places where leading with the marketing section wouldn't get you anywhere, where an author would be better selling based on their idea and their credentials rather than their impressive Rolodex." Note that neither editor is saying you don't need to mention your book's potential audience, but that this discussion is of secondary importance to the book itself. Andrew Miller admits to skipping the marketing section entirely. Despite our reputations for being far more focused on commerce than art, many well-respected agents also eschew marketing sections. My colleague Sarah Burnes, a longtime agent at Gernert, doesn't include them, feeling they are both a burden and a misdirection for clients. "Writers are not good at it and in my opinion, it makes the writer think too much about that and not the work." While the editors and agents mentioned focus on narrative-driven books, even at imprints that focus on prescriptive titles, which tend to have a more targeted purpose and clearly defined audience (Recent college grads! Middle managers! Allergy sufferers!), proposals cluttered with stats make for a less-than-persuasive read. Niki Papadopoulos states, "Social media stats are helpful, but I also have Google. So, don't do that."

So what should you do in lieu of marketing hooks, gimmicks, and stats? Think like a publisher and try to explain the audience of your book in terms of comps, as well as the tools you already have at your disposal to help the publisher reach that audience. If there are specific audiences or communities your publisher might not know about that would be interested in your book, share those too. You can do this in one to three paragraphs.

Let's start with comps (or as I always think of them, "comp co-comp, comp, comp," thank you, Sisqó). Publishers value books almost entirely in relation to other books. While this logic may seem circular and somewhat insular, comparing proposed books to actually published ones makes use of the best available metric we have for estimating a book's possible audience. It's also how every publisher comes up with the advance they'll pay and the publicity and marketing budget.

To choose your comps, start by coming up with your own thorough list of **recent, successful** books on related subjects. Make the list as exhaustive as you like, but then winnow it down to three to five titles. A good way to do so is to write a one-sentence description of why each book on the list is related to yours and see which feels the most apt. To gauge a book's success, use the number of Amazon reviews or note if it was a national bestseller. The importance of recency is to anticipate how publishers themselves value books. In coming up with a profit and loss (P&L) statement for a possible acquisition, publishers largely focus on similar books published within the last three to five years. There's a frustrating bias toward recent titles that might make finding comps more challenging, but the logic behind it is that the market for books from ten or fifteen years ago doesn't reflect the market of the moment, and any book you are proposing will likely come out at least two years after the time of acquisition.

All that said, there's also space to talk about your book's comps a bit more holistically, and in that case, you can look further back. Chris Jackson calls these "soul comps," a term I love. Let's say you're writing a history of urban gardening. You'll want to look at histories of gardening, but if the book that truly inspired you, the one that made you fall in love with gardening, is Frances Hodgson Burnett's *The Secret Garden,* you can say that! Or you could talk about these books outside the comps section, such as in the bio, where you discuss how you came to the project. (Just to be sure to mention a couple of recent, relevant titles as well.) Comps also needn't be solely limited to subject; you can also think about them in terms of approach. If you're writing a book about your mixed Korean American identity, you may want to mention *Crying in H Mart,* but that comp would be equally relevant to a book about grieving the death of a beloved parent.

While you should know about all the books recently published on your subject, **you certainly don't need to mention them all in your proposal.** Remember, it's a selling tool, not a bibliography. Getting the right balance can be particularly challenging if your subject has been widely covered. Let's look again at the "audience section" (my preferred term for the marketing component in a book proposal) from *The Light of Days* to see how Judy Batalion distinguished her book in a very crowded field:

> There is a continued widespread fascination with World War II as well as in recovered histories of heroic women past. Recent bestsellers like the beautifully poetic *The Zookeeper's Wife,* a nonfiction tale of resistance focused on the Warsaw zookeeper's wife who maintained a household of hidden Jews, and the dramatic novel *Lilac Girls,* about three different women including a Pole who had a minor role as a messenger, show that there is popular interest in resistance tales. *A Train in Winter,* about the friendships between women fighters in the French resistance after being imprisoned at a Nazi death camp, was a powerful, popular success, as was *The Lady in Gold,* a riveting story of art, the Holocaust, and a female Jewish muse. *Hidden Figures,* a remarkable group biography of African American women who worked for NASA (and were key in the American World War II and Cold War efforts), and *Radium Girls,* about poisoned radium factory workers who fought to change employment leg-

islation, are both works of narrative nonfiction that chronicle and recover the stories of heroic women lost to history. The newly published *Code Girls,* which unveils the story of women who helped break codes in World War II, is already a national bestseller. Scholarly works, like the foundational *Women in the Holocaust,* address the female experience in war, but do not focus on female fighters; more recent releases, like *Saving One's Own,* elaborate on different types of Jewish rescuers, but not specifically on women's roles or gender in war. The story of *Jewish* resistance is rarely told; we almost never read about female combatants. The tale of Jewish women who fought the Nazis is virtually unknown. Now is the perfect time to reveal the ultimate female fight.

In her audience section, Batalion starts by acknowledging the vastness of the field, which also makes a case for its enduring interest. Because there are so many World War II books, she focuses on ones with a similar style and approach, which helps her to emphasize the strengths of her own book without resorting to excessive self-flattery. She acknowledges the many books written about resistance during World War II, showing she knows her terrain. She then specifies what sets her book apart: none of these other (successful) books focused on Jewish women, and the story of Jewish women battling the Nazis is entirely unknown.

Your comps don't have to be on-the-nose equivalent subjects. Publishers aren't looking to publish carbon copies of previous titles, and if there is a book out there exactly like the one you want to write, you should probably reconsider your own. In trying to determine what counts as a comp, think about books that would make sense next to each other on a bookstore table or on a reading list grouped thematically. Think too about the argument and approach of your book here, as Linda Villarosa did in her comp section:

As in Sheri Fink's depiction of a Katrina-ravaged New Orleans hospital in *Five Days at Memorial* or Rebecca Skloot's rendering of the tale of Henrietta Lacks, I plan to write a deeply human story of our frequently inhumane medical system. *Under the Skin* will be a companion to *Evicted* and *The New Jim Crow* in its exposure of widespread, systemic inequality hiding in plain sight. Like those books, I hope *Under the Skin* changes the terms of debate. It will draw audiences who are interested in race, social justice, and medical narratives as well as readers who appreciate deeply reported narrative nonfiction. There is tremendous hunger for this area of discussion; after each of my last two *New York Times Magazine* stories, I had dozens of reprint requests from college professors and graduate and doctoral students in a wide range of disciplines. This will be the first—and, I hope, definitive—book on race and health disparities. My aim is to write a book that will live on bookshelves and syllabi for years to come.

There was no other recent book on Villarosa's exact subject—racial health disparities in the U.S. health system—so she comped her book by her subject's underlying themes: the often inhumane U.S. medical system and structural inequalities. Like Batalion, she uses comps to highlight her approach: deeply reported, character-driven nonfiction with an element of exposé. Bringing these strands together allows her to name the audience for her book: "audiences who are interested in race, social justice and medical narratives as well as readers who appreciate deeply reported narrative nonfiction." Because Villarosa has been writing on her subject for years, she can also speak to the response to her pieces as further proof of the audience for her work.

In speaking about the comps for his book *The Method*, Isaac Butler first centers entirely on the approach. While his book is specifically about acting, his comps work to underline the interest in cultural histories of performance and group biographies of artists:

The Method will be a narratively driven cultural history of a set of ideas that are so influential to our basic assumptions that we often take them for granted. Similar in approach to James Gleick's *The Information*, it will be a relay race in which artists, eccentrics, geniuses, and crackpots pass a baton forward over more than a century, pulling American popular culture with them. As in Alex Ross's *The Rest Is Noise*, it will be driven by biography but not ruled by any one individual, carefully situating its subjects and their work in historical and cultural contexts. The story of *The Method* will combine high-stakes human drama and behind-the-scenes hijinks with criticism and history, much like Peter Biskind's classic *Easy Riders, Raging Bulls,* or Mark Harris's *Pictures at a Revolution,* making the reader feel simultaneously like they are part of the sweep of paradigmatic change and viewing that change from the vantage point of today.

Butler then performs a tricky but sometimes necessary move: He acknowledges other books on the subject to explain what his own will cover that they don't:

Due to the cultural prominence of the Method, and the number of very famous lives it intersects, there are a range of books that tell pieces of its story. Jean Benedetti, a tireless biographer and translator of Stanislavski, has written several monographs about his life and theories. J. W. Roberts's *Richard Boleslavsky: His Life and Work* tells the story of the man who brought the "system" to the United States. The most well-known book to touch on this story is probably Wendy Smith's classic *Real Life Drama: The Group Theatre and America.* Many of the subjects in this story wrote memoirs, and many of them have been the subjects of biographies. Oddly enough, given how fascinating and complicated Lee Strasberg, the man who codified the Method, is as a character, his sole biography was written by Cindy Adams, and is considered tawdry and unreliable.

Butler wants to position his book as groundbreaking (which it was, hence the National Book Critics Circle Award!); one way he does so is by acknowledging there are disparate pieces of the story he aims to tell out there, but no one has successfully woven them together or viewed them through the lens he is proposing.

You'll also want to detail any means at your disposal for reaching your book's audience, especially if those means aren't readily apparent. Per Niki Papadopoulos, "In the marketing section, I want to hear a story about who your audience is, and how you plan to interact with them." So how might you, a nonfamous person, reach an audience and then persuade them to buy your book? I got more granular on this subject in chapter 2.5 on platform, but to recap, those means might include publications that have already published you (and thus might do so again). If you have a newsletter, blog, podcast, or some other medium you directly control, list that here. If you are very active on social media, with a robust and engaged following, mention that too, though no need to enumerate followers. (And don't include lines like "I plan to start a newsletter to support the launch of the book" or "I'll be active on Facebook to market the publication." It is very, very hard to gain significant social media followers, so intentions don't count for much.) Include your past or present professional activities and associations as well as any institutional resources of your employer. If you regularly do speaking engagements, give details—speaking engagements are particularly persuasive as they put you in front of an interested, captive audience and can move a lot of books. List any awards you have won, either here or in the About the Author section; they show you are recognized by your peers as distinguished in your field, and thus your field will be interested in hearing about your book. If you have any academic, philanthropic, professional, or corporate organizations that might be helpful in promoting your book, list them too. These lists can also help point publishers in the direction of audiences they might overlook. Sizable but not immediately obvious is your sweet spot, especially if you have a direct connection to that audience. Not useful information: "I am writing a cultural history of amusement parks; 75 percent of Americans visit an amusement park in their lifetime." Useful information: "I am the proprietor of a small amusement park in Elysburg, Pennsylvania, which receives 1.4 million visitors each year. Last year, I was the keynote speaker at IAAPA Global Expo, the largest trade show organization for the attractions industry, which attracts nearly 40,000 attendees and has over 250,000 members."

Another way to give publishers a sense of your audience is by listing your relevant personal contacts. Just as being part of a professional organization or on the faculty of an academic institution can help you get word out about your book, so can well-connected people you know: fellow writers, prominent colleagues in your field, former teachers or students, members of the media, anyone with a large social media following. Some authors put these directly in the proposal. I tend not to do this—I feel it gives away too much personal information indiscriminately—but I do have my authors make a list of all their relevant contacts and offer it on request to interested publishers. If you are in the process of querying agents, you can list your contacts in the proposal itself or mention you have one when you pitch and offer it on request. (And to be clear, you certainly don't need to have well-placed friends and family to publish a book; I'm including this advice so you can make the most of every resource in your arsenal.) Some proposal submissions also include blurbs. This is not at all necessary, and soliciting blurbs from other writers before you even have a book deal feels very cart before the horse to me, but if a well-known writer happened to read your work and love it, you can by all means share this info.

CHAPTER SUMMARIES/BOOK OUTLINE, 10–20 PAGES

Finally, your book proposal should include a chapter-by-chapter breakdown of its contents. This serves as proof that you have a plan for how your book will unfold and that you have enough engaging material to carry the reader through to the end. This is usually handled in short two-to-four-paragraph descriptions of each chapter. Let's start with this example from Clint Smith's proposal:

Chapter 2—Through the Eyes of Those Forgotten

Standing in front of the Whitney Plantation one finds themselves surrounded by a tapestry of Spanish moss draping from the branches of two dozen oak trees. In autumn, the leaves change color, fold into themselves, and dress the dirt road in a quilt of red and orange. The Big House, its white facade with a dozen open doors and windows, sits at the end of the road like a skull that has been left hollow, wind slapping the shutters back and forth against the panel. Listed on marble walls that glisten in the southern Louisiana sun, are the names of more than one hundred thousand slaves sold throughout the state. On the porches of the former slaves' quarters sit the clay sculptures molded in the likeness of enslaved children, intricately detailed from the contours of their jaws to the bridges of their noses, reinforcing the sense that these children—or children like them—had once been real. The Whitney was built in 1790 and sits in Wallace, Louisiana, a small town of less than seven hundred people just thirty-five miles west of New Orleans. Purchased nearly two decades ago by John Cummings, an eighty-one-year-old white attorney who would end up spending sixteen years and $10 million of his own money restoring the rundown property, the plantation became, in 2014, the first museum in the United States dedicated solely to memorializing slavery through the perspective of the enslaved. "I knew slaves were here of course, but I had no idea what a commodity they were," Cummings said after purchasing the property and learning of its history. "I had no idea how deprived they were, not by force of circumstance, but by deliberate planning."

Following the purchase of the Whitney Plantation, Cummings has become a student of history in an attempt to more fully understand the institution of slavery and how it has shaped the landscape of our country. He knows, however, that most people won't, or can't, take the time to sit down and read tomes on nineteenth-century American political economy. Cummings believes that the newly designed Whitney can serve as an initial access point to this difficult history, for those who might not otherwise find their way to the scholarship on the subject. "I've seen some of the great empirical studies done but they just sit on the library shelf gathering dust," he said to me on a recent Tuesday afternoon in his kitchen. "We want to bring them to the masses."

This chapter will reflect on the history and significance of the Whitney Plantation—which remains the only museum in the country *singularly* dedicated to slavery—linking it to my own ancestors who were enslaved people in Louisiana and very likely part of the more than one hundred thousand enslaved people captured on the granite walls on the plantation. It will include in-depth interviews with both founder John Cummings—with whom I have already conducted an extensive four-hour interview—as well as director of research Dr. Ibrahima Seck to unpack how the Whitney Plantation's exclusive and unrepentant focus on slavery served as a catalyst for other plantations throughout Louisiana and across the country to reevaluate, and in most cases to simply begin, conveying their relationship to that period of history.

The structure of this summary is a good place to start. Paragraph one introduces the subject of the chapter in broad strokes. Paragraph two goes more in depth, giving a sense of the kind of characters and stories the book will contain. Paragraph three stresses thematics and connects the particulars of this chapter to the book project as a whole.

This last point is particularly important. Because chapter summaries tend to give a lot of detail in a small amount of space, they can get in the weeds awfully quickly. You need to show you know your subject matter, hence the need for all that detail, but you also want to underline why these particular details matter. This is also a good exercise for you as a writer. The chapter summaries are a place where you are forced to ask yourself, and to answer: Why *this* story? Why *this* character?

While you want the details and explanations to be as persuasive as possible, know that the finished result—the actual book—will likely differ considerably from what you lay out in your chapter summaries. A lot can happen between when you sell your book and when you finally write it, and chapters you propose will expand, contract, and change shape. Some may even disappear entirely! Publishing professionals who read your chapter summaries know that too. Here is some liberating advice and context from Rebecca Saletan, editorial director of Riverhead: "Writing outlines or chapter synopses can be daunting when you have not yet written the book. I always tell writers that what an editor is looking for isn't so much a set-in-stone description of the shape of the book, as evidence that the writer is grappling intelligently and creatively with how to organize something as big as a book. In fact, if the finished manuscript comes in exactly in accordance with the structure proposed at the outset, it's often a warning sign that something was not as alive as it should have been in the process. Structure usually shifts and evolves as a writer goes deeper into the research and the writing." Your outline is not a contract in blood; it is a good-faith effort showing you know the scope of your story and you have a provisional plan for writing it.

Given that book proposals are often written at the earliest stage of working on a book and before a lot of the research and reporting has taken place, some writers feel hesitant to give the kind of detail Smith does, knowing it will likely change. If you fall into this camp, I advise you to zoom out just a little bit and think about your book in terms of "acts" instead of chapters. You may not yet be able to summarize the contents of chapter 3, so what if you were instead to think of your book as a three-act play? Describing the arcs of each act, and how those individual arcs help build upon each other to create the whole, can be a very effective means to explain the structure of your book as well as its thematics and narrative engines. Good chapter summaries weave back and forth between incident and plot points and larger thematic concerns. Being mindful of both these requirements will keep you from veering into "and then, and then, and then" territory or falling into too much abstraction.

Katie Salisbury takes the act approach to outline her biography of the legendary film star Anna May Wong. To avoid the "and this happened and then this happened and then this happened" monotony inherent in biographical summary, Salisbury structures Wong's life in terms of five distinct movements. Here is Act I:

Act I: Past Is Prologue

The book opens with the birth of Hollywood, a sleepy farm town first incorporated in 1903, and a speculative new technology-cum-art form: the motion picture. We meet Anna May Wong as a young girl growing up in a multicultural neighborhood in Los Angeles just as major film companies like Paramount, Warner Bros., and Columbia Pictures are opening studios several miles away. Her father, Wong Sam Sing, owns and operates a laundry on Flower Street, a few blocks from Chinatown. All of the Wong children help out at the laundry, whether it's working the counter, ironing in the back, or making deliveries.

Born in America, Anna May does not realize any difference between her and the other kids at school until a group of boys follow her and her sister home, taunting them with yells of "Chink, Chink, Chinaman!" With an increasing aversion to school, she skips class for the cheap movie theatres on Main Street and becomes a regular spectator on the sidelines every

time a Hollywood production rolls into Chinatown—so much
so that crew members begin referring to her as the "Curious
Chinese Child." On one of these occasions, she catches sight
of actress Mae Murray at work and is confused as to why she is
dressed in rags. The young Anna May is disgusted, not realizing
the getup is for a part. "Yet my first ambition to become a film
actress myself was born at this time," she wrote later for *Pictures* magazine. "I'd show Miss Murray how a movie star should
dress." Through her own hustle and bravado, she snatches a part
as an extra in Alla Nazimova's *The Red Lantern* in 1918 at the age
of thirteen.

Despite her parents' disapproval, Anna May continues to
audition for parts with the help of various friends and contacts, like Robert Wagner, a director and screenwriter and one
of her father's laundry customers who petitions on her behalf.
By 1922, she wins her first lead role as Lotus Blossom in the
silent film *The Toll of the Sea,* a variation on *Madame Butterfly.*
But it's not until she secures the "Mongol slave" role in *The
Thief of Bagdad* two years later that she finally gets her breakout
moment. The film, a swashbuckler loosely based on a story from
One Thousand and One Nights, costs $1.1 million, making it one
of the most expensive movies of the 1920s. And everyone wants
to know, of course, who that bewitching Mongol is. Anna May
boards a rocket ship destined for stardom.

The "act" approach allows Salisbury to cherry-pick her details and
moments from a life rich with incident. Act I has thematic specifics—
early Hollywood, the discovery of a vocation, the obstacles of racism outside the home and parental disapproval within, incredible
ambition and bravado—that are illustrated through the well-chosen
details of Wong's life.

While the details and particulars will likely change, your chapter summaries should make clear that your subject is rich enough
to merit a book and that you have put serious thought into how
you'll present its materials. They also give your potential agent or
your editor valuable information on how your mind works. Per Niki
Papadopoulos, your chapter summaries show how you as the author
"think about organizing information and presenting it in front of the

reader, how deep you've gone into the concept and really thought through what each chapter is going to do, what it's going to draw on, and what readers are going to get from it." Still stuck? More than one editor I spoke with suggested thinking of the structure of your book as a syllabus. Per Eamon Dolan, vice president and executive editor of Simon & Schuster, and a structure obsessive, imagine "chapter one as the first week of class. So, what do I need to know to get started?" To steal from Anne Lamott's beloved bird-by-bird advice for tackling a piece of writing, think of each individual chapter as a week's assignment within the master class that is your book.

ON SAMPLE MATERIAL

In addition to the proposal, most submissions also contain sample material. The need for this and the length required can vary. If you are a very widely published writer and/or your book is going to be an expansion on previously published material, you can often use that published material in place of a sample. Otherwise, you will likely want to draft a sample chapter or two. While many publishing professionals skim over parts of the proposal, none of us skip reading any sample material. How you write and how your book will read is *the* most important question, and one even the most hurried of skimmers will want answered. Several editors I spoke with admitted to skipping ahead to the sample chapter before reading anything else.

The sample is where the rubber hits the road, the rubber being the book you propose and the road your ability to pull it off. A painstakingly constructed chapter outline won't mean much if your sample doesn't read well, while an excellent sample can be hugely persuasive. Per Maria Goldverg, senior editor at Liveright:

> The sample is actually quite important, particularly if an author doesn't have a huge platform, or if they've only written short pieces before, or if they're proposing an ambitious book that will be weaving together multiple narratives or telling a long, complicated history. It ends up being the piece that I often point to as evidence that the writer is "up to the task" and "can deliver,"

so to speak. With academics, it shows that they know how to write for the trade. And, to be quite honest, even if someone has published a well-written or well-received trade book before, it's possible that the publisher hasn't read that book and might still be skeptical that the author can pull off what's promised.

Note that Goldverg says the sample is particularly important in certain instances—if you are an entirely unknown writer or you are doing something that mixes genre or is particularly hard to pull off. In those cases, I would lean toward a longer sample rather than a shorter one. I inevitably get asked how long the sample should be, and I inevitably say, "It varies!" I usually advise between five thousand and ten thousand words. (I never give page counts as they also vary depending on how you format your work.) As you are thinking about length, keep in mind why publishers like to see a sample: They want to see that you are capable of executing what you are proposing.

If your book's main selling point is the voice, the sample material should be even more extensive. This is especially true with memoir. For memoirs that are sold on the strength of a truly incredible personal story or a very strong platform—if you were, say, kidnapped by a polygamous cult or once starred in a beloved children's television series until you were kidnapped by a polygamous cult—you can get away with a lot less in terms of sample material. In the likely event that this doesn't apply to you, and if your personal story is compelling largely because of how you'll tell it, you'll want to make sure your sample is as polished and extensive as possible. Front-load your proposal with at least two or three sample chapters (ideally, taken from the beginning, which makes for an easier read) and then follow it with a detailed outline of what the yet-to-be-written parts of the proposal will include as well as the Publisher's Paragraphs and audience section described earlier.

The same general rules apply for essay collections, which, judging from my inbox and the pitches I hear at writers' conferences, many folks reading this book may be trying to write. You'll want to show your work by including sample essays and a clear outline of the other essays the book might contain. I'm often asked how many, if any, previously published essays you should include when pitching a collection. While there is no hard-and-fast rule (a mantra to keep in mind during every phase of your professional writing career!), it's extremely hard to publish an essay collection if you've never published any essays. Unless you are already a very well known and best-selling author (Ta-Nehisi Coates and Patrick Radden Keefe, both *New York Times* bestsellers and major award winners, come to mind), it is also extremely hard to publish an essay collection of material that is mostly previously published. You'll thus want to strike a balance in your submission materials between published essays, which show that you are an established and professionalized writer, and new material that wouldn't be available elsewhere.

HOW TO END IT?

Books need to have conclusions. Proposals, not so much.

KEY TAKEAWAYS

- Your proposal is a selling document, but can and should be as interesting and engaging as the book itself.
- It is perfectly normal to feel overwhelmed; just know that once you learn the process, it is as easy as following the steps.
- What the proposal needs to include, or questions it has to answer:
  o What, precisely, is the book? Be clear, concise, compelling.
  o How will the subject sustain itself over the course of seventy to one hundred thousand words? Or, why is this not a magazine-length article?
- Are you qualified to write it, and if so, why?
  o Instead of a corporate bio, tell the story of how you came to your book's subject in the first place and what makes you uniquely qualified to tackle it.
- Who are the potential readers of the book?
  o Reference comparative titles, called "comps," that will help explain your hoped-for audience. Just remember

that your marketing plans and platform are secondary in importance to the proposed book itself.

- How will the book unfold? Write a summary of chapters, with three- to four-paragraph descriptions for each.
- Throughout every section, you'll be answering the question on every reader's mind (agents, editors, and generally): How do you write? So remember that agents and editors and, ultimately, your audience are looking to see how the book will read.
- The creation of a nonfiction book is unusually collaborative. After you've written a proposal, generally you hone it with the literary agent before sending it to editors, who may want to further craft the idea. Do not be nervous about or against this! While it might not, it often results in a better finished product.

Interview with Brettne Bloom, literary agent and partner at The Book Group, whose titles include *Crying in H Mart* by Michelle Zauner, *Wild Game* by Adrienne Brodeur, *This Happened to Me* by Kate Briggs, and *The Body Keeps the Score* by Bessel van der Kolk

Bloom is, among other accomplishments, an expert in memoir. Nearly all the advice in this book applies to memoir writers, but in a few distinct ways, memoir is a special case. As with fiction, an individual memoir's magic comes down to voice as much as subject matter, and the intimacy, and even collusion, that voice creates with the reader. And unlike much nonfiction, memoir is sometimes sold with a full manuscript rather than a proposal and a partial, though as Bloom makes clear, there is quite a lot of variation in the field. While Bloom's taste, like any good agent's, is distinctly her own, her excellent advice on conceptualizing, structuring, selling, and then publicizing a memoir is broadly applicable.

How much of your list is memoir, nonfiction, fiction?

My list is exactly half fiction, half nonfiction. I've been an agent for twenty-four years. I started out doing a lot of narrative history, biography, psychology, working with doctors, academics, and journalists. Over the years, I realized that I wanted to do more memoir. Personal essays and memoir have always been a passion of mine, but it took a while to figure out exactly how to do it well. My memoir list has definitely grown in the past ten years. It's something that started with reading a lot more memoir, and reading more that were not "story of my life" memoir, but about a very specific experience.

You said it took you a while to figure out how to do memoir well. What did you learn during that process? What didn't you know when you started?

I didn't grasp that memoir could be about a specific experience. In telling this super-specific experience—whether it's facing terminal cancer, having a narcissistic mother, or dealing with the loss of a parent while trying to find yourself—I didn't realize that you could take those and tell a whole story of life using those experiences as a framing device. Then I started reading the big memoirs that came out when I was coming up in the business like *The Glass Castle, Educated,* and *Wild.* They helped shape my understanding of what a good memoir could be. The other thing, too, is that good memoir can read like a novel. You can use some of the same devices that you use in a novel, like three- or four-part structures, crescendo moments, or climactic moments. Even though life doesn't necessarily follow a novelistic framework, you can still think about a way to impose that framework on the story you're trying to tell. I studied it. I also figured out the kinds of memoirs that I thought could do well.

And what kind of memoir is that?

I would call my memoir *the slice of life.* It's usually about one particular relationship or one particular experience and it's telling the whole story of someone's coming of age, coming into oneself, or coming into knowledge about something through the lens of that one experience. I'll give you an example. I worked on an incredible memoir called *Wild Game* by Adrienne Brodeur. That memoir is about how, when Adrienne was fourteen years old, her mother woke her up in the middle of the night and told her that she was starting an affair with Adrienne's stepfather's best friend. Overnight, Adrienne went from being her mother's daughter to being her confidante. That relationship as her confidante lasted for twenty years and shaped Adrienne's life in profound ways. Other things happen to Adrienne along the way, but the memoir was specifically about *this* relationship with *this* thing.

Editorially, how did you figure that out?

I tell my clients who are working on memoir that the most important decision you make when you're writing a memoir is where to open. If Adrienne started that story when her mother lost a child—as her mother did—and talked about her mother's grief and depression after losing that child, then their divorce, and then her starting the affair, you would have sympathy for her mother. This book was not necessarily meant to be a sympathetic portrayal of her mother. This book was a portrayal of a daughter who wanted to dig into the relationship in all its nuances and complexity. And so, deciding to start the book the night this happened to Adrienne, it shifted the lens.

How do you help a writer choose where to start?

You spend a lot of time talking through the dramatic moments—I call them the crescendo moments—of the story. Most projects that I sell on proposal end up staying very true to the shape of the proposal, because we spent so much time figuring out where it should open, how it should open, why it should open there, what happens next, and then mapping it out. I want my clients to go off and write the book knowing they have the road map done.

Is there anything that you could explain to a writer just starting out to help them internalize your wisdom and do for themselves what you did for Adrienne in terms of writing a proposal that would get your attention?

Figuring out, in the narrowest way, what the story is that you're telling. You can always open it up, but I suggest starting small. Think about the memoirs that people love, that people go to again and again—they're about one specific thing. *Glass Castle* is about dysfunctional parents. *Educated* is about wanting to be educated. To spend time figuring out that one specific part of your story, it's important to figure out the voice. Is it reflective? Is it something that happened to you when you were a child, so you're going to stay in a childlike perspective? Or are you an adult looking back on this experience you had as a child with an adult's wisdom? Are you writing in the present tense? In the past tense? It's very useful to be at a point in your life with this thing that's happened to you where—as Truman Capote said—"the tears need to be dry." They don't have to be bone dry, but you need to be at a place where you can look back with clarity.

All the memoirs I work on have a degree of complicity on the part of the writer. You do not want a memoir where someone else is the monster and you're perfect. There's a great line from Vivian Gornick where she talks about how you have to show the cunning of the victim and the humanity of the monster.

I love that line.

A memoir is not about score settling. It's about getting to some universal truth, showing people that you survived something, and they will too. In order to be a fully realized human, you have to acknowledge your faults, your weaknesses, your own complicity, whatever it was that happened. Having some nuance there is important, and having some self-awareness and reflection. Also, realizing that no memoir should ever, ever, ever be the full story of someone's life. It really needs to be thinking more specifically and then drawing on the examples from your life that kind of support that thesis about that thing that happened to you.

How important is it to you that someone who's writing a memoir who isn't famous has publication history? Can someone publish a memoir before anything else?

For me, on the selling side, it's a lot easier to sell something if there's something in the world that's related to the story, but it definitely is possible to do so without it. You have to figure out what your goal is. Because if your goal is just, *I feel this burning desire to tell the story and it doesn't really matter in what form,* then you can look at self-publishing. I have a client who has no publication history but her father was killed in a mass shooting. She's writing a memoir of what it feels like to be touched by gun violence in this country. She's not famous, but she's a beautiful writer, a beautiful person, and has a lot to say about this issue. Because of that, she *could* publish an excerpt before publication [but that wouldn't be mandatory]. Because of the topic, there is public interest.

I hear anxiety from emerging writers that they're going to give the whole story away if they publish any part of it first. Do you think that's a legitimate concern?

Every book I have sold has given the story away. I have teenagers, and both times they read *Romeo and Juliet* for school, I was like, *Oh, my gosh, the prologue gives the whole thing away.* You know exactly what's coming but it's all about how it happens. They're gonna die, he tells you that in the prologue. I think that the flap copy gives the story away. It's all about the experience of reading. I don't worry about that too much.

When you're sending out a memoir, what do your submissions typically look like?

I am somebody who obsesses. I was trained by an incredible agent named Jill Kneerim, who died two years ago, but she was my mentor for fifteen years and really taught me how to be an agent. I apprenticed under her, and she was amazing. She taught me the value of a really detailed proposal. I probably go overboard, but it's served me well helping authors map out what the book should be. I don't want the most exciting day of their life to be the day of the book deal—though I do want that to be great—and then the next day for them to be full of anxiety. I want them to feel like, *Oh, I know exactly what I'm doing.* I'm always happy and feel satisfied when the proposal follows what we've crafted. I have a proposal that always opens with some great scene, then I have the Why this book? Why this author? Why now? Then I usually include two chapters, sometimes an outline, sometimes just a description of the rest. It's usually about fifty pages.

Do you have any other advice for memoir writers, before we transition to general agent advice?

Read as many books as you can in your category and know where you stand on the shelf. Get a sense of different structures, voices, formats. One of the first things I do when I'm working with someone is assign them reading in the category that they're writing. And I'm obsessed with how to open things. I think about it constantly. You can't make anything up, but there's no rule that says you can't move things around. Another exercise I have people do is think about the ten big moments that have to do with the story that they're telling.

What do you do prior to a book's publication when you think it hasn't been set up properly?

I go for one big break, whether it's NPR or one piece placed. You have to throw a lot out there and see what sticks. You can do it strategically, but try different things. I go into every publication with a couple of goals in mind. I have a novel coming out this summer that I love so much and I am like, *I would love these three things.* I'm doing everything I can to make these three things happen. Then my hope is that if one happens, great, but maybe the things that I'm doing to make those three things happen will then in turn help other things happen. I also like to talk to my authors about what their goal is because sometimes their goal is different from my goal. I ask: What do you really want? A hometown reading? Some people just really want me to submit their books to every award you can possibly think of. I represent an author who really wanted to go to festivals and another one really wanted to do something on the *Today* show. Sometimes you don't know until you ask people what would be meaningful.

Then I try to shift the conversation in a subtle way, saying to the author, *Okay, let's put our heads together and figure out everybody that you know, everyone you've ever met in your life.* Let's get a great mailing list together so that you can let people know everything that's going on, how they can help support the book, what they can do. I've been trying lately to get my authors to start thinking about their mailing lists. If I were writing a memoir, I would start with that list. There are probably about two hundred people from all parts of my life who I just want to know that I have a book coming out. For writers just starting out, tell people what they can do to help. Sometimes people want to help, but they don't know what they can do.

You're always so much better connected than you think.

One issue I've been having lately is when authors get frustrated that they're expected to draw on their contacts. That's kind of what the publisher is paying you to do—they're paying you for your literary work, but they're also paying you to be part of the marketing. Also, the reason why we go to the publisher and say, here's all the author's contacts, is because the author is expected to use them!

Any parting wisdom?

Yes. I genuinely believe in the value of sharing our personal stories of growth, struggle, triumph, and transformation in whatever form that takes, no matter what happens on the book side. If your story helps one person feel less alone in this world, whether because they've gone through something similar or feel inspired by what you've experienced—by what you've *survived*—then that's an amazing, amazing thing.

CHAPTER 4

WHAT IS AN AGENT FOR?

On a visit to a university to speak to a group of academics interested in writing books for a general audience, my host decided to have me skip the usual "this is what an agent does" spiel and open with a Q&A. He warned me his group was eager to bombard me with questions, and that they were "very lively," bringing to mind a kindergarten class on a collective sugar high. My host called on the first hand that shot up, a woman about my age, of similar curl type and intensity. "I don't mean this the wrong way," she said, "but what is the point of *you*? I get what editors do, but what is an agent *for*?"

I like to think of myself as the person who asks the question everyone else is thinking. Game recognizing game, I couldn't take umbrage. I knew the curly-haired professor was, in fact, hinting at what many people think, and that the role of agent is viewed with no small amount of suspicion. Agent characters in books and films are almost uniformly well-dressed, status-obsessed, borderline sociopaths who are completely unaware of and/or actively hostile to their clients' tender feelings. The name doesn't help. The word "agent" can bring to mind slightly nefarious connotations: secret agent, undercover agent, double agent. We seem a little too elusive and more than a little too exclusive. A professor friend who invited me to speak to his department told me with refreshing honesty that half his intended purpose in trotting me out was to show his colleagues that agents were normal people, locatable in space-time (or via email) and not some sort of semi-mythical being floating around in the ether. For many aspiring writers, the prospect of selling a book seems so far off and improbable that the necessity of finding and then securing one of those people who sells books for a living—and that you need one of them to actually achieve your dream of publishing—seems both daunting and maybe a little unfair. You need to write a book *and* find an agent? It's just too much to ask. No wonder you resent us.

So why all this trouble, and what is an agent *for*? The simplest explanation is that agents represent authors in selling books to publishers. With very few exceptions, major publishing houses, as well as the larger and midsize independent ones, will consider only book projects submitted by agents. This is, in part, a volume issue, a challenge that has only been exacerbated by industry consolidation. In publishing, we frequently refer to the "Big Five": Penguin Random House, HarperCollins, Simon & Schuster, Macmillan, and Hachette. These multinational conglomerates and their many individual imprints represent over 80 percent of the book publishing market. Agents act as a funnel and a filter for the thousands of aspiring writers who would otherwise be pitching these publishers directly, which would require far more vetting and sorting than the editorial staff of any house could ever handle. While an editor at a publishing house would never be able to read every submission by every writer around the country who would wish to be published by them, the sluicing work of an agent is a barrier to entry meant as a form of quality control. I wish I could gloss over the gatekeeping function of our role, but it's a central—and valued—part of the job. An agented submission comes with an assumed knowledge of the marketplace as well as the imprint and the individual editor being pitched. Our selectivity is part of our value, and one of the reasons agents turn so many things down. (The other just as important reason is the time and attention we try to give to each writer. This varies by agent, but if an agent takes on more clients than they can reasonably manage, some will inevitably be shortchanged.) The more thoughtful and selective an agent is in what she pitches and to whom she pitches it, the more seriously her submissions will be taken by publishers. Once you are represented, this assumption of selectivity works to your advantage.

While an agent's industry knowledge serves publishers, it also serves her clients. An agent must choose not just which imprints to submit to but which individual editors at each imprint. Because you can submit to only one editor at each imprint, an agent's familiarity with editors is valuable. (The Russian-nesting-doll nature of editors at imprints within publishers, and the submission rules governing this structure, are discussed in greater detail in the following chapter on the submissions process.)

Part of an agent's job is to know individual editors' tastes and interests, as well as more personal qualities: who is hungry for new submissions, who is currently ignoring their inbox, who would like to acquire more memoirs or fewer biographies, who spent their junior year in France and loves all things Parisian, who just got off maternity leave and never wants to read another parenting book. This information is accrued over regular meetings with editors over lunch, drinks, and Zoom, and through shared intel among our agency colleagues. (My own company's weekly meeting has time set aside for "People News" and "Gossip," where we discuss all sorts of these intangibles.) This doesn't mean an agent will submit your book without your feedback or buy-in, or that your opinions don't matter. You should by all means discuss with your agent what characteristics your dream editor and publisher would have, though I would urge you to think as much about your ideal publishing experience and editorial relationship as you do an imprint's prestige and reputation. While a publisher with lots of prizewinners and bestsellers can make a good case for themselves as your partner, your agent can help you think through other, less obvious criteria, e.g., how hands-on or overwhelmed an editor might be, the strength of a publisher's publicity, marketing, and sales departments, and how you would fit into their overall list.

Your agent also manages the business side of your relationship with your editor and publisher, a dynamic that publishers and the editors who work for them strongly prefer. Publishers do not wish to negotiate terms directly with authors, preferring to keep their relationship with you purely editorial. Ben Greenberg, editor in chief at Random House, lists some reasons why: "From a logistical standpoint, it's far more seamless to negotiate deal points with someone who has a broad, preexisting understanding of industry standards and best practices. But also, agents are, ostensibly, less emotionally invested in the work, since they did not create it, while equally invested financially, which generally leads to a clearer-eyed negotiation for all parties." Publishers see agents as a protective layer between them and the author, to the benefit of both parties. As Rakesh Satyal, executive editor at HarperOne, explains, "This is a business relationship—among the author, the agent, and the publisher—and having a professional well versed in these business matters is most beneficial to the author, not just with a specific book but throughout their career. After all, when you need legal advice, you consult a legal representative. That is an apt analog for the author-agent relationship."

The most important business function an agent serves is negotiating the advance for your book, with the aim of getting you the best deal possible at the publisher who is the best fit. Your agent will also negotiate and vet the particulars of your book contract, which will contain finer-print details of the terms of publication. Most established agencies have rigorously negotiated contracts already in place with publishers, called boilerplates. Because agencies are continually doing deals with the same set of publishers, and publishers want access to the clients they represent, agencies have leverage to negotiate stronger, more writer-friendly contracts. In competitive situations, agents can sometimes win improvements on their own boilerplate terms. At the very least, this boilerplate contract will be better than any you can negotiate on your own.

While the most significant negotiation an agent does for a client is the advance and deal points of your book contract, a good agent should remain your advocate and sounding board throughout the publication process. I always tell my authors, "I exist so you don't have to have any difficult business conversations with your publisher, and thus can focus solely on your editorial and creative relationship with them." This is not to say that you and your editor won't have disagreements or that you shouldn't get into the editorial nitty-gritty with your editor. The editorial nitty-gritty is, in fact, where you should put your energy. However, the publishing process is much bigger than what happens on the page, and this is where your agent can step in. Getting down to brass tacks, this could mean anything from nixing a proposed jacket an author hates, advocating for a bigger marketing investment or more publicity support from the publisher (or pushing back on paltry publicity and marketing efforts), chasing down money owed you, or coordinating and advising on the exploitation of other rights (foreign, audio, film/TV, podcast), among many other things. My own literary agent, Meredith Kaffel Simonoff, frames it thusly: "Part of an agent's job is to exert a palpable day-to-day presence from the outset of any publishing relationship, which in turn contributes to keeping publishers on track and pushes them to maximize their efforts and be as collaborative as possible with the author. It's also our job to be an elegant version of the 'heavy' when it comes to situations that are problematic or that we sense are actively running toward trouble and need a strong hand (and light touch) to intervene." If your editor has gone MIA, if the marketing plan for your book is nonexistent, if the publicity messaging is insensitive to your concerns, if payments are late, your agent can and should step in on your behalf. When people outside the industry find out I have a book deal, they often ask whether—or even assume—I was my own agent. It never even occurred to me to hire myself. I knew I needed a sounding board, an advocate, a fixer, and a buffer. When my own book was "orphaned" because the editor who acquired it moved to a different publisher, I had a mild freakout rather than a major one because I knew Meredith would step in to make sure I had a great editor reassigned to my book as soon as possible. I share this not to toot our own horns or overstate our workloads, but so you know that you should feel comfortable seeking your agent's help and advice when any trouble arises, or even if you just have questions and concerns. In fact, a good agent can sometimes help prevent said trouble from arising in the first place, because knowing what you're worrying about can help us avoid bumps preemptively for you and ensure a smoother ride.

This does not mean, however, that your agent can or should intervene in every dispute, or simply do your bidding. Eamon Dolan at Simon & Schuster believes there are two types of agents. One "takes an author's side in any matter reflexively, ignoring the publisher's experience and often their own. The other supports the author in a subtler and more powerful way by guiding them toward the best approach." Dolan strongly prefers working with the latter type, so much so that when he himself became an author, it was this sort of agent-as-author-adviser, rather than agent-as-publisher-adversary, that he sought out. As much as it may seem otherwise, constant badgering by your agent on your behalf would not be in your best interest. More often than not, a too-squeaky wheel's emails go unanswered; you don't want to have that agent, much less be that author. Your editor, publisher, and marketer will work all the harder for you if the working relationship is respectful and collegial, and if they feel your expectations are ambitious but within the realm of reality. (I can't tell you how many times, when I was working as a book publicist, my fellow publicists would go above and beyond—making one more call, sending one more pitch, trying for one more event—for the authors who were the sweethearts of the season.) Given their experience with other publications, an agent can help you put your dreams for your book and attendant anxieties into context. Perhaps you've long fantasized about going on an author tour and speaking at indie bookstores across the country. You and your agent *could* ask why your publisher isn't sending you to San Francisco, but your agent can also tell you if such a request is the best use of what I call your "ask ammo," which is never an unlimited resource. Perhaps a Goodreads giveaway or stylized book mailing sent to big shots in your field are a better use of publisher resources instead. Your agent should be able to advise on what should be prioritized in your publication, as well as what can and can't be controlled. And publishers know we know all this, which is why, when we step in with a strongly worded request, it carries weight.

I want to underline, though, that while an agent can and should work on your behalf throughout your publication, our interventions are not magic. I know it's an incredible feeling to get signed by an agent, a major step as a writer, a sign of faith in one's writing, and a sharing of the yoke of your career. Just because an agent asks for something—a higher advance, a bigger marketing budget, another deadline extension, a different publicist—does not mean they will get it. Do agents have a better chance than an author working alone at having reasonable requests honored and authors' wishes taken seriously? Yes! Do we rule by fiat? Good lord, I wish that were true. And no matter how powerful the power agent, our name alone can't sell a book. The quality of the book and the whims of the market will always be the most decisive factors. We also have one specific role within the publishing industry, and the scope of work of an agent doesn't also mean "publicity" and "marketing." An agent wouldn't be the one to get you on NPR or the *Today* show (that would be a publicist's purview) or to craft your social media campaign (that's marketing's job). Once your book is sold, your publisher will assign you a publicist and a marketer, though their work doesn't kick into gear until several months before publication. We'll cover these details in chapter 6, on the publication process.

A good agent, however, can dramatically improve a book's quality and its positioning in the market before the book is even sold. This is where the editorial aspect of our job comes into play, and where our role and our skill set overlap a bit with those of editors. In both fiction and nonfiction, agents work closely on editing manuscripts (in the case of fiction and some memoir) and proposals and sample materials (in the case of most nonfiction) before submitting them to publishers. Especially with nonfiction proposals, an agent often works with the author on the structure and shape of the book itself before actually selling it, helping the author at the earliest stages to build the book project from the ground up. While agents differ in how editorially involved they are, your agent should be able to offer editorial input on your book and have a good sense of how to position it to publishers.

HOW DO WE MAKE OUR MONEY? AND WHY DOES THAT MATTER TO YOU?

One of the questions I get asked most often when I tell nonpublishing people what I do for a living is "Do you work at a publisher?" Nope! No agent does; that would be self-dealing. Agents work at agencies, which can vary widely in size from one-person shops in someone's living room to multinational talent agencies like CAA, WME, and UTA, which represent every kind of "creative," from actors to directors to athletes, in addition to writers. No matter the size of the outfit, it is the job of the book agents who work there to sell writing *to* book publishers; you, the writer, are our clients. Publishers are our customers.

Agents work on commission only, and that commission rate is standardized across the industry. An agency receives 15 percent of a U.S. book advance, and this money is usually split between the agency the agent works for and the individual agent. The same 15 percent commission applies to all future royalties that book might earn, while a 20 percent commission rate is charged for monies earned from sales of foreign rights. The latter rate is higher because U.S.-based book agents often work with coagents based in other countries to sell books internationally. Those two agents' agencies typically split that 20 percent commission fifty-fifty. The same goes for film and television deals; a book agent works with a coagent to sell a book's dramatic rights, and their two agencies split a 20 percent commission. **No agent should charge you up front for reading your manuscript or doing any editorial work on it.** The Association of American Literary Agents Canon of Ethics says that agents can offer paid editorial services only to clients who approach them for that specific purpose, and not for literary representation. They prohibit agents from charging for editorial work up front unless the agent makes clear **that offering paid editorial work is *not* an offer of representation, nor a condition of it.** If an aspiring writer does become an agency client after an agent has undertaken paid editorial work on the writer's book, the agent must agree to reimburse the client all editorial fees. This distinction must be clear from the outset. There should be no "I'll consider representing your book. No, actually, pay me to edit it." This would be a bait and switch that muddies the agent's role. An agency that charges for editorial work *and* sells books on commission is by far the exception, not the rule, among established agents and agencies. If any agent charges you to read your submission, walk away.

Which brings us back to the initial question I was asked by my curly-haired interlocutor: She understood what an editor does, but what is the difference between that job and the job of an agent? The most obvious difference is structural. While an agent may do editorial work on your proposal or manuscript, they work for you. They are your fiduciary, meaning they are appointed (by you) to act on your behalf and to put your interests before your editor's or publisher's. This means they are not able to operate without your consent. They earn commission only by selling your book rights, which is why many of us describe the job as "You eat what you kill." The editor, by contrast, works at your publisher, and once you have a book deal, you essentially work for them. The process works thusly at its most rudimentary: You and an agent decide to work together; once you both feel the editorial work between the two of you has concluded and your proposal or manuscript is ready to be considered by publishers, your agent submits it to editors at publishing houses; your agent manages the sale of the book; and, should it sell, the publisher will pay you for it, and the agent's agency will commission that payment at 15 percent.

SO HOW DO YOU FIND AN AGENT?

Go to a bookstore. No, we are not usually lurking in the aisles (though we might be), but we are reliably found in the acknowledgments section at the back of a book. The front of the store will be stocked with bestsellers and new releases, so head back to the section with books that seem like they'd be shelved or displayed next to yours and take a look at the shout-outs in the final pages. Go to your own bookshelf at home and do the same with your favorite titles. Finally, do this with all the comps you mention in your proposal. All of these acknowledgments sections will help you build a list of agents to pitch.

The two richest resources for finding info about agents are *Poets & Writers,* a magazine and website, and the web-only database Publishers Marketplace. *Poets & Writers* has a detailed directory of agents and the magazine often publishes profiles of agents as well as advice from them. Publishers Marketplace tracks and announces agents' recent deals, which is a great way to see which categories an agent is currently selling. Particularly with nonfiction, where there is often a multiyear gap between the deal and publication, looking at published books is invaluable, but those books reflect deals that happened at least two years earlier, if not more. Publishers Marketplace can give you information on newer and junior agents who may have done a few deals but whose books aren't yet out in the world, though know that even Publishers Marketplace might not give the full picture on what a "baby agent" (as we lovingly call them, though you never should!) might bring to the table. The agent Rayhané Sanders offers helpful, detailed advice on why researching junior agents is worth your while, which reflects my experiences as a baby agent as well:

Publishing is an old-school industry in that if an assistant has been given the green light to start building a list, it means that she has likely worked on very many published books behind the scenes/without credit. Which is to say that even if you don't see Junior Agent's name show up on very many Publishers Marketplace deal reports, even if you don't see her name thanked in the acknowledgments sections of your favorite comps, that doesn't mean she isn't ready and able to represent you and get you a book deal. Junior agents at agencies are still building their own lists while they make the transition out of working in other administrative capacities—they are frequently younger, have more time both personally and professionally to devote to your debut, and they are hungry. When I was starting out as a baby agent, I took on manuscripts that needed a lot of work—manuscripts I probably wouldn't touch today. I don't have the same kind of time, and my plate is fuller now that I'm older and more established. But at the time, I'd go four, five, ten rounds with an author before taking a book to market. I'd cowrite proposals. I'd spend a lot of time because I was hungry to build my list.

I always advise emerging writers to cull their dream agent list for querying, then slash half the names and replace them with junior agents at their dream agent's firm. You can find bios and wishlists of junior agents on many agency websites, and you can always do some online sleuthing on Publishers Marketplace or even Google to find out if assistants at agencies have acquired a project or two yet. What you need at this stage of the game is someone who believes in you and wants to go in on a dream together with you, even if you don't have a long résumé quite yet. A young, hungry agent with a lot of time for you and space on her plate to fill is sometimes exactly what you want.

Having once been a baby agent and now, as a more experienced one, seeing how aggressively my junior colleagues must work to build their lists from scratch, I couldn't agree more wholeheartedly, though that appeal can be hard to see when you are in the trenches. Writers, especially when roving in packs at writers' conferences and readings, can get a little name-droppy about their agents. I think of it as the equivalent of walking around with a recognizably expensive designer handbag—right on the line of tacky-but-impressive! Know that dropping a fancy name indicates next to nothing about the quality or the future of the relationship in question. I took on some of my most beloved (and successful!) clients when I was still a baby agent, and a very special bond develops between author and agent if you grow your careers together. It can be a really fulfilling way to work with a person who may be with you for your entire writing career. (And working with a future power agent at the beginning of her career can have its own "I saw the Velvet Underground in 1965" cachet; in time, you'll be the one with bragging rights.)

It's absolutely true that a well-established and prominent agent will have deeper publishing relationships than a newer one. A writer may be concerned that a less experienced or younger agent won't be taken seriously by publishers. As someone who says the quiet part out loud, I saw a bit of myself in the aspiring writer I met at a writers' conference—when I was still a fresh-faced late thirtysomething—who asked me somewhat dubiously, "But do editors actually get back to you?" Perhaps keep this question to yourself, but also take a good look at the agency where any junior agent works and the books that agency has sold. Junior agents can draw on the relationships their agency (and their boss) has with publishers. If an editor receives a submission from a newer agent at an agency with whom they have previously done deals, they will likely take it seriously out of respect for the agency relationship. As I have heard from editor after editor, they are also often delighted to have new blood in the game. This doesn't mean you shouldn't pitch more senior agents or the power agent of your dreams. Agent Sarah Bowlin of Aevitas has excellent advice on how to balance your submission list between established and emerging agents:

> I usually tell people to make three different groups—the "stars" or "dream" agents, the really good people who might be more available, and the assistants or early career agents who are newly building a list—and then query a few agents from each group every round. So, if you get feedback that makes you revise or change something between rounds, you still have some people from each group to go back to.

While simultaneous submissions (the industry term for sending out queries to different agents at the same time) are acceptable and even expected, avoid simultaneously querying multiple agents at the same agency. Agents don't like to have to compete with their colleagues for projects. The process of signing up clients is already competitive enough, and the agency itself works best as a place of collaboration and mutual support, not internal competition. If two agents at the same agency were interested in repping you, one would have to defer to the other, and possibly be pissed about it. (We spend enough of our day being pissed at *publishers,* so we best not turn on each other.) Additionally, if you carpet-bomb an agency with your submission, it may look like you are throwing spaghetti against the wall to see what sticks rather than doing your research in advance to make a thoughtful choice. If a particular agent does pass, you can certainly query another agent at the same shop.

About those passes: They are an inevitability, and you will of course be disappointed, especially if they come from an agent you've dreamed about working with. First, know that the most successful agent-author relationships are just like any other one: They work best if both parties have equal passion. Second, take comfort in knowing that all agents carry around a haunting set of names of writers we passed on who went on to great success. And remember what author and legal scholar Dorothy Brown said about passes in chapter 1—a pass doesn't mean you'll *never* be published, just *not now, with this person.* Finally, many agents don't send passes at all. I apologize on our behalf; I know it is upsetting, but it is certainly not personal. For many of us, the hours in the work week don't permit us to carefully read all unsolicited submissions *and* provide good service to the clients we already have, which is always our top priority. A nonresponse can mean a pass, though there is no hard or fast rule about the amount of silence that means "not for me." You can certainly follow up, though I would avoid sending more than two or three follow-up emails. Many agency websites specify how long the agents take to reply and whether they reply to submissions they aren't interested in.

WHAT GOES IN A QUERY?

There's no single formula for how to craft a query. In polling just the agents in my office on how they'd advise authors to write one, one colleague responded, "I'm personally opposed to 'formulas' of any kind." I know this process would be easier if I could simply say A + B + C = Q(uery) & Offer of Representation, but rest assured that all agents say their own version of the same thing when explaining how to query. As with a book proposal, there isn't so much an industry-wide agreed-upon structure as there are questions your query should answer. My colleague Chris "I'm Personally Opposed to 'Formulas' of Any Kind" Parris-Lamb advises, "I always say writers should open with something that tells me why they're querying me; then no more than one paragraph describing the project; then a graf about the books they think theirs is in conversation with, or will share readers with, and/or why they think there's an audience for it; and finally a bio whose focus is less to summarize their CV than to show why they have the authority (and platform, if applicable) to write this book." My colleague Seth "I Love an Itemized List" Fishman, by contrast, gets a little more into the details, while not diverging from Parris-Lamb's advice:

1. The purpose of the query letter is to get me to turn the page to your ms. Keep it simple, no gimmicks.
2. Do your research. Know who you're writing to, know the spelling of their name and gender, know if they represent your category.
3. Keep it to just three paragraphs on one page, ideally. They amount to: Why, What, Who.
   (a) Why: One to two sentences, WHY I AM WRITING YOU, e.g., "I understand you represent Ann Leckie, I met you at Tad's dinner party, My friend Sam Miller recommended . . ."
   (b) What: One paragraph, ideally, on WHAT I AM WRITING. A brief synopsis. You don't need to introduce every character and the entire plot. Cut yourself some slack here and don't overproduce. Comp titles can go here or in "Why."
   (c) Who: One paragraph. WHO ARE YOU. Include your job or hobbies if they directly relate (i.e., I am a coal miner, and my book is set in a mine). Include publications (if you have more than three, list your

top three and say "among others"), list awards of note, MFAs, etc.

Bonus info: Don't include the word count. There is zero benefit for you in doing so, but there *are* detriments. Every agent has these kinds of tips. Instead of focusing on them, though, focus on the writing, and making the query letter simple and easy and a vehicle to the work itself.

I share these examples because while Parris-Lamb and Fishman don't offer identical guidance, they are seeking the same information from a query, which is the answer to four main questions:

- WHAT is the book about?
- WHY does it matter?
- WHO is writing the book and what makes you qualified to do so?
- For WHOM is it written?

In the interest of keeping it real, not all the queries I've included in this book, all of which eventually resulted in a published book, even answer these questions. This is not to say you should skip answering them—your query will only be stronger for doing so—but to show the successful range of variation in the wild.

Agency guidelines differ on how much material, if any, they ask writers to submit when they query, so check each respective agent's website first. If you are querying, though, you should be prepared to submit a book proposal, if asked, and ideally at least one sample chapter. If you have already published on the subject of your book, clips of that writing can also serve as samples.

Query #1

This query for a parenting book came in to a colleague over the transom. While it's longer than the norm, its length allows us to see the range of what a query can cover. The colleague did end up signing the writers and selling the book to Workman. It was published as *Raising a Kid Who Can* in 2023.

Dear Anna,

This has not been a great 15 months for human beings; as a parent, it's been even harder for you.[*] As mental health professionals on the front lines and moms ourselves, we know families need something to help them dig out of this mental health morass. But the post-pandemic period is a rare opportunity.[†] If we do this right, we will create the kind of psychological strength that could turn our kids into a new Greatest Generation: more resilient, more balanced, more courageous. But how can already overloaded and exhausted parents turn what feels like such a roadblock into an advantage?[‡]

Enter *The Parenting Playbook: The Skimmable Guide to Raising Kids in a Post-Pandemic World,* a 53k-word how-to manual for parenting, backed by the latest scientific research and a deep knowledge of human development, broken down into bite-size, illustrated chunks.[§] If Rick Steves and Emily Oster collaborated on a parenting

---

[*] This query was sent in the middle of the COVID-19 pandemic. It is about parenting and mental health, and the authors targeted agents who were parents. The first line is a direct address to Anna on that count.

[†] This pitch is for a prescriptive book, aka one that offers a solution to a problem. The first paragraph paints the problem in broad strokes; that is, the "WHY does it matter?" as well as "For WHOM is it written?" before it actually explains "WHAT is the book about?" This creates a bit of suspense in the letter. The solution—the WHAT of the book—is held back just a bit until after the problem is revealed.

[‡] A classic framing of a prescriptive book and of a nonfiction project more broadly: XYZ bad thing is, in fact, an opportunity for XYZ good thing.

[§] The always-helpful one-sentence description of WTF the book actually is.

book and had Jeff Kinney illustrate it, the result would look a lot like *The Parenting Playbook*.*

The *Playbook* is for this moment and beyond, since all the parenting we do from now on is post-pandemic parenting. We boil parenting down to Ten Essentials and offer concrete tips and tools for what parents can do, how they can do it, and why it matters. Each chapter starts with a section called What's the Deal? followed by What's the Science? But you can also skip straight to Just Tell Me What to Do or In the Trenches, and come back at your leisure to Points to Ponder. There's something for everyone here, whether you want to think deeply about your parenting philosophy or just need help in the moment with the problem of the day.† While the *Playbook* has helpful information for parenting children of all ages, our core audience is parents of kids ages three to sixteen. We provide examples of our strategies for a range of ages so that parents can easily identify and apply the tools regardless of their child's age. It's a different approach to a parenting book—one we believe will be a breath of fresh air to parents with good intentions but short attention spans.‡

Our vision is to become the trusted go-to resource for busy parents who want concise, evidence-based, mission-critical information they can refer to time and again, a *How to Talk So Kids Will Listen* for this generation. *The Parenting Playbook* is filled with playful drawings, infographics, and font changes to both keep readers engaged and help

---

* Here is what I call a "vibes comp." Rick Steves is a travel writer who specializes in off-the-beaten-path journeys; Jeff Kinney's books are for kids and illustrated in a playful minimalist way. Oster is an economist who has written several bestsellers about parenting through an economics lens. Seeing these three seemingly disparate names together gives one a feel for the tone of the book: unexpected, approachable, but science based.

† Not all query letters contain a section on how the book will be structured, but I think including a few sentences on that is very helpful. This is a good model of how to do so without getting into the weeds.

‡ Further specifies the book's readership.

them remember the important stuff. We believe high-quality information in an easy-to-digest format also has tremendous potential to launch a brand and series of deeper dives, by age such as toddler or teen, or by subject matter such as motivation or anxiety. All three of us are popular speakers in the D.C. metro area, with a wide network to promote the *Playbook* to parents, teachers, and other professionals who are hungry for our extremely usable guide.[*]

We think *The Parenting Playbook* will appeal to parents who always mean to read books like *The Whole Brain Child* by Daniel J. Siegel and Tina Payne Bryson, *The Teenage Brain* by Frances E. Jensen and Amy Ellis Nutt, and *How to Raise an Adult* by Julie Lythcott-Haims but never quite have the time. Our audience is readers who have graduated from Emily Oster's amazing books *Expecting Better* and *Cribsheet* and are looking for their next step. Think of the *Playbook* as SparkNotes for parenting.[†]

We know the challenges and we have the solutions, developed over more than sixty-five combined years working with tens of thousands of families from three different vantage points: expertise in the brain (psychiatrist Catherine), behavior (psychologist Heather), and emotions (psychotherapist Jennifer). We are also parents ourselves, so we share our own struggles in each chapter. Parenting often happens on the fly, so we need to help each other keep an open perspective and a sense of humor.[‡]

---

[*] This addresses why the authors are qualified to write the book while also giving us a bit of info about their platform or how they will promote it.

[†] Here the authors list comps, which is another way to explain the book's audience. These comps are more straightforward than the vibes comps. They show the recent readership for books on the same topic while also differentiating the book they are proposing from previous hits.

[‡] Here is more detail about who is writing the book. Because this book has three authors, this detail is kept fairly minimal. The force is in the combined experience of three different parenting experts with three different areas of expertise.

We have a book proposal and full manuscript at the ready that we would love to share with you. We welcome the opportunity to discuss our project with you at your convenience and we appreciate your consideration. Please find attached the proposal including sample chapters.

Best regards,

Catherine McCarthy, MD, Heather Tedesco, Ph.D., and Jennifer Weaver, MSW, LCSW

Query #2

This is a query I received from Joseph V. Lee, who once worked in publishing as an assistant and is now my client. Our connection when he wrote this was pretty tangential—we'd never met in person—but Lee wisely still used it. If you are querying an agent you, say, met at a writers' conference or saw on a panel, by all means, mention that!

Dear Alia,

I hope you're doing well. We were in touch when I was working at Little, Brown as XYZ's assistant. I'm reaching out because during that time I came to really admire your nonfiction list and am hoping that you will be interested in my proposal. *Nothing More of This Land* is a narrative nonfiction book about the untold story of my tribe—the Aquinnah Wampanoag—and our fight to build a casino on our ancestral homeland of Martha's Vineyard.

To tell this unique story of modern Native American life, *Nothing More of This Land* will follow the linked narratives of the tribe's struggles and my family history.[*] Capitalizing on the island's rapid development into an iconic vacation destination in the 1970s, my family opened a souvenir shop. The industry that my family came to rely on, however, quickly divided the tribe and threatened to destroy our homeland. In the face of these dramatic changes, the tribe made a bold land reclamation attempt, which provoked a strong response from wealthy white summer residents. On Martha's Vineyard, familiar aspects of Native history—loss of land, cultural extinction,

---

[*] Here is the WHAT of the book.

racism—are very real dramas being played out on pristine beaches, not mere historical context. And with some of the most coveted real estate in the country and thousands of years of history at stake, allegiances frequently cross racial and even family lines. Through the tribe's stories and my own struggle to find my place within the tribe, *Nothing More of This Land* will reveal how the current casino controversy is the culmination of fifty years of conflict.[*]

I am a member of the Aquinnah Wampanoag Tribe of Gay Head (Aquinnah) and have an MFA in nonfiction writing from Columbia University. My essays and journalism have been published in *Tin House, Electric Literature, Rewire News, Avidly,* and more. I also write a column on Native identity for *Catapult.* I can reach out to a broad network of writers for endorsements and support, including Leslie Jamison, Adrian Nicole Leblanc, Margo Jefferson, and Colm Tóibín.[†] Thank you for reading and please let me know if you'd like to see the full proposal.

Best,
Joseph

Query #3

This is the query Heather Radke used when first looking for an agent. The template she created could be tweaked and varied for each agent.

Dear XX,

I hope this note finds you well. I am a nonfiction writer seeking representation and am reaching out with the hope that you may be interested in my work. I am a huge fan of so many clients that you represent, including the wonderful X and Y.[‡]

---

[*] And here is the why it matters.

[†] Lee also explains why he is uniquely qualified to write this book. His qualifications are both personal and professional.

[‡] Always good to mention writers the agent reps, especially if they work in similar categories.

Butts is a book-length cultural history that takes as its premise that in our bodies, we carry histories. We carry the histories of our families and of our own lives, but also of the many centuries of evolution and culture that have shaped how we see ourselves and how others see us.* The book describes and analyzes historical moments in the history of the female butt starting with Sarah Bartman's arrival in England in 1810 and going through the so-called "crossover butt" of Jennifer Lopez in the 1990s and ensuing butt renaissance. It also uses magazine-style reportage to examine the butt in contemporary American culture and includes chapters on butt augmentation, fetish, and evolutionary psychology.† The goal of the book is to provide a deeply researched and thoughtfully analytic understanding of how our most private feelings about our own bodies emerge from larger historical and cultural forces, and how and why certain kinds of bodies come in and out of fashion.‡

PERSONALIZED COMP/Audience section§

A bit about me:¶ I'm finishing up my MFA in nonfiction writing at Columbia this year, and my work has been published or is forthcoming in *The White Review, The Paris Review, Guernica, Topic, Longreads,* and *The Believer.* Before coming to Columbia, I lived in Chicago for almost a decade, where I worked as a museum cura-

---

* Here is the WHAT of the book, framed not just as the subject itself—in this case, butts—but also its argument.

† Helpful but not too-in-the-weeds details about how the book unfolds.

‡ And this is the WHY the book matters section.

§ Comps are a great way to personalize each letter for each respective agent you are querying.

¶ It's okay to be a little informal if it reflects your writing style and subject! Radke is proposing a book about butts and being too buttoned-up might not suit.

tor at the Jane Addams Hull-House Museum and an audio producer for Radiolab and WBEZ-Chicago. I have contributed essays
to books on social practice art and the history of Chicago and have
lectured nationally on Jane Addams, social practice art, and innova-
tive museum practice.[*]

I've attached a full book proposal for *Butts*, including an overview
essay, chapter outlines, and sample chapter. I've also attached an essay
on ponies and gender that will be in the Jan/Feb issue of *The Believer*.

ON NOT WRITING QUERIES

Real talk: Pulling together these queries was the biggest sample material challenge in writing this book. The majority of the nonfiction
writers on my list never formally queried me, and the same is true
for most of the agents I interviewed. In truth, we found the bulk of
our clients through our own direct outreach or referrals, something I
think is inherently true for a lot of nonfiction. This isn't to discourage
you from querying agents. In fact, few things brighten my day more
than seeing a well-thought-out book idea in my inbox from an excellent writer. It means less work for me in that I might have something
great to sell without having to architect it from the ground up. I share
how I found my clients to reemphasize the reason I started this book
with the chapter on pitching articles. **The first step in a nonfiction
author's career is rarely signing with an agent, and the first publication is rarely a book.** Almost all agents—from newbies to more
established ones—are regularly reading literary magazines and other
media to look for new talent. I know the assumption of many writers is that you need to have an agent to place pieces in such outlets,
but the reality is you really, really don't. Aside from *The New Yorker*,
which is hard to crack without an agent as an intermediary, nearly all
publications not only take submissions directly from writers but, in

---

[*] This is, loosely speaking, Radke's platform. She has an MFA, has been
published in respected literary magazines, and includes the interesting
career experience of being a museum curator. She makes no mention
of social media, and she still got an agent and a book deal.

fact, prefer *not* to have them come via an agent. (For an exhaustive list of great literary magazines, check out the directory of the Community of Literary Magazines and Presses.) As I discussed in my section on pitching a memoir, writers sometimes worry that publishing a piece from a future book would give too much away, making that book difficult to sell. To that I say, if your whole book could be best expressed in seven thousand words rather than seventy thousand, it probably isn't a book, so go ahead and try to place that great piece. And if you have a ton to say on a given subject (say, seventy to one hundred thousand words' worth), it's always in your best interest to get a teaser out there. It serves as a calling card for you and a proof of concept for agents and publishers.

The one qualification to my advice on needing to publish shorter work before trying to sell a book is if you are writing something prescriptive, i.e., a how-to and advice book. If your main job is not "being a writer" but rather being an expert in a given field, and your proposed book is based on that expertise, it's far less important to prove your writing chops by publishing your writing. You will want to get your name out there, though, because agents who focus on expert-driven books do the same sort of talent hunting. Per John Maas at Park & Fine, an agency that represents many bestselling authors in the prescriptive space, around 25 percent of his agency's clients are signed because an agent there found their work and reached out. To that end, you need to be discoverable. Some ways to do so are by having your work appear in outlets specific to your field, through social media, through self-publishing, and through being mentioned by peers. (For more from Maas and others on this, see chapter 2.5.)

Another major resource for agents finding clients is referrals. I know this can sound discouraging if you aren't institutionally connected to other writers or if you prefer to spend your time at home reading your books and thinking your sweet little thoughts. The latter is true for most writers, including this one. (I am writing this chapter in my favorite place, which is my bed, with my dog at my feet, having once again canceled drinks plans.) The plus side of networking among fellow bookish introverts means a little bit can go a long way—none of us really want to talk *that* much. Start locally and see if there are any writers' groups in your community. Writers' groups also regularly feature in-person and online panel discussions with agents and editors. (The *Poets & Writers* website has a long, detailed list of writers' groups with contact information as well as guides on how to choose one.) Many of the best writing programs in the country also offer online workshops and continuing education courses. Writers' conferences offer many of the same benefits of an MFA, with a much lower time and money commitment. In all these instances, prioritize getting to know your fellow writers as much as—if not more than—elbowing your way over to the agent everyone is dying to talk to. Other writers, both established and emergent, are a rich and varied resource in getting information about agents, editors, and publication opportunities. Don't assume that networking with other unpublished writers is a waste of time. Life is long, and fortunes change. If you are in a writing class and you like a classmate's work, don't begrudge them; befriend them. Everyone loves encouragement but perhaps no one more than an unpublished writer. That said, don't be too intimidated by the ones who *are* published. Send a fan letter to your favorite writers. Introduce yourself at a reading. I wouldn't suggest including a request for an introduction to their agent (or at least not on the first date), but do know that most writers appreciate appreciation just like the rest of us, and you never know when that can be paid forward.

You also needn't be connected to writers with a capital *W* to form the connections you need to be referred to an agent. Just as useful, particularly if the book you want to sell is based more on your expertise than your prose artistry, is to have your work known by your peers. Circulate your work informally within your industry and also through recognized professional channels, such as journals and conferences. If a colleague is active on social media or has a significant following, don't be shy about asking them if they'd be open to sharing your work. And as always, try to get to know other writers publishing in your space. Published writers know other writers and quite possibly agents and editors interested in exactly what you are doing—they just don't know you yet.

SO, AN AGENT IS INTERESTED IN YOUR WORK!

Congrats! An agent responded to your query. Perhaps they asked if you have more work to share. If you have it, share it. If not, be honest about where you are in your process and don't slap together some pages in the interest of seeming like you have more in the kitty than you do. Perhaps they asked to chat. Even better! Very few offers of representation are made without some sort of conversation, so this is an auspicious overture. The agent likely wants to hear more about your book but also to get to know you as a person. Use the call to do the same. You will of course want to weigh the agent's track record and experience, but you'll also want to get a sense of whether you have a shared vision for your book and if this agent is one you'd feel comfortable asking for help when you are stuck, confused, or worried. Your agent isn't your therapist, but they shouldn't make you feel like you've been called into the principal's office.

Don't be surprised if the agent asks you questions that are answered in your proposal or sample material. It may be that we missed something, but it is more likely an attempt to get you talking about your book. The agent will want to know how you talk about it because that will come into play when you are trying to sell and promote it. The agent may also have editorial feedback or suggested changes. My strong suggestion is to listen to these with equanimity. First, they may be useful, even if you disagree with them. Second, and more instrumentally, you want to hear the agent's honest, unvarnished opinion. You won't get that if you immediately bristle at the thought of edits. If the edits are bonkers, you don't have to work with them! You have lost nothing, though, by hearing them out.

You'll also have a chance to ask the agent questions. I'm going to quote from Publishers Marketplace's interview with agent Vicky Bijur, as it's a perfect list of questions to ask:

1. Will you keep me reasonably informed throughout the process of selling my book? For example, can we discuss the list of publishers to whom you would submit my project? If I ask, will you send me the responses you've received?
2. How involved do you get in a book's publication after the

contract is negotiated? That is, how do you see your role?

3. How do you handle foreign rights? Film rights?
4. Do you have an Agency Agreement that you and your client each sign?
5. Will you provide editorial feedback on my work before you submit it?
6. What kind of future charges might there be? Am I responsible for legal fees in case I need a lawyer for a film deal? Or suppose I need a freelance editor or book doctor—am I responsible for those fees?
7. Suppose the first book I do is on labor relations but then I want to do a children's book—do you handle all kinds of books?
8. Feel free to ask a prospective agent how long they've been agenting and what they did before.

I also think it's worth asking the agent for an example of a book they loved working on, or an author they loved working with. Just as they want to hear how you talk about books, you'll want to hear how they communicate interest in what they rep. Hearing about a client they love will help you be a client they love too, always a good spot to be in. And because the core of a good agent-author relationship is communication, you may also want to ask how they prefer to communicate and how quickly you can expect to hear from them.

If you have an offer of representation in hand, you can use that to follow up with other agents still considering. This will signal to us that the clock is really ticking. I find it helpful if a writer in these cases gives me a deadline. You can say something like, "I've just received an offer of representation, but I would love to have the chance to work with you. Would you kindly let me know by the end of next week if you are interested?" If you do go this route, don't then jump the gun and sign with Agent #1 before your own professed deadline. We agents have all been in a situation where we dropped everything to read a manuscript after getting such an email, loved it, let the author know we were interested before the deadline, only to receive a note back saying, "Oh, thank you, but I ended up signing with XYZ!" I know it's very exciting to receive an offer of representation, but you shouldn't feel rushed—nor should you rush yourself—in making the decision. And if an interested agent tries to rush *you,* take that as a not-very-good indicator of what they'd be like as a business partner.

Once you decide to work together, your agent will likely (but not always—individual agents and agencies differ in their signing protocol and paperwork formality levels) have you sign a representation agreement. There can be a bit of a courtship dance, especially with nonfiction, which often requires some developmental work, before you get to this point. You can certainly ask an interested agent if they will confirm that they want to represent you and, if so, what paperwork is involved. The "rep" agreement itself should serve as a clarification of terms for both parties: It will outline how you, and the agent, can terminate the relationship, as well as confirming commission amounts. While these agreements are usually chock-full of legalese, they shouldn't be a lifetime commitment or blood oath. Always feel free to ask your agent for clarifications of terms.

SO YOU WANT TO FIRE YOUR AGENT

I am sorry to hear that! It's stressful and upsetting for both parties. My first bit of (admittedly biased) advice is don't make a habit of it. The publishing world is small and authors who cycle through multiple agents can earn the reputation of being difficult to please. I would also advise against seeking to level up to a bigger agency or more celebrated agent *just* because your book was a success. This isn't just because I am a big believer in dancing with the one who brung you, but also because that agent who was part of making you a success will be deeply invested in your career and ideally, both your careers will flourish in tandem. Today's baby agent is tomorrow's superstar, and if you were lucky enough to get in there early, you will become a central part of their business and their list—always a good thing to be.

If you want to part with your agent because your book didn't sell to publishers, it's slightly trickier. Changing agents doesn't wipe the slate clean in terms of where you can submit. If Farrar, Straus and Giroux passed on your book when Agent X tried to sell it to them, you don't get a second shot at selling the same project to them, even if you try a different editor there, just because Agent Y now represents you. If you leave your agent before your book is sold, be sure to ask your first agent for a full list of who considered it and what their responses were so no one ends up in the awkward position of receiving an email saying, "Yeah, we already said no to this one." It's a bad look for all involved.

In considering parting ways with your agent, I would advise you to think less about your book's sale, advance size, or market performance, and more about your agent's service. Most books, even those that garner huge advances and rigorous promotion, don't do well commercially. We—agent, author, editor, publisher—often have very little control over that. We do, however, have control over how we behave. Your agent should be clear, kind, and responsive. You should have a reasonably shared vision of your book. Above all, you should trust them to act in your best interest. We can't magic you into best-sellerdom, but you shouldn't doubt that your agent is on your team.

In parting ways, you should also be clear and kind. Don't draw out the process and don't relitigate the past. If your agent asks why you are changing representation, you are under no obligation to get too specific. It's okay to secure representation with another agent before moving on, and it is also okay, and sometimes unavoidable, to share the new agent's name with your old one. There's also no hard-and-fast rule on how to pull the trigger, so I'd advise choosing whatever form of communication feels most comfortable and nonconfrontational. Another reason to keep things collegial is that the money for any deals your erstwhile agent negotiated will flow through their office in perpetuity. There's no need to burn bridges with someone who sends you checks.

KEY TAKEAWAYS

- An agent represents authors in selling books to publishers. And, lest you think you don't need one, with very few exceptions, the Big Five publishing houses as well as the larger and midsize independents consider only book projects submitted by agents.
- Literary agents are both the architect and the real estate broker, working closely on editing manuscripts, proposals,

and sample materials before submitting to publishers. An agent will work with the author on the structure and shape of the book before selling it, helping at the earliest stages to build the project from the ground up.

- An agent works for the author (you), who works for the editor and publisher. But it is your agent who manages the business side of your relationship with your editor and publisher. Publishers do not wish to negotiate terms directly with authors, preferring to keep their relationship with authors purely editorial.
- A good agent will remain your advocate and sounding board throughout the publication process—one that is much bigger than what happens on the page—and make sure you don't have to have any of the hard conversations with your publisher directly.
- Agents have a specific job, but it does *not* entail "publicity" and "marketing."
- Agents work on commission only, and that commission rate is standardized. An agent gets 15 percent of a U.S. book advance, and all future royalties that book might earn, and 20 percent of money from sales of foreign rights.
- You can find agents in the acknowledgments section of your favorite books or, better yet, Publishers Marketplace. No agent should charge you up front for reading your manuscript or doing any editorial work on it.
- Established agents are great, but up-and-coming agents are a good place for new authors to look.
- The majority of nonfiction writers do not formally query agents. In truth, most agents find the bulk of their clients by reaching out to them first.
- The first step in a nonfiction author's career is rarely signing with an agent, and the first publication is rarely a book.

CHAPTER 5

THE SUBMISSION PROCESS, OR THIS IS WHERE IT HURTS

When I was little, I hated having my blood drawn. Nurse after exasperated nurse tried to reassure me that it didn't hurt and I would be just fine, which is an easy thing to say when you are the one holding the needle. The standard advice was to close my eyes and it'd be over in a second. I inevitably howled. Of course, it wasn't the pain that hurt but the anticipation of it. As a budding hypochondriac (one of the reasons I spent my childhood getting a lot of blood drawn), my worry was that a routine medical test would reveal all the things that were wrong with me, and one of those things was assuredly imminent death. I eventually met my morbid match when I got a phlebotomist who gave it to me straight. First, she told me she loved drawing blood. I couldn't believe someone would enjoy an act I found so unpleasant, but her delight in blood and needles was the good kind of infectious. Second, she narrated every part of the procedure: "Now I am making a tourniquet. This helps me find a vein." "Now I have found a vein. Looks like you have a good one!" "Now take a deep breath. This is where it hurts." At the end, she gave me the requisite sticker and asked if I'd like to see the vial of my own blood. When I said yes, she brandished the vial with glee. Seeing my own blood in a plastic tube suddenly made the procedure seem both miraculous and reassuringly routine. I didn't get over my dislike of having my blood drawn—it's kind of creepy and it hurts!—but having the process handled by someone who enjoyed it, who appreciated its awe and saw the importance of explaining its mechanisms—made my fear manageable.

You see where I am going here. The submission process is extremely unpleasant for authors, and this is not an irrational response. To extend my metaphor, you are sending a sample of one of the most intimate parts of yourself out into the world for evaluation and diagnosis. You don't know what the result might be, but when you really want to sell a book, learning no one wants to publish that book can feel like a fate nearly as catastrophic as imminent death. Of course you are terrified.

I am a bit like the sanguineous phlebotomist. I *love* being on submission—not because I am a sadist (or at least not consciously so), but because I relish bringing what my author and I have been working on, just the two of us, to the wider world. The only way I can explain the tingle I feel the night before I go on submission with something I love is that it feels like the eve of opening night. But because I'm more Mama Rose than Gypsy Rose Lee, I know my giddiness is probably mine alone. I don't think I'll ever be able to fully feel the anxiety my authors do while we are on submission (this book notwithstanding), but I've come to believe the phlebotomist's approach goes a long way, and that it's the author's due as they enter not just a creative collaboration but an extended business relationship. While I will go into detail about the submission process, I hope this chapter will also empower you, the author, to ask your agent appropriate questions throughout. In this way you'll be able to obtain the necessary clarity to weather the ordeal, and perhaps even be the stronger for it.

One of the reasons the submission process is so excruciating is because of all the components of a writing career, this one is where you are faced with the most variables and where you have the least control. The less you try to control it, the better off you will be. I can't emphasize this enough: You need to hand the reins over to your agent here. Hopefully, this won't be hard to do, because at this point in the process, real trust should be established, and it's the agent's job to foster that trust. Submitting and selling a book is at the very center of an agent's job, and during this part of the publishing process, publishers want to deal with them, not you. No matter how much you know about the industry, your agent—even if they are relatively new to the business—will know more. Precisely because the submission process has so many variables and because agents don't want authors to read too much into either initial silence or early but noncommittal shows of interest, your agent likely won't share everything blow-by-blow. That said, you are entitled to transparency and clear communication, and knowing how the submission process works will help you know what to ask.

Your agent's first step is writing a pitch letter. This letter often draws from your proposal and even from your own initial pitch, especially if the project has remained essentially the same. Some agents share their pitch letters with clients, some don't, but you are certainly allowed to ask to see it. Feel welcome to ask questions about how the book is being described and positioned and to offer suggestions, but also trust that your agent likely knows more about the market and the intended audience (in this case, a select group of editors) than you do. This is why it's so important to talk with a prospective agent before signing with them about your shared sense of your book's market and audience. By the time you go out on submission, you should know you are on the same page.

Second is the submission list. Your agent will put together the list of editors to whom they will send your proposal for consideration. There are informal but strictly observed rules that govern this process. An agent can submit to only one editor per imprint for each respective submission, but can submit to more than one imprint per Big Five publisher. Confusing, I know, but it helps to think of it a bit like a Matryoshka doll, with little companies inside bigger ones.

On the following page is a chart of the current Big Five publishing houses (HarperCollins, Macmillan, Simon & Schuster, Penguin Random House, and Hachette). On the right is a list of some of the most prominent independent publishers, or "indies." Under the Big Five I've listed some sample imprints that operate within them. PRH, the largest of these conglomerates, gets double umbrellas because of how they bid. There are divisions within that company (Random House group, Knopf Doubleday, Penguin), and then imprints within these divisions. If more than one imprint within a given division is interested in bidding on your book, they will bid collectively in what is known as a "house bid." To complicate matters further, in the era of mergers, acquisitions, and just plain folding, this tree changes fairly often. It's your agent's job to know about the movements within the industry; regardless of the details, though, the rules tend to remain largely unchanged.

Let's use my own book as an example of the process of navigating this tree and the submission rules it requires. In my case, my agent submitted my proposal to many editors, including Maria Goldverg at Pantheon, an imprint at Penguin Random House and part of the Knopf Doubleday Publishing Group, who ultimately acquired it. Note I mentioned that Pantheon is in the Knopf Doubleday group. Each of the other imprints under that divisional umbrella (in this case, Knopf, Doubleday, Schocken, and Vintage Books, among others) at PRH would have also been fair game to submit to. The same goes for any other imprint at PRH, any imprint at any of the other Big Five conglomerates, and any indie. What my agent would *not* have been allowed to do is submit to more than one editor at Pantheon though. It was Maria or bust where Pantheon was concerned.

Because an agent can submit to only one editor per imprint per project, part of her job is knowing which editor at each given imprint might be the best fit. If you have any relationships with book editors, you should absolutely share them! But more likely than not, your agent will have a far better sense of individual editors' mandates and tastes than you can glean from publicly available information. Agents regularly meet with editors to discuss what the former is selling and the latter is buying. During these meetings, an agent might also gauge interest in your project; when an editor's ears perk up over lunch about an upcoming submission, it lays the groundwork for what's to come. Meredith Kaffel Simonoff did exactly this kind of prep when selling the book you are reading, and it's an illustrative example. Over coffee one afternoon, as she tells it, she asked Maria Goldverg about her publishing origin story while reflecting on her recent job move, which evolved into a conversation about the industry's opacity and how that can fail to serve authors and their books. Meredith discovered in Maria a shared desire for greater transparency in the business and also had the opportunity to discuss her then-new colleagues at Gernert, which allowed her to pivot to the little-known fact that I was writing a book about this very subject and that she was representing it. The conversation was apparently off to the races from there. The same was true when the time came to find me a new editor at Pantheon, after Maria left; Denise Oswald stepped easily into the role with much the same shared mission and collaborative spirit.

Because a submission list is often based on an agent's personal relationships and contacts, and because it is likely full of names you don't know, not all agents share their submission lists with clients. Don't be surprised if your agent doesn't, but by all means ask to see it if you wish. As in any close relationship, you should never have that creeping feeling you're unnecessarily being left in the dark. If there are publishers whose books you love, go ahead and share those thoughts with your agent. You can certainly give feedback on their submission list if you have strong feelings about any of the imprints listed. In almost all cases, the submission is sent out simultaneously, meaning a range of editors get the materials within a day or two, almost always over email.

The number of imprints and editors an agent submits to will also vary based on the project and an agent's approach. In some cases, it might make sense to do a wide submission, which can include fifteen to twenty names. In other cases, a tighter submission is in order. Given that you *can* send to, say, twenty people, why would an agent only send to ten? The latter can be in service of the reputational long game for both the author and the agent. An agent wants to have the reputation of being judicious and considered, not scattershot and random. Consistently sending editors projects that are good fits gains an agent respect and means their submissions are read quickly and considered seriously. You want this kind of agent. An agent may also decide to do a submission in rounds, or widening circles. Because you get only a single shot with one editor at each imprint, you don't want to blow it. In some cases, especially with debut authors, it can be helpful to cautiously test the waters. If there is significant interest early on, an agent can then always send out more widely. If there are only passes but they come with constructive and consistent editorial feedback, the agent and author can reassess the current iteration of a project. I'm sharing this info not so you can help your agent strategize (my guess is that would be as unwelcome as telling your dentist how to fill your tooth), but so you don't get anxious if, say, you compare notes with friends and their agent had a totally different plan of attack.

The length of time before submitting and getting responses varies widely, but it can be anywhere from a couple of days with well-known authors to a couple of weeks to over a month. While you are waiting for news, you'll be dying to check in with your agent, but more likely than not, if there was good news, you'd be the first to know! Be prepared for the passes to come in before the expressions of interest. It takes longer to get to "yes" than "no," not because an interested editor would be deliberating for weeks but because an editor can never make an offer on a book without buy-in from their colleagues and their superiors (most likely, the editor in chief and publisher). Thus, when an editor reads a proposal or manuscript they like, the next step is to share it with their colleagues for reads. Sometimes an editor will communicate that they are getting reads on a project to the agent; sometimes the agent will communicate that to you. Often an agent will use any early expression of interest from one editor to follow up with the others considering it in order to move the process along. In service of managing expectations, your agent likely won't communicate any of these little ripples of interest until they have something firmer in hand. This is typically the point at which an editor is interested in talking directly to you.

ON PUBLISHER MEETINGS

If an editor is seriously interested in acquiring your book, they will likely ask your agent to set up a meeting with you. Writers sometimes feel that such a request is the publishing equivalent of being called to the principal's office. This is not the case at all! A meeting with you is, more often than not, a prerequisite for a publisher making an offer. It's always a good sign, never a reason to panic, and can result in crucial information gathering for all parties involved. Publishing a book together is a long and deeply collaborative relationship and, at least on the publisher's side, a financially risky one. The legendary editor Daniel Menaker once compared acquiring a book to a night at a casino. The publisher hands you a chunk of money up front and there's a high probability they will never earn it back. Before anyone gives a writer a contract and some cash, they'll want to know a bit about the recipient. The editorial fit is important for both sides. Especially with nonfiction, which is largely sold on proposal, there are inevitably editorial questions. If you think of a proposal as a road map for a book, the collaboration between author and editor fills in the topography. (Do road maps already have topography? I never claimed to be a cartographer, just a lover of extended metaphors.) That initial meeting might involve addressing what that topography will be, but it's primarily to see if you both feel comfortable figuring it out together.

Authors often want to know what level of interest a meeting indicates. The submission process would create much less anxiety if the meeting were a universally agreed-upon overture. I'd say it's a bit like a first date (they wouldn't ask you if they weren't interested!), albeit one on *The Bachelor*. One ride on horseback can be all it takes to arrive at a pretty heavy and very public commitment. In advance of any formidable commitment, you should come prepared. I like to send my authors bios (and if I have them, publicly available photos) of every editor they will meet with so they can prepare and differentiate. Not every agent does this, but you can certainly ask yours for information in advance on the editors you'll meet. The publisher's website, the editor's social media, and especially Publishers Marketplace can all give you information about an editor's list, though as with agents, it's far from complete. Can a meeting determine whether or not a publisher will make an offer? Again, it varies. Often a publisher goes into a meeting knowing that they will offer, but a good meeting can heighten their interest (and increase their financial commitment). If there are editorial reservations, a meeting can be determinative. Sometimes an editor will propose a very different version of the book than the one you put forth yourself. If the version they are proposing is substantially different from your own, and if you really want to work with them, you may be asked to submit a revised proposal, but in most cases, these editorial differences are resolved in the meeting. If you can both agree on the editorial direction, the meeting can be make or break. Given the collaborative nature of the relationship, the initial meeting between prospective editor and author is often as much about editors selling themselves to you as it is about selling yourself to them. In most meetings, the editor will tell you about their imprint and the kind of books they publish. Now is not the time to show your prowess as a literary critic, so save any criticism about those books for the debrief with your agent. Listen with respect and (for the sake of politeness, and your bank account) express enthusiasm for their work and their list. No one is going to force you to work with an editor you don't like or respect (and the meeting's purpose is in part to determine these preferences), but the more interest you have, the more offers you'll get—and an offer from a publisher you don't want to work with can drive up the price from one you do. (Don't tell any editors I told you that.) The same is true when the editor discusses your submission. Letting an editor speak their mind unreservedly about your own book also serves you in terms of finding a good collaborator, so do not dismiss any editorial feedback out of hand. You want to get their unvarnished opinion to make the best decision possible, especially if you are lucky enough to choose among multiple parties. If an author immediately shuts down any proffered editorial advice, an editor may not be fully honest about what they think. Such resistance to editorial collaboration can also be a red flag for an editor. Editors, after all, do want to edit.

In terms of tone, if you have ever fantasized in the shower about holding forth on public radio, now is your time to play pretend with a willing partner. "What would I say on NPR about my book?" is a good question to keep in mind, as publishers will be thinking about it as well. When the time comes to spread the word about your book, you will be its best and most visible representative. In either case, the editor will surely be thinking, "How well will this person be able to talk about their book in public?" As in a media interview, simply talking is half the battle. Editor after editor I've spoken with about the goal of that first meeting has said that it's about getting you talking about the book, in large part to see how you do it and then to let a natural conversation unspool from there. Don't be surprised if you are asked questions that are answered in the proposal, especially right off the bat as conversation starters. Take these softballs as a warmup, and know that it's totally okay to repeat (and ideally expand upon) material you have already shared. Think about book interviews you've listened to, and how their intended audience isn't people who have read the actual book as much as potential readers the author is trying to convince to do so. While the editor in your meeting will have read your proposal, they will also be thinking about how you would explain your book in public to those potential readers. Being able to give a thumbnail description of your book is particularly important if the editor asks colleagues such as the publisher, the editor in chief, publicists, or marketers to join the meeting. As discussed in chapter 3, these secondary readers will be encountering your work as generalists and might have read your proposal only cursorily. Keep this kind of reader in mind as you talk about your work and answer any questions about it.

I wish I could give you a list of likely questions that will be asked, but they vary too widely. That said, the opener is usually something along the lines of "Why this book? Why now?" Again, you may very well have answered that in the proposal (especially if you took notes while reading the proposal chapter!). Don't let this faze you, and remember the editor's number one goal: to get you talking. While you can't control or even anticipate any further questions you'll be asked, you do have some latitude over the range of the conversation. Come up with three to five talking points you'd like to be sure to hit during your meeting. Thinking about stories or examples you'd like to share is helpful too, especially if they go beyond what you have already shared. This kind of prep work will help you in the initial meeting with publishers as well as further down the line when it comes to publicity. If you're stuck, your agent can be helpful in developing these. I sometimes do a mock meeting before our publisher meetings to help a client prepare, and you can certainly ask your agent to do this. If that doesn't feel like an easy ask, recruit willing family and friends.

The format of these meetings is pretty consistent. They usually last an hour, and at their most intimate, it'll be just you and the editor. If an editor asks colleagues to join, the editor will still be the one to run the meeting. Don't read too much into whether or not the editor rolls deep, as it is no indication of the level of interest or the size of a possible offer. Sometimes the meetings are in person (especially if you live in or close to New York City); they can also be held remotely. Agents vary in whether or not they go to these meetings, but if you do want your agent there, by all means, ask them. As for my mother's favorite question—"What should I wear?"—I've heard it said, "The agent should look rich and the author should look poor." I disagree, and don't think you should show up with tin cup in hand. Instead, wear something that makes you feel like the most confident version of yourself. If you have the good fortune to get a lot of meeting requests, take a moment to note your impressions after each one. Once a publisher shows interest, your agent will then follow up with all the other publishers considering to see if they would like to pursue your book. This means the meetings are usually clustered together and happen over the course of only a few days, making it very easy for them to start to blur together. You'll be so excited at meeting one, but by meeting five, you could very well be stuck wondering, "Wait, which one was Penguin?" This is also why I think it can be useful to have your agent join your meetings, as you can debrief together on how they went.

Just as in a job interview, you'll likely be asked if you have any questions yourself. Most writers' default is to ask the editor how they like to work with a writer. This is of course exactly what you'll be most curious to hear, but good luck getting an illuminating answer. In all my experiences of hearing this question asked and answered, the response is almost always some variation on: "I follow the writer's lead! Sometimes writers like to check in as they go and send in chapter by chapter. Others like to go off in a cave for a year and come back with the full manuscript." (Drink every time an editor mentions this proverbial cave.) A more helpful set of questions might be, "How do you envision editing this book?" "What do you think characterized your most successful editorial relationships?" and "What books have you most enjoyed working on?" The last question can be particularly revealing. While an editor's job first and foremost is to edit, their secondary one is to position and sell your book. It's impossible to glean from a phone call what an editor will do on the page, but you *can* learn a bit about how they talk about books they love and the authors they love to work with. You want to know how an editor will talk about your book when you're both ready to bring it to the world.

And as an editor never operates in a vacuum, you may also want to ask how your book fits into the imprint's overall list and if they have published anything with a similar audience. This is especially important if the editor leaves for another job, because your contract will keep you with the publisher they left.

Meanwhile, based on the timing and level of interest in the meetings, your agent will most likely set a closing date by which publishers need to offer. The closing date is usually set for shortly after your last scheduled meeting. Your work is (temporarily) done! Your only job in between the last meeting and the date of your auction is to manage your anxiety to a sufficient degree that your loved ones can remain excited for any good news.

AUCTION ACTION!

Very early in my career as an agent, I heard from a publisher that they were planning to offer on one of my submissions and then that another publisher might be putting an offer together as well. Yeah! I was a real agent at last! I excitedly called up my client to tell him the good news. He responded, "Great! Can we get a little auction action going?"

Auction action . . . I was expected to create auction action? How would I do so? If I didn't, was I a total failure? Would my client be disappointed?

Reader, there was no auction action. (Though now every time I run an auction, I think "Auction action time! Mount up!") This didn't indicate any failure to do my duty as an agent nor did it indicate a lack of interest in my client's book. We sold it to a publisher the author liked for a fair price, and the book did go on to sell quite well. This is to say, while you may have heard about the exciting phenomenon of book auctions, you don't need to have one to sell your book, nor is an auction always the best or most lucrative way to do so. More specifically, an agent doesn't have the ability to materialize an auction out of thin air. First, an auction can happen only if you have enough bidders to run one, and if you are confident multiple bidders will attend. Otherwise, it's like starting a fire with only one stick. Having two definite bidders doesn't necessarily mean an auction is the best route either. The fewer bidders you have, the harder it is to run a successful auction, especially if your agent is uncertain that the parties will bid at the same level.

Finally—and this is an increasingly common scenario in the era of corporate conglomeration—editors at imprints at the same parent company are not allowed to bid against each other if there is not also an outside bidder in the auction. So, returning to the tree from earlier, if Penguin Press and Knopf both want to bid on your book, and if they are the only imprints interested, your agent must disclose to both that only PRH imprints are bidding. Because they are both part of Penguin Random House, they would then have to coordinate and submit a house bid. In cases such as these, if one imprint wants to pursue a project more aggressively than the other (translation: if they were planning to spend more money), the less aggressive party will sometimes defer and drop out. But if editors at both imprints under one Big Five publisher are still interested in offering on your book, the total advance amount and terms of their offers will be identical, and each editor will usually write a letter detailing why they and not their colleague are the right choice. You are never under any obligation to go with the highest bidder, and the highest bidder isn't always the best choice. You'll also want to weigh how well you connected with the individual editors, if you felt aligned with their vision for your book, and if the imprint's list seems like a place you'd feel at home. While it is hard to get too specific about the marketing and publicity plans for a book at the submission stage, and as publicity and marketing budgets are almost never specified in an offer, an editor will often address how they plan to position and market your book. Consider all these things as you are evaluating your options.

Authors sometimes wonder if there is any downside to accepting a large advance. Can it make it harder to get a second book deal if that large advance doesn't earn out? There are a lot of variables to consider in answering this, but generally speaking, not earning out a large advance makes it harder to expect *an advance of a similar size* for future projects. This is because the advance size of your second book is often based on how your first book performed commercially. (As debuts don't necessarily have these ready comparisons, predicting what they'll sell for is always a crapshoot.) That first advance size doesn't set your fee as a writer going forward, but it does set expectations for publishers. The bigger the advance, the more pressure there is on the book to do well, for you, of course, but also for your publisher. In yet another case of the rich getting richer, books that cost more to acquire often have bigger marketing and publicity budgets and receive more bespoke attention from the imprint. This is why, all other things being equal, if one advance is significantly higher than another, I say take the money and run. Writing isn't a particularly remunerative business, and you may never have such a windfall or publishing opportunity again.

The decision gets trickier, though, when all things aren't equal. Let's say the larger advance comes from an editor you didn't like as much or from a publisher with a less impressive list. In those cases, I'd say trust your gut, talk to your agent, and think about how much those preferences are worth to you, emotionally, creatively, and in dollars and cents.

Sometimes the best option is not an auction but instead to accept a preemptive offer. Given how book submissions are typically managed, you and your agent will know everyone who is considering, as well as everyone who passes. The respective publishers, on the other hand, are mostly in the dark. It may be the case that there is one party who is far more interested in your book than anyone else, and, especially if they are a good fit to publish it, encouraging them to take it off the table—which would require them to make an attractive enough bid to forestall conversations with anyone else—is sometimes the best way to go. Pushing the best, most interested publisher to make a blind bid can result in the most appealing offer as they are, in essence, bidding against themselves. When you make the decision to accept a preempt, or to choose one offer over another, it can be hard not to second-guess yourself (or your agent). Would you have gotten more money if your agent had done X instead of Y at Z juncture? Would your dream publisher not have passed if your agent had sent the submission to a different editor? By all means, ask your agent to walk through the pros and cons of your options or any offers, but keep in mind that while it's our job to be well informed and transparent, none of us are psychic. The best way to sell a book is nearly as variable as books themselves, so try not to get too bogged down in comparing your own process to others' or in imagining counterfactuals.

If your agent does decide that an auction is the best route to take, she will then send all the potential bidders rules for an auction. An auction can be structured in a number of ways, and agents often determine how to structure an auction based on the number of parties involved, their best guess on the range each wants to spend, which imprints the agent wants to be sure can bid competitively (usually determined by the author's preferences), and other contingencies. Auction notices can give you some sense of how an auction can be run. Here is a fairly intricate one, but it'll give us a lot to unpack:

Dear X,

Thank you so much for your interest in *The Best Book Ever*.

Should you choose to bid,[*] I welcome your opening offer for North American and standard sub rights by **10 am on Monday, December 8**[†] by email.[‡] The **top eight bidders** will be allowed to continue into the next round. I will then go in rounds from lowest to highest.[§]

We are expecting up to fifteen bidders;[¶] some of those will be grouped as house bids.

---

[*] One of the things that makes auctions such a nail-biting experience for both authors and agents is that you often don't receive confirmation on who will bid until the last minute.

[†] The agent sets when an auction begins.

[‡] Book auctions aren't like *Get Out;* they do not take place in person. Most are conducted via email and phone.

[§] Here we get into the fine art of running a book auction. In this one, I used a structure that incentivized high bids at the outset and then allowed me to narrow the playing field to the most aggressive bidders. There are as many ways to structure an auction, though, as there are agents. Don't tell your agent how to structure theirs!

[¶] An agent doesn't need to disclose to each bidder who else is bidding but we do disclose the expected number of bidders.

We reserve the right to go to best bids at any time[*] and as always, we reserve the right not to choose the highest offer.[†] We also reserve the right to insert a minimum increase, not to exceed 10 percent **of the current high bid.**

I kindly ask that you submit your bid within one hour when[‡] your turn comes up.[§]

Please let me know if you have any questions. In the meantime, thanks again—I look forward to hearing from you.

Yours,

Alia

How long an auction takes depends on the number of bidders and the structure. "Best bids" auctions—which ask all players to make one blind bid—are one-and-done in a day; same with "two rounds best bids," in which each bidder makes one opening bid and then has a second chance to improve it based on the highest bid in the first round. Sometimes agents will structure auctions to have multiple rounds, but all to be finished in a workday, but at other times, you are in for the long haul. I have had round-robin-style auctions that lasted for over a week! It's a nerve-racking time, to be sure, and agents vary in how much they share each movement. The best thing you can do while your agent is at auction is give her space to do her job.

Once the auction concludes, you will be presented with all the best

---

[*] As an auction nears its end and folks begin to drop out, an agent will at some point ask for best and final bids.

[†] The most important thing to note: Authors are under no obligation to go with the highest bidder! Many authors, in fact, chose an under-bidder because they prefer the editor and imprint. An auction works to get the best offer possible out of the bidder you prefer.

[‡] Me trying to regulate. It never works.

[§] In auctions that have multiple rounds, the bidders are told the level of the highest bid.

and final bids. During the auction, publishers usually focus just on the advance level. The final offer will include any additional bells and whistles, but these tend not to be anything too surprising or outré. Here is a composite example of a final offer so you can see what one may include:

Dear Alia,

Anonymous Publisher couldn't be more excited to share our best final offer for *The Best Book Ever*. We are delighted to offer $100,000, in quarters, plus a $25,000 earnout bonus.

Advance: $100,000[*]
Payout: In quarters—on signing, D&A, pub, and 12 months after pub[†]
Bonus: $25,000—if the book earns out in the first 18 months[‡]
Royalties: Standard—10% to the first 5,000 copies sold, 12.5% to 10,000, and 15% thereafter.[§]

---

[*] This is the total amount of the advance, against which any royalties will be set. As long as your book is finished and accepted by the publisher, this amount is guaranteed.

[†] This is a standard payout of an advance. In a highly competitive situation, an agent can sometimes get more money on signing than evenly split quarters, and with smaller advances, authors are sometimes offered thirds or even halves, but quarters is the default.

[‡] A bonus is extra money on top of advance and royalties that a publisher pays if a book hits a certain threshold, usually a dollar amount of earnings in a given time period. It functions a bit like a second advance. It's a predetermined amount of money set against future royalties. Unlike royalties, which are earned in a drip drip fashion over the course of royalty periods set six months apart, a bonus is paid in one fell swoop.

[§] Final offers also include the royalty rate. The ones listed here are industry standard. Anything below these you should absolutely

Rights: All standard including audio and ebook rights[*]
Territory: World
Delivery: 18 months
Word count: 80,000 words

Please let me know what you think—I'd also be more than happy to get on the phone with you and/or the author at some point, or have him speak with other members of the team as well. I'd so love to work with him on this and on his future books, and to have another book with you at Anonymous Publisher!
    With thanks,
    Editor

The initial or final offer may also include an editorial letter and even a publishing plan. As for the latter, remember that it is still early days for your book. While it is good to see a publisher's publicity and marketing intentions, if they are coming at the auction stage, they are a guesstimate. It's very rare to specify a dollar amount in any proposed publicity or marketing spends, or to make any ironclad commitments.
    Once all of the final bids are in, it's decision time!
    Many authors don't anticipate the difficulty of making this choice. You're usually allowed to sleep on it, but it's expected that you won't take more than a day (or the weekend if the auction is on a Friday) to come to your decision. When you do, your agent will break the good news and the bad news. Typically, this is when the editor you have chosen is put in touch with you directly. Prior to that, especially during the auction, all communication should go through your agent. As for the disappointed parties, keep in mind that life is long and publishing is a small, gossipy world. A personalized note of appreciation is always a nice touch; your agent can instruct you on how to send it.

---

question. In very competitive situations, an agent may be able to get a slightly improved royalty rate, but that is quite rare.

[*] Audiobook and ebook royalty rates are also standardized across the industry at 25 percent of net receipts.

WHAT'S NEXT? WAITING!

Yeah, you have a book deal! Go ahead and tell your friends, though wait for your publisher's go-ahead to publicly announce it. Publishers will often formally announce a deal through industry media outlets like Publishers Marketplace and *Publishers Weekly*. They'll work with you and your agent on the language used to make sure it meets your approval. Once the announcement is made, you are free to share any way you wish.

Note that the public announcement often comes *before* the actual contract, and the contract can take over a month to be ready for signature. This wait time between the handshake deal and the signed contract often makes writers nervous. We all love to see it in writing (especially writers!), but the honor system of agreeing to an offer is strictly held by all parties. Auctions couldn't happen without them, and because agents work with the same imprints, editors, and publishers again and again, anyone backing out on a deal risks being blackballed by the rest of the industry. In my entire agenting career, I have never heard of it happening. It's also totally fine, and even typical, to start working with your editor before the contract is signed.

A draft of the contract will route to your agent. This is true of all business and money communications from your publisher. Contracts, royalty statements, and money go to your agent's office for review and are then sent to you. Your agent will vet the contract when it comes in. This can sometimes make authors nervous. *What if there is something surprising in the contract?* Rest assured there almost never is, at least if it's with a publisher your agent or agency has done business with before, and given that there are only five major publishing conglomerates and a relatively small number of independent publishers, this is unlikely. Your book contract, if you are repped by an agent, will be based on the "boilerplate" agreement between the publisher and the agency. Per publishing lawyer Jonathan Lyons, "A boilerplate is a 'form' agreement used between parties which includes language that has been negotiated between the parties in prior agreements. In the publishing context, a boilerplate is established over time in multiple negotiations between a literary agency and a book publisher." The draft of the contract your agent receives will reflect these previously negotiated changes (and will thus be much stronger than an unagented contract). These changes often appear in bold in contracts and are a helpful thing to focus on when reviewing yours as they usually concern the issues that most affect authors. Your agent's suggested changes to the contract will focus on matters specific to you and your book. Jonathan Lyons adds, "Terms that are specific to a certain project, such as the scope of grant of rights, advances, and royalties, are not boilerplate and need to be negotiated each time. A boilerplate expedites the contracting process between the parties, as they need not negotiate each issue every time a deal is made." So, after waiting for your agent to receive the contract, you'll have to wait for them to review it and negotiate any changes. Once this process is finished, it will route to you for review and signature. This is almost always done electronically.

You (finally) get paid once the contract is signed. Let's do a quick review of how publishing money works. We'll use a pretend $100,000 advance for the sake of round numbers and a standard payout, which is quarters. You would get $25,000 on signing, minus your agent's 15 percent commission, so the check issued to you would be for $21,250. You will receive the same amount at delivery and acceptance of the manuscript, at publication of the hardcover, and again twelve months after *or* at publication of the paperback edition, whichever comes first. These payments are guaranteed to you, even if the book sells zero copies. You will start receiving royalties only should the book earn out. Here is a formula to get to your earnout number (it assumes a traditional initial publication in hardcover and standard escalating royalties that are broken into three tiers: a 10 percent royalty on the first 5,000 hardcover copies (meaning 10 percent of the money from the first 5,000 copies goes toward paying off the advance), a 12.5 percent royalty on the next 5,000, and a 15 percent royalty after that):

Advance (1st-tier royalty units x (list price x royalty rate))—
   (2nd-tier royalty units x (list price x royalty rate)) = remaining advance
Remaining advance / (cover price x royalty rate) = number of copies to earn out for tier 3
Number of copies to earn out for tier 3 + tier 1 units + tier 2 units = total units needed to earn out

And here's an example of that using our $100,000 advance, a
$27.00 list price, and those standard royalties:

$100,000 − (5,000 x ($27 x 0.10)) − (5,000 x ($27 x 0.125)) =
    $69,625
$69,625 / ($27 x 0.15) = 17,191
17,191 + 5,000 + 5,000 = **27,191**

All of which makes sense when you already know what you're
doing, so let's walk through it. We'll start with the $27 list price mul-
tiplied by 0.10 (our 10 percent royalty), which equals $2.70 (the dol-
lar amount per book going toward paying off the author's advance for
the first 5,000 copies).

Take that $2.70 and multiply it by 5,000 (the first-tier royalty
units) and that gives you $13,500 (which is the amount in royal-
ties that the author will make—and which will be put toward the
advance—from the first 5,000 copies sold).

Repeat this using the next tier royalty:

$27 list price x 0.125 (12.5 percent royalty) = $3.375 (dollar amount
per book going toward earning out for the second 5,000 copies).

$3.375 x 5,000 = $16,875 (the amount in royalties that the author
will make from the second 5,000 copies sold).

Take the total advance of $100,000 and subtract both $13,500 and
$16,875 and you are left with $69,625 (the amount remaining to
earn out after first 10,000 copies are sold).

Then multiply the $27 list price by 0.15 (aka 15% royalty) and you
get $4.05 (the dollar amount per book going toward paying off the
author's advance for all copies after 10,000).

Divide $69,625 (remaining advance) by $4.05 (dollar amount per
book going toward the author), and you are left with 17,191 copies.

Add that to the 10,000 copies sold across the first two tiers before
reaching the 15 percent royalty threshold, and **the number you are
left with (27,191) is the amount of copies the author would need
to sell in order to earn out a $100,000 advance.**

Easy, right? Not really (and I got help from some more mathemati-
cal colleagues on this equation) so for back-of-the-envelope calculations, I'd suggest just using this formula with the top 15 percent per
book royalty rate and not messing around with the escalators:

TOTAL ADVANCE ÷ (LIST PRICE x ROYALTY RATE) = NUMBER OF COPIES THAT NEED TO BE SOLD.

A few other things to note: I used hardcover royalties for ease, but your book will sell in four different formats—ebook, audiobook, hardcover, and eventually, paperback. Each of these has a different royalty rate. I know the number of books that need to be sold seems high (or it doesn't, which means you haven't been checking the Book-Scan numbers for recent bestsellers and wondering dispiritedly how we keep the lights on). **Note that a book does not need to earn out for it to be profitable for the publisher!** A book reaches profitability long before it earns out. A very rough rule of thumb is to cut that earnout number of copies in half, and that will give you an approximate idea of when profitability is reached. (This will vary by publisher, and is impacted by advance level, royalties, and production costs, but for a typical work of nonfiction or fiction without any elaborate design bells and whistles, it provides a reasonable estimate.) Also note the "A" in D&A, which is for "acceptance." You do not receive that second payment of the advance on first submitting your manuscript to your editor. You get paid only after you reach a final, edited version that's deemed ready for production. If your book is getting a legal read, not uncommon in nonfiction, the D&A payment will likely be held until that is completed. The editorial process can take months, even longer than waiting for the contract, so keep this in mind as you make plans about what to do with that delicious D&A money. Money for any deals negotiated by your agent will be paid to their agency first, commissioned, and then sent to you. Your agency will also send you the necessary income tax information, royalty statements, and any royalty payments. (Typically, publishers send these to your agent two times a year; your contract will have details about the royalty schedule.) Have money questions? Ask your agent, not your publisher.

A secondary revenue stream for book writers is subsidiary rights, particularly dramatic rights and foreign rights. Dramatic rights (that is, adaptation for television and film) are almost always reserved to the author in a book deal and thus yours to sell separately. This is typically done with your agent working in conjunction with a book-to-film coagent. If you hear you have film interest, congrats, but don't start moodboarding your pool house. Contrary to popular belief (and every movie about publishing ever made), film/TV options are often sold for far less money than book rights. The real upside to them is if a film or TV show actually gets made, an admittedly slim chance, but one that, when it happens, often results in very strong book sales.

Foreign rights deals are just as exciting and even more drawn out. Authors often ask, "Will my book be available in the UK?" or "How do I get it in France?" I wish we could make these things happen through simply wishing them so, but in reality, a book appears in other countries only if a publisher in those countries buys the rights to publish and distribute it. The selling of those rights is done either by your agency or by your U.S. publisher, depending on the terms of your book deal. A U.S. book deal grants one of three types of rights: North American rights (these are the primary ones and the rights sold in the process outlined in this chapter), World English rights (North America and UK/Commonwealth rights), and World rights (North America, UK/Commonwealth, and the entire translation market, including Spanish, French, Chinese, etc.). In some cases, the agent sells only North American rights to the publisher; in others, the book deal includes UK/Commonwealth rights and/or translation rights. If your agent reserves the foreign rights, your agency can sell them on your behalf and you will receive moneys from them directly. If your book deal included foreign rights, your publisher is in charge of selling them and any moneys received will be applied directly to earning out your advance. Foreign-rights sales are never a guarantee. As my colleague Rebecca Gardner, The Gernert Company's foreign rights director always says, "Foreign deals should be considered cream on top." They *may* happen when the book is sold in the United States, but can also happen later down the line. As Gardner explains, "There is no set or specific timeframe as to exactly when deals might happen. Foreign rights can be sold throughout a project's publishing life— sometimes from first concept, to proposal and manuscript stages, and often in the run-up to and during U.S. publication and beyond. News of positioning, marketing, publicity, and sales in the U.S. are important factors to international editors choosing which projects they'd aim to translate and publish for themselves." For more intricate detail about the foreign rights side of the business, see the Q&A with Rebecca Gardner on foreign rights in appendix C.

Nonfiction editors work in a variety of ways and there are no hard-

and-fast rules on how the two of you will work together to get you to a finished book. Sometimes an editor will ask you to write a detailed outline of the book before starting to draft your chapters, which may have you thinking, "Wait, didn't I already do that for the proposal?" Yes and no. The outline you wrote for the proposal was to give publishers a road map for your book. The outline you do with your editor is to give you a more detailed guide to help you along. If you don't already have it in your proposal, you might figure out story beats for each chapter or characters for each section, reporting priorities, or a preliminary schedule. All of these things can be tremendously helpful.

As mentioned earlier, editors often give a different version of the same answer to the question of how they like to work with authors and simply say they will defer to you. This is meant to be an author-friendly approach. It's your book and you are the boss of it. That said, I've found that in the most successful editorial relationships, an author sends in some material for review and signoff, especially as they first start writing, before submitting the final manuscript. Doing so prevents you from writing a whole book your editor hates. By sending in those early chapters, you are getting buy-in and support as you go along. It can also be a protective measure. Very occasionally, an editor will feel that the final book submitted is not the one they contracted and this can lead to tricky editorial disputes. If they see early chapters and approve them, you will avoid such disputes at the end. Check-ins throughout your writing process help ensure you two are on the same page and avoid any surprises. For what it's worth, this is the approach I took in writing this book, based on what I've seen works best over the years.

Agents vary in how involved they are editorially after the book is sold. I compare the author-agent relationship to sending your kid off to kindergarten. (You are the kid.) You're now in the hands of your teacher for much of the day, and you have to learn to trust them, but you started with your agent, and they will likely be your primary and most consistent publishing relationship. If home is the place where, if you have to go there, they have to take you in, your agent always has to take your calls and be there to offer support. As an agent, I try to defer to the editor's instincts and stay out of their lane as that is usually best for the book and for the editor-author relationship, but I am there to counsel and support the author in any editorial disputes. I also often serve as a second reader for the author, a role that can be particularly useful in the early stages of writing. I'll read early chapters before my authors hand them in or review the final manuscript before it is sent off to the editor, and my own agent did the same. This helps the author turn in the best version possible to their editor and helps me foresee and forestall any problems.

An agent may also step in should there be changes at the publisher to ensure a smooth transition. The most common of these is an editor leaving for another imprint. If this happens, you will be assigned a new editor. The best thing you can do in this case is try to develop a good relationship with your new editor. Ask your agent to set up a meeting and use this meeting to get your editor up to speed on where you are in writing and to get to know her. You'll want your new editor's feedback on your work-in-progress as well as her investment in its development, but keep in mind that when these reshufflings happen, the remaining staff often finds themselves with an even thicker to-be-read pile. Be prepared to set up a new editorial schedule, to ask your editor what would work best for her, and to be patient as everyone adjusts.

Authors sometimes ask me what they can do to support their book's publication in the period between when a book is sold and when it is published. Truly, the best thing you can do is write the best book possible. Easy advice, I know, but keep it in mind when you find yourself distracted by thoughts of book promotion. It is not your responsibility to think about that while you are writing your book, nor does it serve you. Give yourself permission to concern yourself with publicity, marketing, and all its attendant responsibilities after your book is delivered. If you do get any media or event requests, it's a good idea to share them with your publisher. Sometimes, your publisher will suggest you hold on doing any media to save it for the book's publication. In other cases, such appearances can help position you as an expert and help you network. Your publisher can work with you to decide this, and having them hear about such interest will help them reach your audience once the time comes. Keep track of any media or events you do and the contact information of all involved to share with your publicist and marketer as they plan your book's promotion.

It's not uncommon for a nonfiction book to be late. Everyone who works on the publishing side of nonfiction understands that the delivery date in your contract is an educated guess. Don't assume, though, that "all nonfiction books are late!" and then be glib about your delivery. You are under contract, and even though industry conventions overlook and often expect lateness, your publisher is contractually allowed to cancel your book for it. Stay out ahead of this problem. If you think your book will be late, try to tell your agent at least three months before it's due. She can then ask for a contract extension, which will give you legal cover for your delay. Alerting the publisher is also a courtesy to them. Books are scheduled for publication based on when they are expected to deliver, so your publisher knowing they might need to move your book from the fall list to the spring one is helpful intel as they make publishing plans for you. Publishers want to publish your book at the best time for its success and not run up against competition from other houses or even inside the imprint itself. Alerting your editor about any significant delays in writing can help ensure it gets breathing room on the list. If you do need to ask for an extension, keep in mind that, ideally, you want to make such an ask once. Therefore, ask for as much time as you realistically need, not for the amount of time you would finish by in a perfect world. The world will never be perfect, so cover your own contractual ass.

WHAT IF MY BOOK DOESN'T SELL

The last section laid out the best-case scenario. Of course, there is always the possibility that your book won't sell. This is always a deeply disappointing result, and I would never underplay how shitty it feels. It really, really does. Know that if a publisher passes on your proposed book, nothing prevents you from trying with them on another project further down the line. In case you switch agents in between selling book projects, make sure you have a list of the editors who considered your first book. This will help your new agent determine whom to submit to (and whom to skip) in a second submission. Switching agents doesn't mean you can now submit the same project to a different editor at the same imprint. There are limits on the magic, if any, that changing representation can affect. Once an imprint has passed on the book, that door is closed unless—and this happens occasionally—they say they would consider a revision. And remember this above all: Not selling a book doesn't mean your writing career is over! It has happened to many, many successful writers during the course of their careers, and who doesn't love a comeback story?

KEY TAKEAWAYS

- Know that the submission process is unpleasant for authors and not without reason. A good agent, however, relishes bringing into the wider world what they and the author have been working on.
- The less you try to control the submission process, the better off you will be. And I can't emphasize this enough: You need to hand the reins over to your agent.
- The current Big Five publishers are HarperCollins, Macmillan, Simon & Schuster, Penguin Random House, and Hachette. And within each of these are multiple imprints, sometimes grouped into different divisions. An agent can submit to only one editor per imprint for each submission. The process may cast a wide net or it may use small targeted submissions. The agent's job is to decide which is the best way to approach submissions for your book.
- Buckle up for variability and waiting. The length of time before submitting and getting responses can be anywhere from a couple of days with well-known authors, to a couple of weeks, to over a month.
- If an editor is seriously interested in acquiring your book, they will ask your agent to set up a meeting. A meeting is often a prerequisite for a publisher making an offer, and to see if you both feel comfortable working on the project together.
- Practice how you want to talk about your book. "What would I say to Terry Gross on NPR about my book?" is a good question to keep in mind. Publishers will be wondering the same thing.

- Offers can come preemptively, through auctions, or any number of different ways. Trust your agent through this process, as it is nuanced and they will have navigated it before.
- A draft of the contract will route to your agent. This is true of all business and money communications from your publisher. Contracts, royalty statements, and money go to your agent's office for review and are then sent to you.
- Payments arrive in quarters—at signing, at delivery and acceptance, at publication, and twelve months after the publication date. An agent's cut is 15 percent.
- There is always the possibility that your book won't sell. This is a deeply disappointing result, and I would never underplay how shitty it feels. It really, really does, but that does not mean all hope is lost! It just means you submit to a new round of editors, or you start working on a new proposal.

CHAPTER 6

THE PUBLICATION PROCESS

I have an exercise I ask my authors to do before pub day, and I am going to make you do it too. Get a nice piece of paper (maybe even get your own custom stationery—this chapter will also include advice on how to use it) and write yourself a list of the top five things you want your book's publication to achieve. That list might include big-ticket items (a major award, a sticker from Oprah), although, after all is said and done, the authors I know who felt best about their publication experiences used this exercise to think about more personal and fundamental things, ones less determined by external validation (or things over which they have zero control). One, a first-time writer and practicing physician, wanted his book to allow him to meet and network with other writers, as he didn't meet very many at medical conferences or in his teaching hospital. Another wanted to do as many events as possible at Black-owned bookstores and ended up selling hundreds of copies at his own local, Black-owned indie. A third desperately wanted an event in her hometown, a small midwestern city rarely graced with author visits. We had a book event at her high school auditorium, crowded with old friends, alums, and curious young people who had never seen a published author in the flesh. She was interviewed onstage by the high school history teacher who changed her life, and the mayor gave her a key to the city. Her book went on to become a *New York Times* bestseller (also a top five goal of hers), but I am certain, of all her publication experiences, that night meant the most to her.

Coming up with your own definitions of success isn't just so you can give yourself a participation trophy no matter how your book is received, though you may think, if you are reading this as an author who hasn't yet published a book, that holding your book in your own hands is trophy enough. I wish I could assure you that will be the case, but the publication process is where even the most gentle-tempered authors can break bad. Markers of success seem to proliferate and endlessly shift, and the weight of things can be hard to determine. There is something about your book going unmentioned on Lit Hub's "Most Anticipated Scorpio Season Titles!" that can make you certain it will be a total failure or that your publicist didn't actually do the galley mailing or that after all this work and time and heartbreak, you are still not in the cool kids' club. There is something about getting on Wisconsin Public Radio that makes you want to email your publicist at 9:00 p.m. on a Friday to check in yet again on the status of *Fresh Air*. If you think you would never, ever become this person, spend twenty-four hours in a publicist's inbox.

Having concrete and you-specific goals in mind is a good form of protection against the inevitable disappointments of your book meeting the wider world (there will be disappointments; no one ever gets All the Things), the dopamine addiction we all develop in response to recognition we *do* receive, and the feeling of competitiveness with other writers—all of which you will of course feel. It also allows you to focus on what you may actually have your hand in shaping. The publication experience is the least solitary part of a writer's career. Nearly every publishing professional I interviewed for this book repeated some version of the phrase "publishing is a team sport." The corollary to this is that having your book do well means you need to be an excellent team player. My aim with this chapter is to help you get as much publicity and marketing as possible without driving yourself and your loved ones completely crazy in the process—*and* while remaining an author your editor, publisher, publicist, and agent want to fight for and would love to work with again. Maintaining your equanimity and perspective during the publication process not only serves your well-being and that of others; it also serves your career.

In this chapter, I will be honest about the real challenges of book publicity and marketing, giving you guidance about what you can expect, ask for, and control, and what you can't, and to help you—through years of my own context and experience, as well as that of the colleagues I've interviewed—discern the difference. A former coworker of mine once introduced me to the phrase "the calm before the calm" to describe the week before a book publishes. (She also called her bookshelf of clients' titles "the boulevard of broken dreams." She left agenting.) I share these rather depressing bon mots because the unfortunate truth is that it can be really hard to get publicity for books. Invariably, no matter how much attention your book receives, it's nearly impossible not to have the nagging sense that it could be getting even more. Relatedly, it's also impossible not to be excruciatingly aware of all the other books that seem to be getting plaudits you haven't. My goal is to help you shape your ambitions into manageable actions while keeping some perspective on the shifting nature of publishing success. I'll cover what to expect from the publication process, explaining the players involved, their responsibilities, what happens when, and most crucially for our purposes, what you can do to help along the way.

While the publicity and marketing team at your publisher will be the ones running the show in the lead-up to publication, the more proactive and responsive you are, the better your publication will be. Per Clint Smith, whose first nonfiction book debuted at number one on *The New York Times* bestseller list, "The biggest thing that many authors don't realize is that in order to sell their books, they need to be their own biggest marketing hustler. A great publicist can go a long way, but success is also about tapping into your own networks (college alumni chapters, church and civic organizations you're a part of, friends who can host book dinner parties for you, etc.). So much of it is pushing the book yourself in networks of people who want the opportunity to support you."

This chapter will introduce you to the key and supporting players and then be structured as a run-of-show leading up to your book's publication. The clock will start nine to twelve months before pub (as you'll see, it takes a really long time to publish a book, and in most cases, the more time you have, the better) and take you through publication day and (just) beyond. I'll be giving you a lot of detail, so at the end of this chapter, there is a down-and-dirty calendar of the book publication process for quick and easy reference.

THE PLAYERS

The most important new character in your book publishing life is your assigned publicist; she will increasingly become your primary contact as your pub date nears. You will likely meet her at your first meeting with the publicity and marketing team, described in more detail later. Understanding publicity's purview, and how it differs from marketing's, which I'll cover in just a bit, will help you know how to work with each department effectively and whom to go to with your ideas and questions. **Your publicist is in charge of "earned" media coverage and appearances, e.g., interviews, reviews, and book events.** Your participation is needed for many of these things, both in terms of logistics and ideation, hence the regular communication as the publicity campaign kicks into gear. Your publicist will be crafting your press kit, which includes the pitch letters that try to persuade the media to cover you, the press release that explains to the media what your book is and why it matters, and ancillary materials like an author Q&A or archival photographs that enhance the pitch. In most cases, your publicist will have a general pitch and press release that goes out every time she sends someone your book, as well as more personalized pitches tailored to specific individuals, markets, and outlets. If your book is about baseball, she'll create pitches specific to sports media and perhaps another to a book reviewer she happens to know is a huge baseball fan. Authors can be tremendously useful in helping their publicist develop their pitches, coming up with talking points to include with pitch letters, and suggesting media that might be interested. (Let's say, for example, you happen to know that the hometown of a popular podcaster features in your book.) Just as with your agent and your editor, this relationship works best if approached in the spirit of respectful and enthusiastic collaboration. Lean more toward "What do you think about trying this?" rather than "Can you do this for me?" or worse, "Did you get this done?"

Next up is your assigned marketer. The publicity and marketing departments work closely together and at points overlap; the key distinction is **marketing largely concerns itself with *paid* opportunities: advertising in print, on radio, podcasts, and social media; digital advertising; promotion through accounts such as Amazon, Barnes & Noble, indie booksellers, and big-box retailers; collabo-**

rations with places like Goodreads, Meta, Audible, and Spotify; outreach to social media influencers, and creation of a suite of promotional assets for the author to use. Sometimes marketers create merch (think the Instagram-famous Sally Rooney bucket hat) and swag bags to send to social media and industry bigmouths, some known by the authors, often just from their own mailing lists. You'll work most closely with marketing on two aspects of their campaign, and these are also where you can be most useful. First, marketing works to identify particular niches and communities that an author's work appeals to and then either generates in-house content for, or pitches author access to, those communities. A maxim to keep in mind during the entirety of the publicity and marketing campaign: You are your own best expert on the content of your book, as well its audiences. You can help your marketer pinpoint and connect with these communities and work with her on how to best reach and address them.

Note I used the word "assigned" when talking about your publicist and marketer. Unlike editors, who pick and choose their authors and projects, publicists and marketers have far less say in what they work on. I share this as I think it can help you in approaching these members of your team. They are sometimes able to call dibs on individual books that interest them and may even tell you so when you meet them—always a good sign but not necessary for a great working relationship. Unlike your editor, though, your publicist didn't chase down your book and then throw money at it, and unlike your agent, she doesn't work for you—she works for the publisher and has to service all the authors assigned to her, while balancing their competing emails. While you have no control over whether or not your publicist likes your book, you do have quite a bit of control over whether or not she likes *you*. Publicists in particular can get a bad rap, which I think has to do with a cultural discomfort with the icky necessity of self-promotion and the mercantile side of the book business—as well as the need for someone to blame when that business doesn't go as well as everyone hoped. Remember those competing demands and make it a goal to be your publicist's favorite author of the season. This, more than any "Just following up!" email you want to send while feeling anxious at 8:00 p.m. on a Tuesday night, will bump you to the front of the line.

In the background, but just as important as the publicist and the marketer, is the sales department. Those who work in sales are in charge of selling copies of the book to accounts; that is, retailers who in turn sell books to consumers. (NB: Although you can buy a publisher's books directly from their website, this is not where most book readers go to purchase them.) The reps aren't assigned to individual titles; instead, they sell to specific accounts or regional territories—ranging from Amazon to Barnes & Noble to Costco to Northern California independent bookstores. Like so much in publishing, personal relationships are part of the business dealings, including between sales reps and the accounts they service. They know the retailers' tastes, demands, and quirks—and often those of the flesh-and-blood person who actually decides if Barnes & Noble will take twenty copies of your book or two thousand. (These are accurate representative numbers of a nationwide Barnes & Noble initial order. Bookstores usually put in very conservative orders of books by authors who don't yet have a proven track record.) A good sales rep will know the sensibilities of Amazon's true-crime buyer or which indies in Texas sell a lot of food-related titles. You likely won't work directly with sales, but you may be privy to important feedback they receive from accounts—say, if Target thinks the exposed nipple on your jacket doesn't work for their market, a thinly veiled (ha) incident from one of my own recent work days. Take this feedback seriously.

Meanwhile, the editor you already know and hopefully trust isn't going anywhere. While publicity and marketing work in a more front-facing way in the run-up to publication, your editor functions as a kind of project manager for your book's release, liaising between all the departments, and often between the publisher and the author and agent. You can absolutely communicate with your publicist and marketer directly, but your editor is a great resource anytime you need general help or have questions about the publication process.

Ditto your agent, who shouldn't be going anywhere either. Your agent will be joining all key meetings and should be kept in the loop about all developments. Your agent should be your trusted adviser and advocate throughout this process, especially when you don't like the way something is going or simply have reservations you'd like to talk through. Remember the advice from chapter 4: Your agent exists so you don't have to have any difficult conversations with your publisher. If you find yourself desirous of firing off a salty email, ask your agent first. They'll probably do it for you so you can remain your sweet, appreciative self.

RUN OF SHOW

The Nine to Twelve Months Before Publication
(Henceforth Referred to as "Pub Date")

The road from finished manuscript to published book is longer than most people think, and definitely not as seen on television, where an author can hope to walk past her book in a gleaming window display moments after receiving that life-changing phone call. In publishing, we often use the phrase "making a book." To us, "making a book" doesn't mean its physical production, though that in itself is (increasingly) time-consuming thanks to the closing of domestic printing presses, which means many books are now shipped from overseas on a literal slow boat from China. Making a book instead refers to the groundwork that the editorial, publicity, marketing, and sales departments at your publisher must lay down in order to introduce your book to retailers, the media, and the public in hopes of it being successful. In real life, it takes nine months to a year for a book to transform from a finished manuscript in your editor's inbox to one your mom can hand out to her friends, in large part because of that groundwork.

Your book's birthday, or pub date, is also determined by your publishers' corporate calendar and the larger book-buying patterns of the American public. Publishers divide up the year into seasons (original!) and your book will be slotted into one of their two to three sales seasons, which are typically fall, winter, and spring or just fall and spring. The back-to-school energy of September and October means book sales rise so lots of new books get published then, especially by already well-known authors. Once we get past Thanksgiving, the holiday season is usually too cacophonous for a new title to get attention, but it's also chock-full of "Best-of" lists in newspapers and magazines, and awards announcements (hence the tendency to publish serious award contenders in early fall). From January through May, another big rush of books comes out. The dead of summer tends to be light on new books, with readers distracted by travel and childcare and vacation, unless your book is a beach read, in which case, please slip it directly into my tote bag. It's less likely for nonfiction to be published in this period.

Scheduling your book is one of the first important decisions your publisher will make about the details of its publication. Sometimes it's simple: Your book is delivered and it fits perfectly into their calendar for publication twelve months later. More often, it's about vibes. January is prime for self-help and "New year! New you!," one of several seasonal promotional hooks used by booksellers and the media. Dark and scary feels like fall. Publishers also like to take advantage of holidays and anniversaries that could give your book a news hook and possibly more media attention. The danger of this is the inevitable glut of books by Black authors published every February and Juneteenth, books by women for Women's History Month, and by queer authors for Pride, all fighting for attention. This in turn inspires counterprogramming decisions: Escapism during election season! A high-brow beach read! The "fuck off!" to becoming a new person on January 1! (To be clear, all of these have been successful strategies to create bestsellers.) No matter what, your publisher will put serious thought into whether following or bucking these modalities makes the most sense.

Your publisher will also need to position your book in relation to other titles it is publishing as well as other books it may know about that could be competitive. You don't want two memoirs about being bipolar to come out in the same month. (I know because I was once the beleaguered publicist for one of them.) I share these behind-the-scenes machinations not to overwhelm you but so you have a sense of the work that goes into the seemingly arbitrary decision of when your book comes out. **It's usually not a decision you have a lot of control over, but you are allowed to offer feedback and suggestions.** If, for example, you know of a useful anniversary or news hook tied to your book, by all means share it. (I repped a book about the inner workings of the Supreme Court, and the author strongly suggested we publish it in May, when key court decisions would be handed down. It worked: the author was tapped as an expert to speak on MSNBC and public radio about important cases, propelling the book to the bestseller list.) You're also allowed to ask about the reasoning for your book's pub date; it could be helpful to hear as it will shed light on its positioning.

Positioning—how your publisher is thinking about your book's readers, peers, and predecessors—is a key concern as your publisher lays the early groundwork for introducing your work to the public. You did some positioning yourself in your book proposal when you discussed the book's audience and your comp titles, and now it's the publisher's job to revisit how your book will be presented and explained to the world. The team at your publisher—editorial, sales, publicity, and marketing—will become collaborators in this process.

The initial steps in doing so happen at two tentpole events that occur at every publisher two to three times a year. The first is "launch," where your editor presents your book to everyone else they work with—sales, publicity, marketing, and design, as well as their editorial colleagues—for the first time since its acquisition. This meeting happens roughly nine to twelve months before a book is set to publish, depending on where the book falls within the season. The launch meeting is important because up until this moment, you and your editor have been working in a silo, but you will soon be part of a team. The rest of the company needs to know about your book in order to sell, publicize, and market it. While those other players won't have a say on its content, they may very well have useful feedback about how to sell the book to the public; e.g., media outlets to target, tour cities to visit, communities that may want to support your book. While you don't participate in launch, the feedback you might hear from it can be helpful to keep in mind as you start to think about how you will present your book to the public as well.

The second tentpole meeting is "sales conference," and it occurs about three months after launch. By then, the positioning and pitch for the book have been refined, the title and subtitle have been tweaked as necessary, a cover has been designed, and marketing plans have come together. This is the moment just before the sales force goes out and makes their first pitch to their accounts, including Amazon, Barnes & Noble, schools and libraries, and independent booksellers. A helpful way to think about launch then sales conference comes from Yaniv Soha, an executive editor at Atria: "Launch is like the table read of a new play while you're still sort of tinkering with the script. Sales conference is more like the final rehearsal of that same play." Both exist so you can get things as right as possible before opening night, so if you do hear feedback from launch or sales conference about tweaking the cover copy or the jacket or the marketing for your book, don't be alarmed. This is precisely the reason for rehearsing.

The launch to sales conference season at the publisher is largely a fallow one for the author, but a good time to start thinking about your lists. First, draw up that wish list for your book that I mentioned at the top of this chapter. Especially with media and event goals, it will be helpful to share these with your publicist when you meet her, which you will be doing soon. Also make a list of everyone you want to know about your book: friends and family; current and former colleagues; current and former teachers and students; anyone in the media you know; groups, institutions, and organizations you may be involved with; and all who have helped and supported you in your writing career along the way. Gather their email and snail-mail addresses if applicable in one well-organized place. You'll be coming back to this list again soon.

If you are thinking about hiring a freelance publicist, a year to nine months before publication is when you should begin researching and reaching out to them. It's unlikely you will have met your in-house publicist by this time, so it may feel a little soon to address this very expensive question. (As of this writing, freelance book publicists charge between $20,000 and $50,000 for a full campaign.) Hiring a freelance publicist can seem like a choice between working with the one the publisher assigns to you versus paying money for your own, but ideally, both publicists will work in tandem. Deciding early is not about slighting the in-house publicist; it's because many freelance publicists book well in advance, and the top ones are *choosy*. Much like agents, this choosiness gives freelance publicists some of their power. They take on only a handful of carefully selected books each year, so when the media hears from them (and the good ones have excellent media contacts), they pay attention. And given the small size of their lists, freelance publicists can in turn give you more attention than any in-house publicist might be able to do.

Being able to choose your own publicist is one of the biggest draws in hiring a freelancer, so investigate and ask questions before writing any large checks. Lena Little, a former in-house publicist and current freelancer, suggests taking a look at the previous campaigns of any freelance publicist you are thinking of hiring. Per Little, "When you search for their books, what are you seeing? Are you seeing a lot of media hits? And are these the kind of places that you would like to be in? What are the subjects of the books that they've worked on? It's not such a large world that you probably can't find someone who has worked with them." If you do get to talk to one of their former clients (and you can also ask for references; as an agent, I often offer references to potential clients), Little advises asking about how the publicist communicates, how transparent they are, and how they handled any difficulties in not getting media. Her advice echoes what I would tell writers considering an agent: "Anyone guaranteeing you results is a red flag rather than a good sign." As with an agent, a publicist—in-house or freelance—should be able to guarantee pursuing leads, supporting your book, and giving you information and context. They cannot promise securing you media. It *is* worth looking at the overall arc of success that they've been able to get for their writers in the past, just as you would in considering an agent or a publisher. Think in terms of the company you'd like to keep.

You'll also want to have your author photo taken in this time window. The author typically arranges this and pays for it. Because your author photo will be used with the promotional materials your publisher will soon be generating, aim to have it at the ready as soon as the publisher needs it. Author photographer Beowulf Sheehan explains a bit more how the photo is used at this early stage: "The photograph isn't needed only for the book itself and promotions to the public. There are promotions of the book by the publisher to booksellers and by the publisher and literary agents to foreign publishers. They're saying, 'Hey, this thing is in the pipeline.' People who are considered critical influencers respond and get a sense of who the author is from the picture in the publisher's catalog. Having the author portrait on the galley is also critical, because it builds momentum for the author's work. It's not the end of the world if the author portrait isn't on it, but why would you say no to a further opportunity to promote your work?" I love this explanation, not only because it explains why you need to get your shit together (at least in terms of your author photograph), but also Sheehan captures all the paddling beneath the surface that happens before your book magically appears on the shelves. Sheehan has more wisdom to share on how to use your author photo when you have it, and his suggestions apply to so many other aspects of how you can support your book's rollout with a little "show and tell." He continues:

> When it comes to selling something, timing is critical. It's only natural that when something new happens for us, we want to share that information. We grow up being taught to play the game of show and tell. It's the first game we play in kindergarten, and to some extent, we play it our entire lives. Writing a book and getting that book published is one of the highest forms of the game of show and tell. When an author portrait is made, I often have the experience of the writer wanting to take that photograph and put it on his/her/their social media right away. I appreciate the enthusiasm. That's wonderful, but let's hold off. Hold off and wait until it is possible for your social media followers, for your loved ones, for your community, for that circle of people in your life, to be able to push one further button on your website and preorder the book. Having information is one thing, but it's so much more valuable to be able to act on that information. What if you post on your channels, "Hey, everybody, here's my author portrait! I love it so very much!" before your book can be bought? What happens if you get excited about something, and you can't act on that excitement? All you can do is sit with that feeling and wait for that feeling to dissipate. You want to build on that excitement instead. Novelty is great. Novelty works. Let it work for your book and you.

Sheehan's advice is a great reminder that every time you have new information about your book, especially if that information has a visual component, you can use it to ramp up the excitement among those who you hope will support it.

Six to Nine Months Before Publication:
Galleys, Jacket Wars, and Blurbs

While sales, publicity, editorial, and marketing are coordinating on launch and sales conference, production (which is exactly what it sounds like) and the art department are working with your editor on designing and setting your physical book. This includes the actual pages—you'll see proofs of these at different stages for sign-off—and most significantly, the jacket. The goal is to get the jacket designed in time to use it on the bound galleys. A galley is an early, uncorrected proof of your book, printed with the jacket image on a glossy paperback cover, roughly six months before a book is published, four months at the latest. (**If you're at the five-month mark and don't yet have a galley run date, ask your agent to follow up.**) If you've seen one of these around, it likely says something like "Uncorrected Proof—Not for Resale" somewhere on the cover. Publishers create galleys in a limited number to get copies of the book to those who need to read it early: primarily booksellers, librarians, (sometimes) blurbers, national book clubs, and long-lead media. Ideally, the jacket will be designed before galleys are printed and mailed so your book in its earliest incarnation will come out of the box looking distinctive. If a jacket isn't decided upon in time for the galley, the galley will be jacketed with a plain cover with just its title.

The jacket, where art tries to marry commerce and doesn't always succeed, is often the first point of authorial frustration in the publishing process. I think that's due to a fundamental misunderstanding on the author's side of how jackets get designed, in large part because of how they are unveiled to you. One day a few months after your manuscript is finished, you'll find an email in your inbox from your editor with a proposed jacket or, in some cases, two or three. The editor will say some enthusiastic words about the jacket, usually indicating a preference if they are sharing more than one. You are reasonably left with the impression that the publisher designed only a couple of jackets, liked them, and sent them your way. In reality, the art department likely designed multiple jackets and ran those past your editor and the publisher, and in some cases, publicity and marketing. They also likely disagreed among themselves. After much back-and-forth and jacket wars between these parties, they arrived not at a jacket that in a perfect world they all loved but, quite possibly, one they agreed they could live with. They then sent this jacket to you and your agent. Their team feels they are at the end of the process, while you, understandably, feel like this is just the beginning.

While the publisher leads the charge in designing the cover, they want you to like it, and most book contracts stipulate that the author is given reasonable consideration or approval of the jacket. In some cases, your editor will solicit your ideas about your jacket before the design process kicks off. **To be proactive about the process, make a list of covers of other books you find appealing, ideally ones in your category that sold well. Spend some time trying to articulate why these jackets appeal to you.** What are their color palettes? How would you describe the typographic elements? Do they use any images, and if so, what kind? How do these images work with the type? It's helpful, too, to think about what you absolutely *don't* want on your cover. Are there visual images so overly associated with your subject you'd rather die than see on your jacket? It's better to let your publisher know this in advance to prevent your jacket designer from wasting time on something that won't work for you.

If your publisher proposes a jacket you don't like, try to respond with specifics rather than a simple thumbs-up or thumbs-down. Having vocabulary and referents from jackets you love will make this easier. Keep in mind how you experience jackets in the wild as you evaluate proposed covers. No one will examine your book jacket as closely as you do, so think in terms of, "If I saw this jacket at a bookstore, would I be drawn to it?" Try not to be too literal. If the bike in your book is green but appears red on the cover, think less about the actual bike and more about the overall visual effect. Your jacket is so important to how you feel about your book, and you are stuck with it for life, but the jacket war hurdle comes early in the publishing process and is often your first introduction to the larger team, so pick your battles over the particulars wisely. If your publisher has strong feelings about a font or a color or an image, hear them out. Your goal in all of this should be to get a cover you like without completely alienating everyone working on your behalf in the event you don't like what they present you. Once the jacket is finalized, you will likely want to share it. Coordinate the cover reveal with your publisher to make the most of it. You'll want to wait to do so until your book is available for preorder; your publisher can provide you with links and help you set this up.

Around this time, your publishing team will also start the process of soliciting blurbs. The job of soliciting blurbs is typically divided between the author, the editor, and sometimes the agent, depending in large part on who, if anyone, has a relationship with the person being asked. If you happen to know an author who'd be a good blurber, steel yourself to make a personal request. Authors are inundated with requests from people inside the industry, which means requests from someone they know personally or don't regularly hear from carry more weight. Ideally, you'll have at least one blurb secured before the galleys are printed so it can appear on its jacket, but if you don't, don't stress. It's more important to have blurbs for the finished book, which is usually finalized and printed two to three months before publication. (Most books are now printed and shipped from overseas, and thus take months to get to the United States.) You and your publisher will want to shoot for at least three blurbs total. Quotes from early trade reviews—i.e., the ones that run in publications like *Publishers Weekly* and *Library Journal,* which are industry-facing—may also be used as blurbs on the jacket if they come in on time. This is one of the reasons it's so important to get the galley out well before your book publishes.

As production works to finalize the interior of your book, you will be asked to review and sign off first on the copyedited manuscript, and then on page proofs (typeset pages). Because it takes so long to make a physical book, delays in your returning the copyedited manuscript or page proofs can result in a delay getting galleys or finished books. The same is true in asking for substantial changes to the text. Generally speaking, once you and your editor have finished the developmental stage of the editing process, the book goes into copyediting. From that point on, you should be looking to make as few changes as possible, though it is permissible to make some during the copyedit and first-pass review. First pass is generally speaking your last opportunity to make textual changes, but even then, they should be minor. Any changes that come after first pass should be limited to fixing factual or other key errors. This is in part because once a book reaches second pass the pagination needs to be set so it can be indexed. You will inevitably see things in the text you'd like to tweak (I've never met a writer who didn't), but the closer you get to publication, the riskier that is; ask yourself if those changes are worth creating a delay. Most times they are not.

As you're finalizing the interior pages, you will be asked to write the acknowledgments section, that useful part at a book's end where I sent you to hunt down agents and editors several chapters back. Because this part of the process comes so late in the writing stage, when you are often very, very tired of writing, it can get rushed. It's worth it to make a list of the names of everyone who helped with your book and to check it twice, lest you become like the author of an agent friend of mine. His agent coauthored the proposal and his editor did a heavy lift as well, but both went unmentioned in the acknowledgments section. He did remember to give his dog a shout-out, to whom he wrote: "Daddy loves you, bow wow!" Absurdity aside, this was hurtful to the people who worked on his book. Don't hurt feelings and don't end up being the author everyone at your publisher calls "Lil' Bow Wow."

Six Months Before Publication: Meeting Your Publicist and Marketer, Organizing Contacts, and Mailing Galleys

I'll be covering a lot of ground in this section and introducing a lot of new information and to-do items. You'll be shaping your book's talking points and how it will be pitched and presented to the media and readers. You'll be organizing and marshaling your personal contacts in hopes they will support the book. Most important, you'll be meeting your publicity and marketing team and establishing your working relationship with them. This is the part of the process where you truly begin to share the reins with your team, and how well you do that will determine your book's success as much as your own individual efforts. I'd suggest taking a page from Chloé Cooper Jones, author of *Easy Beauty*, whose interview appears on pages 63–70 of this book. I'd initially reached out to Jones both because her book was one of my favorites in the year it was published, and because everyone on her publishing team kept telling me how much they adored working with her. Given how Jones approached the publication process, this should have been no surprise. I love her philosophy, so I'll quote at length:

Before *Easy Beauty* came out, I was starting to get anxious about so many things and my brain was suddenly swirling. I sat down and made a very specific list of things that I could have any control and influence over and things that I could not have any control or influence over. Reviews? I have no control over that. Book sales? I have no control over that. I have no control over any external response. Goodreads? Definitely no control over that. Twitter? No control.

On the other side of the list were things that I *did* have control over. Number one was writing the absolute best book I could write. Doing my most serious, diligent work with my edits. The big one was being a really good colleague to the team that was helping me put the book together, a team that I was *equally* a part of. Which meant figuring out with my agent what I could do to support the book, speaking eloquently about the book, saying yes to as much good PR work as I could, understanding the limitations of the jobs that a PR person has, and not making their life harder.

When I made that list, I felt like it was really easy for me to let go of all that—I don't look at any of that. Of course, I want my book to sell well. That has a direct relation to my life. I can look at my Amazon ranking all day long, and see if it's going up or down, or I can do a really thoughtful, serious amount of work to prepare for this podcast that I'm doing. I can show up really ready, I can think about what I want to say, I can try to be as articulate as possible, and I can hope that doing well with those things generates book sales, which it did. Why look at the thing that I have no influence over? All I can do is be an amazing ambassador for my book.

I can also be the kind of person that my entire publishing team roots for. I want to be their favorite person—because I'm answering your emails, because I'm respectful of their time, because I'm saying yes when I can, because I'm jumping in and being a team player, because I'm offering ideas, because I'm handling things for myself, because I'm staying calm, because I'm not getting on their last nerve. It translates—seeing myself as a colleague, and not as the star.

You can be a help throughout your publicist's pitch process by, to borrow from sex columnist Dan Savage, being "game, giving, and good." Say yes to all that you can, no matter how small potatoes it may seem. This will engender goodwill with your team, and the more interviews and events you do, the better you'll be at it. Give helpful feedback, pitch ideas, and suggestions, and respond to all emails in a timely manner. Do the very best you can with every opportunity. Come to any interviews prepared. Listen to the program a few times or read the writers' work before an interview. Practice your talking points and don't worry if you repeat yourself at different venues or during different interviews. Unless you're the Grateful Dead, you are likely talking to an entirely new audience each time, and if you have managed to acquire some groupies along the way, they will want you to play the hits.

Meeting Your Publicity and Marketing Team

Six to nine months before your book is set to publish, you'll have your first meeting with the publicist and marketer assigned to you. (If, when you're near the six-months-till-pub point you haven't heard anything about a publicity and marketing meeting, ask your agent to set one up.) This is when you will also begin the process of becoming your publicist's favorite author of the season. The first meeting is largely a meet-and-greet. Because it comes well before publication, and often not soon after you have delivered the final manuscript, the publicity and marketing team may not have read the entire book, though they should have a working knowledge of its subject and scope. Their plans for it, at this early stage, will necessarily be quite general, especially as the publicity components—reviews, interviews, and other coverage—don't often get confirmed until just before a book comes out. (Nerve-racking, I know, though you are not alone in the nail biting.) I'd suggest thinking about this meeting as a place to give information rather than get it. Come prepared to talk. If you have ideas for pitches your publicist could make or for pieces you could write yourself, share them. Doing so will also set the precedent for a collaborative relationship going forward. Not all authors ask to see pitch letters and publicity material, but I think it can be really helpful. While your publicist will have ideas about which media outlets, and specific media contacts in particular, are worth pursuing, you can also share your own publicity goals and, if applicable, your wish list for your dream publication. This serves you but also your publicist. Per Michael Goldsmith at Doubleday, "A successful intro meeting with an author is one where they're taking a little bit of time to reflect on what their vision for success is with the publicity campaign, because the more clarity the publicist can have around that, the more they can try to realistically meet an author where they want to be while also operating within a realm of rational optimism." It's so important to articulate your hopes and dreams early because good publicity takes time and disappointments are too often articulated when it's too late to course correct. Per Jynne Dilling Martin of Riverhead, "Often when there's disappointment, or a disconnect, it rears up too late, right before on-sale, or right after on-sale. I want to know, early on before it's way too late, what are the most important things to you? If I have concerns about how likely or realistic any of them are, I want to have that conversation early. I don't want you going seven months in your heart hoping the phone's going to ring and it's going to say a thing that I know is probably not ever going to happen. [Or if it's something that's possible] I want to know that early so we can make sure it does happen for you."

In a similar spirit and keeping with my list-making directives, you can steal a page from my first boss, legendary publicity director Lori Glazer, and make a list of your top five hits: the five top places that, in a perfect (but not implausible) world, would cover your book. Looking at the coverage of your comp titles is a helpful way to reverse-engineer this list. Ask the publicist if and how they are approaching these outlets, and if you have any hooks in mind, suggest specific pitches for each. You likely won't get all of your top five wish list, but they are good, shared goals to keep front of mind. If you have any specific ideas for book publicity and marketing, or any questions, don't hesitate to bring them up. Brainstorm any of this with your agent if you'd find that helpful. While the first meeting is too early in the process for publicity confirmations, you can certainly ask where your publicist will be pitching, though even that will be quite general at this point.

Just as in your initial meeting with your publisher, you'll again be sized up for your ability to talk about your book in person. Your publicist will be thinking (though she would never dare say it), "How would this person do on podcasts? At a book festival? On television?" If you're like most writers I know, you would love to have these opportunities and feel no more than a little terrified of them. (And if you wouldn't like to have them, that's okay too. There are certainly publicity-averse writers out there, but I'd be lying to you if I said being so doesn't make it that much harder to make a living as a writer.) Prepare for the meeting by listing for yourself what talking points you want to get across about the book, just as you did when you prepared for your initial meetings with publishers. Coming to the publicity and marketing meeting with your own talking points will ensure it is also an opportunity for you to shape how your book is presented to the public.

At this initial meeting, you will also meet your marketer and hear about their initial plans. As with publicity, these will mostly be very general at this stage. They may discuss advertising plans, which often sound quite technical and inscrutable. I find it helpful to get these plans in writing (and ask your agent to follow up on this if they aren't forthcoming). Ditto for your own responsibilities.

I would frame this in terms of timeline—thus, not just what you should be doing, but what you should be doing *when*.

On Using (and Sharing) Your Personal Contacts

By the six-month mark, you want to have organized any relevant contacts and have shared them with your team. Ideally, you'll do this before that first publicity and marketing meeting, and if not, you'll do so shortly thereafter. The mention of "personal contacts" sometimes makes authors anxious, especially if you don't work in the media (and most authors don't) and thus don't have a long list. Let me underline this: **You are *not* in charge of sending out publicity copies of your book, of getting reviews for it, of getting it into bookstores and libraries, or of booking your own media. Your publisher is.** But if you *do* know someone at NPR or have a friend who is a widely followed Booktokker and/or think a former professor would be delighted to have you back to campus to give a talk, this info will only help your publisher build their campaign.

This may seem like a redundant effort: At some point early in the publishing process, your publisher likely asked you to fill out an author questionnaire, often referred to as the AQ. In the AQ, you are given prompts such as, "Are there topics currently in the news, or that will be at the time of publication, that might tie in with your book, such as a significant anniversary?" "Please list any media contacts you may have that we can contact for publicity," "Please list any national/local organizations, institutions, etc., that might be interested in purchasing your book," and "Please include any contacts you may have." You'll want to complete the AQ in detail to the best of your abilities, but I am not convinced it's the best way to share your contacts. When I was a publicist, I found the AQ to be an unwieldy and imprecise tool. Names without context don't inspire strategic thinking, and this isn't about deciding who gets a Christmas card this year. I suggest that my authors make a spreadsheet instead, listing each contact, how you know them, where they work, and what you'd like to ask them to do for the book. One of the columns should be to indicate whether the author or the publicist will contact a given person on this list. If you feel comfortable doing so, reach out directly to your personal contacts first, and if the contact is interested in covering the book, you can loop in your publicist to follow up. Here's a mock example of what that template might look like:

Last Name	First Name	Email	Outlet/Institution	Position	For what?	Galley/Finished Copy	City	Connection?	Who Should Contact?
Bronte	Anne	anne.bronte@gmail.com	*Poets & Writers*	editor	coverage	galley	Portland, OR	edited college lit mag together	Author
Bronte	Charlotte	charlotte.bronte@condenast.com	UT-Austin	writing teacher	campus event	galley	Austin, TX	former professor	Author
Bronte	Emily	emily.bronte@gmail.com	TikTok	Booktokker	post	finished copy	Lawrence, KS	worked together at Left Bank Books	Author
Dickens	Charles	charles.dickens@hotmail.com	Pickwick Papers	editor	interview	finished copy	NYC	via Liz Gaskell	Publicist
Gaskell	Elizabeth	mrs.gaskell@gmail.com	*O, The Oprah Magazine*	editor	coverage	finished book	Los Angeles, CA	friend	Author

Whom should you list? Force yourself to cast as wide a net as possible. Think of friends and also congenial friends of friends, former teachers, students and classmates, colleagues and bosses, folks who follow you on social media, anyone who has reached out to you, ever, about your work. This may feel uncomfortably transactional, but if there was ever a time to adopt the mantra "Don't ask, don't get," it's when you have a book about to come out. Imagine if the shoe was on the other foot; my guess is you wouldn't be at all offended by such an ask—and you could very well be on the receiving end soon enough. Especially after you are published, friends and acquaintances may ask you to read their book, perhaps for a blurb, perhaps to cohost an event with them, perhaps simply to give them a shout-out on social media. My hunch is you would of course understand their need to do so, and my hope is that you will pay it forward.

On Your Book's Social Media Campaign and Preorders

Once you are in touch with your publicity and marketing people, you'll want to start working in earnest on your book's social media campaign. To be clear, the six-month mark *isn't* the time for you to suddenly make an Instagram account or start networking with authors you like on social media or building a following around your area of expertise. While authors don't need to have a robust social media presence to be successful, nor does having one guarantee success, if you do want to build a social media platform to support your writing career, you want to start working toward that as early as possible and definitely before your book is being sent off to the printer. (For more on this, see chapter 2.5.) The efforts toward selling your specific book, however, need a book to sell, and this work can begin in earnest once you have digital images of the jacket and preorder links. Your marketing can provide you with all this and more. While your marketer will be the architect of your book's social media campaign, you are the implementer. Note that she can't generate a social media presence for you from scratch and won't be able to gain you new followers or craft you a social media platform out of thin air. Marketing *can* and should work with you on making the most of the audience you already have. This part of the process often fills authors with dread: "What should I post? How often should I do so? How do I promote in a way that doesn't alienate my followers?" Your marketer will generate things for you to post and can also provide you with a calendar and prompts for you to do so. If your marketer doesn't volunteer this, by all means ask!

As for doing so in a tasteful and engaging way, good social media promotion means you don't want to just slap those assets on Instagram and call it a day. Nobody wants to see that. Instead, personalize the content your marketer creates with your own comments and framing. It's okay to be funny or awkward or irreverent or excited about all of it, and to share those emotions with your followers. Book readers, particularly those who follow an author's doings of their own free will, *like* seeing what happens behind the scenes of bringing a book into the world. If you don't know what to say about your book on social media, I'd suggest mixing the publisher-generated content with your own sincere reactions to and explanations of your book's journey into the wider world. You'll also want to use your social media to encourage preorders (advance purchases by consumers from a bookseller before the book is released), and your marketer can work with you on strategies and assets for doing so. If they don't organically bring this up, be sure to ask about it yourself. Racking up even just a modest number of preorders sends the signal to both retailers and the publisher that there is interest in your book. Importantly, preorders count toward your book's first week's sales, which is a bit like its opening box office, on a much, much, much smaller scale. Just as in Hollywood, you want that first week of sales to be as strong as possible, as that will make your publisher all the more eager to support your book and retailers all the more likely to order more copies. One of the most effective preorder campaign strategies I've seen is also one of the simplest, which is offering signed copies through your favorite independent bookstore and then posting about it on social media. Book readers like to support indies, indies like to support authors (and will promote you without your publisher having to buy advertising, which isn't always true with larger corporate retailers), and indies often have their own robust social media accounts that in turn can boost you. It will also help you develop a relationship with your indie, and that can lead to support for the rest of your writing career. Coordinating with an indie can be a win-win for the little guy on two counts. If your publisher doesn't suggest this, you can suggest it to them.

The Galley Mailing

Either shortly before the meet-and-greet with your publicity and marketing team, or shortly thereafter, they will begin sending out early copies of your book. Note that the columns in my media contacts sheet divide those contacts into those who receive galleys versus those who receive a finished book. This distinction is helpful not just for activating your own contacts but in understanding book publicity and marketing as a whole. The print run for galleys is much smaller than that for finished books, and for that reason, and because they are actually more expensive to produce than the mass-produced finished books, they are more valuable. Publishers are thus much more selective about who receives them. (There is also the option to send an e-galley, but some readers will always prefer print, and where possible, that request should be honored.) Booksellers are galley-worthy, as they need to decide if they will carry the book, and if so, how many copies they will take. Marketing needs galleys not just to get your book into stores, but if possible, to get it primary placement. Every month, Amazon, Barnes & Noble, and the indies select a few titles to showcase and the marketing department advocates for theirs to be among the chosen. If this happens to you, fantastic! If not, know that only an infinitesimal number of the books published each month get touched by this particular magic wand and that even getting your book into a retailer is a win, as they all have limited shelf space. Publishers also market to booksellers and librarians at in-person conferences throughout the year, another reason for the need to have three to six months between your book being in galleys and its appearing on shelves. Sometimes authors are invited to appear at these conferences. If you are an experienced and compelling public speaker, it's worth bringing up this possibility or having your agent do so.

Publicity uses the galleys to reach out to long-lead media, e.g., those who produce content months before it is set to run. Foremost among these are the trade magazines, such as *Publishers Weekly, Library Journal, Booklist,* and *Kirkus,* which are primarily read by booksellers and librarians. They also use them for their initial outreach to top-tier print and broadcast media, such as glossy print magazines, *The New York Times*, NPR, podcasts, and television shows that feature authors. Don't expect to have any of this media confirmed at the galley stage. Outreach to top-tier media starts months before your book comes out because they take months to reach a decision, and getting them to say yes often requires multiple rounds of follow-up from your publicist. Quite often, you will have such appearances firmed up only a few short weeks before your pub day.

As your book is now (at last!) being considered by media for coverage, you will be tempted to follow up with your publicist to "hear if she heard." It's okay to be a bit of a squeaky wheel, and for your agent to be one too, but continually nudging your publicist will accomplish only one thing, which is making her dread opening your emails. Ask yourself, before sending such an email, if you really need to know something or if you are just managing your anxiety. It's okay to send some "I am struggling to manage my anxiety" emails too; I've sent plenty myself. But perhaps limit how many of these you send per month, and remember this advice from Jynne Dilling Martin: that for a publicist "to write the reassuring email to the author is ten minutes less that they're doing the rest of their work. And if you need that email every couple of days, or even once a week, you are actually cutting into work that could be being done on your book." To the frustration of some authors, most publicists don't give updates on whom they've pitched because they pitch so many people so often and they are also often repeatedly following up with the same targets. As Michael Goldsmith explains, "Rejection, silence doesn't necessarily mean that a book isn't worthy, or the publicist's efforts are in vain. Sometimes it's just a consequence of the material conditions of our industry that are bigger than we can all deal with. We just keep an ongoing drumbeat, maintaining these conversations in people's inboxes using any sort of excuse to go back to them that we have. If I get a new blurb in, or we get a new prepublication quote, or we get a new national media book hit, I'm going back and continuing those pitch sessions." Your publicist isn't going to tell you that they used the great *PW* review you got to follow up with *Weekend Edition, Fresh Air*, and *All Things Considered*. They may also not give you updates on media that are interested in your book but not confirmed in order to "manage your expectations"—aka not get your hopes up only to be disappointed. I can all but guarantee that all good news will make it to you in good time.

Three to Five Months Before Publication: Locking Down Events, Long Leads, and First Serial

The Illusive Allure of Book Events

Book events are often the thing that authors most want to do, and the publicity tool that publishers are increasingly least likely to employ. The frustration created by this mismatch is only exacerbated by the fact that your friends, family, and near strangers may very well ask you about your book tour, in part because they want to see you in person and in part because that's what book publications look like on TV. If as many people who asked anxious authors about their book tour actually showed up at their local Barnes & Noble to support authors they don't know personally, publishers might be more willing to front the cost. The reality is that publishers see book events as offering a low return on their investment. It can cost four figures to fly an author into a major metropolitan area and put them up for the night, but when the likelihood is that a bookstore event will sell only a few dozen copies, it's hard to make the case for such a spend, particularly when the money could be put to better use elsewhere. It's also not a given that a bookstore will want to host. Especially in major markets like New York, D.C., Los Angeles, and San Francisco, stores can be quite choosy about whom they invite to fill up their calendars.

Your publicist is the person in charge of setting up events for you, and the publisher determines the budget for event travel. There are some things you can do, though, to have a more effective book event and to persuade your publisher to send you to more locations. First, let your publisher know if there are any cities where you think you can draw a good crowd, either because of personal connections or because it contains a particularly good market for your book. Second, think about groups and organizations that can cohost (and thus copromote) your events through their own social media and mailing lists. There may also be institutions—colleges and universities, professional organizations, tech campuses, churches, synagogues, and

JCCs—with whom you have relationships that could partner with a local bookseller to cosponsor an event. Note, though, that wherever possible, you want to have a bookseller sell your books rather than the publisher, and your publisher will want the same. Bookseller sales count toward bestseller lists and BookScan (the data provider the book industry uses to track sales) numbers, while direct sales from publishers do not. For the sake of your publishing career, you want your BookScan number to be as high as possible. Third, most book events work best as conversations rather than thirty-minute readings. Brainstorm other authors or experts who would be good to tap as discussion partners for events. People come to book events to have a more immediate and intimate experience with an author, one that goes beyond what they can get on the page, and a good way to create this immediacy is to share material that didn't make it into the book, either through your own remarks or with your conversation partner. Keep Chloé Cooper-Jones's advice in mind and prep well for your book events. Practice and time your (short) reading and ask your editor which parts of your book would work best. Leave plenty of time for a Q&A at the end. Most folks love nothing more than hearing themselves talk.

In the three-to-five-months-out window, you'll also be working on securing first serial, the excerpt of the book that runs before it publishes. (Second serial refers to any excerpt that runs after publication; these are usually short and almost entirely for promotional purposes.) Sometimes you and your agent retain first serial rights and sometimes they are sold to the publisher in your book contract. If you retained rights to first serial, the contract and money go through your agency. If the rights were sold when your book contract was negotiated, the money goes to your publisher, with 90 percent of it being applied to your advance. No matter who has the rights, deciding whom to pitch for first serial and which excerpt to choose is always a collaborative process. The money one is paid for an excerpt is often quite modest and not the primary purpose of first serial, which is to create buzz for the book. A good first serial can also help your publicist to follow up with and reapproach media that have been sitting on the fence. In choosing an excerpt, pick something that draws readers in but doesn't give the whole story away. If your publisher or agent doesn't bring up first serial, by all means, bring it up yourself.

Finally, if your publicist hasn't nailed down any long-lead media (monthly magazines, NPR, national television) during this period, think of ways to reapproach your contacts. Follow the news closely in case your book ties into any news hooks or calendar items like anniversaries and holidays and alert your publicist if it does. You can also always suggest new pitch ideas to your publicist.

One to Two Months Before Publication: Following Up, Revisiting Your Pitches, and Activating Friends and Family

Your finished books will arrive a couple of weeks before your pub date. Now is the time to break out that stationery I mentioned earlier. Revisit the contact list you shared with your publicist, and think about who would appreciate receiving a copy of your book with a note from you. Especially if you are sending a book to someone who receives a lot of them, this personal touch is a great way to ensure the receiver takes notice. Meanwhile, your publicist will be sending finished books to everyone who received the galleys, following up with media she hasn't heard from, and pitching short-lead media—daily newspapers, digital publications, radio, podcasts, and regional media. Your marketer will be doing similar outreach and following up with social media influencers and accounts.

This is also the moment to mobilize your friends and family who want to support the book. It's time to shine for anyone who has ever asked you "How's the book going?" or "When's your book party?" I suggest my authors send an "I have a book coming and here's how to support it!" email to all such folks. Give them links to buy the book, let them know about any upcoming events, kindly encourage them to preorder copies and, if they are so inspired, to post reviews on Amazon, Goodreads, or the platform of their choice. (And maybe to keep their opinions to themselves if they really hated it.) It can also be helpful to give a quick explainer as to why such things are important: Publishers follow a book's early sales closely, as do bookseller accounts. Strong early sales mean a bookseller is more likely to order additional copies of a book and to feature it more prominently. They also signal to a publisher that a book has the potential to do well, making them all the more eager to support it, and if demand warrants, to push the button on a reprint. The more reviews a book has on Amazon, the more likely it is to appear in searches. Data analytics show that the higher a book's star rating, the more likely people are to purchase it. I hate being the bearer of algorithmic bad news, but I've found that sharing it with nonpublishing industry people makes them all the more eager to help you beat the matrix.

This is also the period when your publicist will be pitching short leads and firming up long leads. Check in with the publicist on where they are with your dream top five hits. A lot will still be up in the air one to two months out, but you should be able to get a status report, and if you aren't yet getting any commitments, work together on fresh ideas for pitching. You can think about Op-Ed ideas and other original pitches that would work well on a short time frame, and the possibility of writing Op-Eds is another reason to closely follow the news. Share any ideas with your publicist and editor for workshopping and editing. If you and your publicist haven't worked up some talking points for interviews, suggest you do so, and if you already have, now is a good time to revisit them, particularly if your book is in any way timely or current-events related. You want to be sure any interviews you give fit the moment.

Four Weeks Before Publication: Finished Book Mailing

The publicist is now drafting the press materials for the finished book mailing. The more specific the pitches, the better they'll be, and this is where you can help. Ask to see the finished-book press materials before they are sent out to make sure you are all on the same page with how the book is being pitched, and know that you are welcome to offer (kindly phrased) feedback. Good press kits make the media's job as easy as possible, so make sure yours includes talking points. Suggest your publicist include a Q&A with you in the press materials and offer to draft one. If you have any relevant photos or images, offer those up too.

This may also be the time to revise your expectations. If the publisher hasn't nailed down any of the top five, come up with a B-list: These may be digital versions of print or broadcast outlets, NPR podcasts instead of flagship shows, local public radio instead of national, etc. Remember that a bird in the hand is better than bitterly cursing out Terry Gross from your sofa.

If you have any events planned, make lists of friends, family, and professional contacts in each tour city to invite. Paperless Post is a good way to make bespoke invites for each event, and sometimes the publisher or bookstore will help create or send out invites as well. Your team can also make digital tour cards with your event details to share on social media. If you have a personal website, make sure to list and update all your events and to add media as it appears. Same goes for all your social media accounts. If someone does encounter your book and googles you, you want them to be able to find where they can meet you in person.

One to Two Weeks Before Publication: The Calm Before the Calm

This period is challenging: You will be nervous and you're often in a holding pattern waiting to hear if and where the book will be covered. Authors expect to be busy in this period, but, in fact, you are likely not doing events or media much before pub day. Be available to your publishing team but know that it is normal for these weeks to feel rather quiet.

It will be hard to keep yourself from obsessively checking your email, and no one but you needs to know what you do in the dark, but to stop yourself from spiraling too much during the calm before the calm, take a few moments to remember the big picture. Revisit your initial wish list for your book. If you have items unchecked, and you surely will, think about what you'd like to happen in the next two weeks and what you can do to make that possible. This is also a good time to thank your team. Your editor, publicist, marketer, and agent would certainly appreciate a thank-you note. If someone did a particularly spectacular job, think about writing to their boss as well.

Speaking more strategically, revisit the top five hits, or, if you have one, the top five B-list to see what you've gotten and who you can feasibly reapproach—on your own, if necessary, and if the publicist has been unsuccessful. Remember the advice from the first chapter of this book: You are allowed to pitch yourself directly. When you have a book coming out, you should cede this duty to the publicist, but if there are media you haven't gotten, and really, really want, you will likely rest easier if you also gave it a try yourself. National broadcast media and the major book reviews prefer to hear from publicists, but regional media are more open to hearing directly from authors, as are podcasts. I know it's awkward to pitch yourself for interviews. Here is a good example of how to do so from two authors who were able to secure multiple podcast appearances through customized versions of this pitch:

Dear Derek,

My name is Rachel Wiseman, and I am the managing editor of *The Point,* a magazine of philosophical writing on everyday life, culture, and politics. I'm writing to pitch you on an episode for *Plain English* about my and Anastasia Berg's forthcoming book, *What Are Children For?* (out June 11 with St. Martin's Press).[*] The book analyzes the rising personal and cultural ambivalence about having children and asks whether it is possible to overcome it. We argue that in asking whether or not we should have children we are asking a profound philosophical question, namely, whether human life is valuable in the present and in the future.[†]

We are big fans of *Plain English*—we love how it brings big ideas into contact with the world as we live in it, and flips received cultural narratives on their head—and we think *What Are Children For?* would be a great fit for the show.[‡]

Here's a brief overview of the book:

Becoming[§] a parent, once the expected outcome of adulthood, is increasingly viewed as a potential threat to the most basic goals and aspirations of modern life. We seek self-fulfillment; we want to liberate women to find meaning and self-worth outside the household; we

---

[*] The authors quickly say precisely why they are writing.

[†] And then offer their elevator pitch of the book.

[‡] Here they explain why their book would be a good fit for this particular pod.

[§] Here they give more detail on exactly what they would discuss, aka the talking points. These can also be presented as bullet points.

wish to protect the planet from the ravages of human-caused climate change; we must do what we can to protect others from senseless suffering. Weighing the pros and cons of having children, young people today are finding it increasingly hard to judge in its favor. *What Are Children For?* seeks to loosen the grip of the shallow narratives that either lament smaller families and growing childlessness as marks of cultural decline or celebrate them as unambiguous evidence of social progress. Exploring the nuances of our collective contemporary anxiety about having children, the book offers those struggling with the decision themselves the philosophical guidance necessary to move beyond their uncertainty.

What do material concerns—about money, career, and the desire for autonomy and flexibility—reveal about our priorities and what "happiness" has come to mean to us? What do people look for in love today, and how do these pursuits align or conflict with the possibility of one day starting a family? Is the choice to become a mother the fulfillment of a feminist ethos or a betrayal of it? Where do men fit in? Isn't it perverse that the question of parenthood is so frequently treated as only a women's issue? How do we acknowledge ambivalence without letting it make the choice for us? And, above all, for all its cruelty, for all the suffering it entails, is human life still worth the trouble?

Peeling back the layers of resistance, *What Are Children For?* argues that when we make the individual decision whether or not to have children we confront a profound philosophical question, that of the goodness of our form of life itself. How can we justify perpetuating human life given the catastrophic harm and suffering of which we are always at once both victims and perpetrators? If we wish to meet this challenge without succumbing to naivete about our predicament, we must, we argue, uncover a capacity to grasp the fundamental goodness of human life—not only theoretically but practically in the actual lives we lead today.

There are a few exciting angles the conversation could take. One that we thought might be of particular interest to you and your audience concerns the question: In our politically and ecologically degrading world, is there any way to justify the decision to have children from a secular, liberal/progressive point of view?

I'm attaching a digital copy and a publicity sheet, which outlines some of the main claims and arguments of the book. I'd love to send you a hard copy—just let me know where to send it.

All our best,

Rachel & Anastasia

You can always pitch your own original pieces, especially if it ties to a news hook, but keep your publicist in the loop so you are not working at cross purposes.

Pub Day!!

Happy Pub Day!! Celebrate yourself.

I mean that quite literally. When you think of your pub day, you probably imagine a book party. I know I do, which is why I am setting aside a little money from my book advance to pay for the wine and cheese. I'm going to once again disabuse you of the movie version of book publishing and tell you what I so often have to tell my authors, which is that publishers rarely, if ever, pay for book parties. A few years back, a publisher threw a pub-day party for one of our agency's authors, and this was such an unusual occurrence that it was covered by *The New York Times*. One guest was quoted as saying, "I can't remember the last time a book launch felt like a proper party!" The book went on to win the Pulitzer Prize. My takeaway from this is parties can really work in certain contexts (the author was a well-connected and beloved journalist and thus his guest list was extensive and impressive), and I wish publishers would foot the bill for parties more often, especially for mine. In most cases, though, funding a party is not at the top of the list of sensible publicity investments.

Until publishers come around to my pro-party platform, take the advice of my client Lauren Oyler, who says, "It's important to manufacture a celebration because otherwise, even if your book is very successful, it will be anticlimactic." Oyler's first book came out during COVID, so we met up with her editor in an outdoor dining shed for champagne and oysters on a freezing cold night and toasted her book with our mittens on. These were dollars well spent.

You will hopefully have a book-reading event on or about your pub day. You'll likely receive congratulatory messages from family and friends. But know that if your pub date doesn't feel like a ticker-tape parade, you are not alone. Book publicity happens on a (slowly) rolling basis. Media hits are sometimes scheduled on pub day, but just as often they occur before or after. The same is true for book events. This is in part because almost all books in the United States are published on Tuesdays, so bookstores can't schedule all book events on every author's pub day itself, nor can media or reviews accommodate that one day of the week for every new book. As my client Ben Purkert explains, "I don't think I'd fully internalized the extent to which it's never just *your* pub day. The way publishing works, your book is bound to come out the same day as many others, and if you've especially angered the gods, many really big names. Your pub day is 100 percent yours to celebrate, but that doesn't mean that every bookseller will necessarily be putting your book on the front table, or even has it in stock." Traffic jams like these mean your book may very well get reviewed a few days or even weeks before or after it is officially published. One easy way to celebrate your day is to stop into your local bookstore(s) and ask to sign stock—though have your publicist check first to make sure they have it. You can do this in every city you visit on a book tour, again with your publicist calling first to give accounts a heads-up. Stock signing is fun, but also useful. Introducing yourself to any booksellers allows them to put a face to a name. You want them to keep your book top of mind and front of tables and, fingers crossed, to read it and recommend it to customers.

Once your book pubs, you will likely be asked by well-meaning people how it is doing. A book's success isn't easily determinable (though I'll be sharing a helpful rubric for doing so from one of my favorite editors in just a bit), which can make the weeks after your book comes out all the more anxiety producing. You'll be able to get a good estimate of book sales within a week of its publication, and you'll be able to see firsthand how well attended your events are, but even the sales of very successful books are often much, much lower than a nonpublishing person would expect. Per BookScan the week I am writing this, the fifteenth-bestselling title on the Hardcover Nonfiction bestseller list in *The New York Times* sold a little over two thousand copies in hardcover; the tenth-bestselling book sold around twenty-eight hundred. You can see why you might not want to offer up your book's sales figures to family and friends, unless they are asking you for money. (You can also respond to anyone who asks you how your book is doing by asking if they bought a copy or three.)

This is where having other writer friends can be particularly helpful, especially those who are at the same point in their career and the publishing calendar as you are. Ben Purkert used the fact that his book came out at a crowded time as an opportunity and shares, "One thing I found really helpful, both for my own sanity and also for the spirit of community, was becoming very close friends with another writer who pubbed at the same time. We could champion each other's work and celebrate each other's successes. It made the whole process way less lonely. It was fun cheerleading!"

Keeping track of what you do—and what you feel—may also help you maintain your perspective on your book's perceived success or failure. Very, very few titles achieve the distinction of becoming a *New York Times* bestseller or a major award winner, so try to reorient your own definition of success to more personal watermarks. Per Clint Smith, who achieved both bestseller status and major award recognition, "The best advice I have is to keep a journal for each day of the experience. Having something that can serve as a space for your gratitude and a space for your nerves is really helpful. The physical act of writing down how excited you were to appear on your local radio station, or how nervous you were that not many people would show up to a certain stop on your book tour, allows you to live in, record, and remember the emotional roller coaster of putting a book out into the world. It's something really incredible, and it can be something really scary. Don't run from that, sit with all of it." In addition to journaling about your publication experience, keep track of all your media appearances, reviews, interviews, and any email addresses and contact information associated with them as well. If you have a personal website, be sure to add these as they come in. This is not just for self-promotion but for easy future reference. I hope you have many books in you, which could mean many different publishing teams. Having this information all in one place will make crafting future spreadsheets all the easier.

My favorite rubric for publishing success comes from Kathy Belden, editorial director at Scribner. It has four criteria:

First, it's a good book. And that's the most important one. And people should feel proud, if they achieve that. It's really hard to write a good book. The second is good attention. Maybe 60 percent of the books I work on achieve those two. The third is good sales. The number of books that achieve all three drops rapidly—it's maybe less than 20 percent? The fourth is profit, which is different from sales. A book can sell well and still not turn a profit. And I would bet there are fewer than twenty that I've worked on that have achieved all four. That's not a lot across a couple decades of mostly doing twelve books a year.

Belden guesses she'd have a better chance at hitting a ball thrown by a major league pitcher than achieving that superfecta. I don't know enough about statistics or baseball to judge whether she's wrong or right, but I know enough about publishing to say with certainty that getting to publish a book is a rare occurrence indeed, and that only 35 percent of books are profitable, and far fewer earn out. If you take one message from this chapter, I hope it will be to enter the publication process with your own rubric of success.

A Second Life in Paperback

A few weeks after your book comes out, things will likely be fairly quiet again. Don't take the fact that you're hearing from your publicist or editor less as evidence that they no longer care about you or your book; prepublication, information flows from publisher to author. As time goes on, and upcoming books become your publishing team's focus, you'll want to be proactive about keeping your publisher in the loop. New books are more exigent, but everyone has a shared interest in your book continuing to sell. Let your editor and publisher know about any events, appearances, invites, and writing you do. This will help them make the most of opportunities to support your book. Knowing about any continued interest in your book will also help your publisher shape their plans for the paperback.

As your pub date recedes into the distance, it will become harder to get your book publicity attention. The primary way you can get a book attention after its pub date is by positioning yourself as an expert on its topic, *the* person on call if and when it's relevant to the news. Continue to pitch Op-Eds and original articles. If you think you would speak well to a particular topic or event—say, your book is about the 1918 flu pandemic and another once-in-a-century virus surfaces—let your publicist know so they in turn can pitch you to broadcast media. Don't be shy about pitching yourself. If you get asked to do any events, be sure to loop in your publicist so they can make sure to have plenty of books on site for sale, ideally vending through a local bookseller.

The paperback edition of a book originally published in hard-cover usually appears one year after the original publication. Not all books get published in paperback—doing so is largely at the publisher's discretion. Because of the lower price point, the paperback is an opportunity to reach a different audience, and your jacket, as well as the positioning and cover copy, may change. Sometimes you will be asked to add a bit of new information to the book, especially if it covers a timely topic, or to write a new afterword or foreword. The publication process for paperbacks is much less publicity focused. Most don't get new press, and unless the book was an extraordinary success, fewer events are planned. There's a general feeling that by the time the paperback edition appears, the die has already been cast. While it's true that it's hard to completely rebrand a book, your thinking about your book may very well have changed since its original publication—perhaps through talking to people or seeing how it was reviewed, perhaps simply because of the inevitable changes a year can bring to one's life and one's world. I would thus suggest, even if you haven't been asked to write a new foreword or afterword for your book, you do so anyway. It may not be included in the paperback, but it will become part of the story you tell about your publication to the public and to yourself. You are the author of your own publishing story.

A MUCH-ABBREVIATED BOOK PUBLICATION TIMELINE

Six Months Before Publication: Meeting Your Publicist and Marketer, Organizing Contacts, and Mailing Galleys

The publicist and marketer should be assigned by now. Request a meeting if they haven't yet reached out.

Organize your personal contacts and think about how to use them, when they should be contacted, and who should do the outreach.

Galleys should be ready to go by the six-month mark (ideally), and at the four-month mark at the latest. Ask to see the galley mailing list as well as the galley letter to get a sense of how the publisher is pitching the book. It's okay to give feedback! You know your book better than anyone else.

As soon as the book is available for preorder, add the preorder link to your social bios if you're active on social media. The publisher can help you set this up.

Come up with a list of top five hits: the five top places that you'd love to cover the book. Look at the coverage of your comp titles for inspiration (and to remain in the realm of the achievable). Ask the publicist if and how they are approaching these outlets and suggest specific pitches for each.

Three- to Five-Month Mark: First Serial, Long Leads, and Events

Even if you don't have first serial rights (a book excerpt that runs before pub), ask to kick off the conversation early, to make sure the publisher is doing all they can to place it.

If you have ideas for original pieces for long-lead publications, now is the time to pitch them. Your publicist, agent, and editor can work collaboratively with you on this.

Make and share a list of cities where they have significant institutional or personal relationships. Such relationships will make the most of any cities you visit and can sometimes be leveraged into more.

Start regularly reminding your social media followers to preorder. Your marketer can work with you on creating a social media calendar and images to share.

One- to Two-Month Mark: Shaping the Pitches, Getting Specific, and Activating Friends and Family

Make sure you have your interview talking points ready to go and that you have workshopped them with your publicist.

Work on Op-Ed ideas and original pitches. If you have ideas for original pieces for short-lead publications, now is the time to start pitching.

Send a friends-and-family email telling everyone about the book, how to support it, and to encourage preorders.

Check in with the publicist on where they are with the top five hits. A lot will still be up in the air one to two months out, but you should be able to get a status report.

If you haven't gotten any NPR booked by now, think about fresh ways to approach.

Four Weeks Out: Finished Book Mailing

The publicist is now drafting the press materials for the finished book mailing. The more specific the pitches, the better they'll be, so offer to help.

Ask to see the finished book press materials before they are sent to make sure you are all on the same page on how the book is being pitched and to offer feedback.

If the publisher hasn't nailed down any of the top five, come up with a B-list, e.g., digital versions of the print or broadcast editions, NPR podcasts instead of flagship shows, local public radio instead of NPR.

If you're going on tour, make lists of invitees, including friends, family, and professional contacts, for each tour city.

One to Two Weeks Out: The Calm Before the Calm

This period is challenging: You will be nervous and you're often in a holding pattern waiting to hear if and where the book will be covered.

Revisit the top five hits, or if you have one, the top five B-list to see what you've gotten and who you can feasibly reapproach—on your own, if necessary and if the publicist has been unsuccessful.

Pub Date and Beyond

On the book's pub date send out another friends-and-family email to remind them to order and support the book.

If going on tour, ask the publicist to set up bookstore drop-ins in each city to sign stock.

Keep all the media for the book—and especially, the media contacts—in one easily findable place, like a Word doc or a Google sheet. Every reviewer, interviewer, segment producer, etc., can be revisited with each future book, and especially if you change publishers, these contacts could be lost.

Interview with Andrea Elliott, an investigative reporter at *The New York Times* and author of *Invisible Child*

In 2013, *The New York Times* published Andrea Elliott's series "Invisible Child," about an eleven-year-old girl named Dasani living in homelessness in New York City, and based on fifteen months of immersive reporting. The series was met with great acclaim, and shortly thereafter, Elliott sold a book proposing to expand it. That book, also titled *Invisible Child,* was published in 2021 and awarded the Pulitzer Prize in General Nonfiction, among many other accolades, making Elliott the first woman to win the Pulitzer in both Letters and Journalism.

Elliott's career illustrates many of the topics and themes the previous pages have explored, and in this interview, she addresses them in great and often inspiring detail. Her answers get into the weeds of writing (she is a weeds person, with the color-coded storyline system to prove it) and reporting a hugely ambitious project, while continually returning to the larger, more existential questions: How do you know if a topic is worthy of a book and if it should be *your* book? What do you do when you feel (and you inevitably will) that you are not cut out to write it? How do you write the damn thing?

Elliott's outsize success and wild ambition are singular (and not disconnected from each other) and perhaps intimidating, but my hope is you also find it inspiring. Her career is testament to what nonfiction can be at its highest level and what you can achieve when you swing for the fences.

I know you pulled out your proposal in advance of our interview, so let's start with that. What was it like to refer to it years later?

It scores high on aspiration and low on practicality. I had no idea what I was taking on. But the scope and vision I had for the book is all here, which surprises me. I'd like to think that some of that scaffolding happened later, but a lot of it was already in place—the plan to delve into Dasani's family history, the narrative detours I would take to explore things like public policy, or the story of the Bloods coming east. It's interesting to go back and look at the seeds of a book. They get planted early.

So if I understand the timeline, the proposal was written after the original articles on Dasani came out?

I'm a tunnel-visioned person. I tend to give all of myself to one thing at a time—for better or for worse. And that one thing, back in 2013, was the Dasani series—reporting it, fact-checking it, taking irate calls from City Hall. It was all I could do until the series went live. I didn't even have an agent. Then it was published, and, suddenly, my phone was ringing off the hook (this was back when we still had desk phones that rang). And one of those first calls was from Kate Medina at Random House, who said, "You had me at the first line." She wanted to know, was this a book? And without even pausing, I heard myself say, "Yes!" As in, zero hesitation whatsoever about a massive, high-stakes commitment. Like, usually, I'm more methodical in the face of big questions. But this was just a full-bodied yes.

Had you thought that, or did it take someone posing it for you?

Clearly it was living inside me, but I hadn't articulated it. What I felt, as I was writing the series, was that her story deserved more space. And this was, at the time, the longest-running investigative project in the history of *The New York Times*. It ran at nearly thirty thousand words. And still, I felt that it had just scratched the surface. I even hinted at this in the series, writing that Dasani's housing projects "hold a legacy so intricate and rich it could fill volumes were it ever told." It's like I was winking at myself. And then, after that call from Kate, I reached out to the agent Tina Bennett—revered by my colleagues—and she instantly took me on board, over the phone. And within a few weeks, we had a deal (with Kate, no less). It all happened so fast. I wrote the proposal over a weekend. Nothing about this process was typical, which I knew because I'd been the student of Sam Freedman, who teaches the famous book-writing class at Columbia's School of Journalism. He taught us how to write a strong proposal, how to compare it to other books in the market, etc. I bet you're now going to ask me how my book differs from the proposal. Here's how it differs. The funniest line relates to my reporting plan. I wrote, "I began reporting on Dasani and her family in September 2012. And I will continue to follow them until September 2014." I was giving myself two years for a project that wound up taking nearly a decade.

[Elliott reading from her proposal] "I'm still exploring a precise structure, but I'm leaning toward a book that begins when I started following Dasani through the series. It then moves back in time to the Brooklyn of her parents, to the rise of modern homelessness in the

1980s, Legal Aid Society's ongoing battles with the city over Auburn Housing, Dasani's parents in the nineties, then Bloomberg's reign and then back to Dasani's own coming-of-age, landing back in 2012."

All of that found its way into the book. But there was so much more that I couldn't have foreseen. Reading the proposal now, as my older, wiser, travel-weary self, I think, "Oh, this kid was ambitious. She had such major heights to climb, and she was game, she was ready. But she had no idea what it would take, which is probably a good thing." The delivery process was still a mystery to me. My proposal—and maybe every proposal is like this—poses far more questions than it answers. It's almost like a proposal of marriage; the answer comes in the marriage itself. In fact, I often compare the book leap to marriage. You know it's going to be hard, so you better be in love. The reason I didn't even have an agent is that I hadn't fallen for the right book. Over the years, I had toyed with this or that idea, but nothing grabbed me in the gut. Nothing knocked me flat. That all changed with Dasani and her family's epic story. It wasn't even a choice. I just felt like I had to write this book. I also knew, from talking to other authors, that it was going to test me like nothing I had ever done. So why sign up for that? Because the heart says yes. That's what carried me through. I had never gotten that feeling from another story. I couldn't NOT write this book.

I couldn't agree with you more. What I'm going to try to gently prevent and something I see a lot as an agent—is writers casting about for a book idea. I don't think there's anything wrong with that kind of generative questioning, but it isn't necessarily the way to write a great book. The best books I know came about when someone who has the skills, and has the ability, and has the chops, then has a story or a topic that can't quit.

I was that journalist who, for years, was casting about trying to find a book through my longtime beat, Islam in America. And when nothing materialized it felt like a failure. In retrospect, I'm relieved that I waited. But at the time, I was weighed down by the expectation of what I "should" do. And here's the thing: A book worth doing doesn't feel like a "should"; it's a "must." That's an important distinction. A "should" is never what fires me up in the morning.

When you look at that proposal, and you think, "Man, this kid didn't know what delivery really involved," was it simply the scope of work? What else didn't you know?

There are so many ways to answer that. I knew myself well enough to predict that I would chase certain facts to exhaustion. Like many of my peers, I tend to go down rabbit holes making sure that I've got it right, and this applies not just to reporting on institutions but to understanding history. I found myself reading an entire book to write one paragraph. I'd always been really careful as a reporter. Some stories took longer than expected, but never this much longer. Two years turned into four, then eight (actually, nine, because the pandemic hit). Some writers tell you to double whatever amount of time you think it will take. I find formulas irritating. What is absolutely true is that my book took the time it needed. I never felt like I slowed down, or had the luxury of stepping away for stretches. It was full throttle, year after year, because so many dramatic things kept happening. I wrote the end of the book three different times. All three scenes are in the book.

When I tell people this backstory, they inevitably ask how I stayed the course. I don't think authors keep going out of some lofty ideal or mission. It's more elemental than that. For me, it probably comes down to the fact that I'm a ridiculous optimist. I'm a cup-is-half-full, I'm going to get this, I'm going to wear that person down kind of reporter. It's the way I work. But what I didn't know going in is that it's also okay to be panicked.

I remember when I suddenly realized this was not just a story about one girl experiencing poverty in the wealthiest city in the world, but also a story about race in America, a story about real estate, a story about sleep deprivation, a story that dealt with neuroscience, a story about so many things. . . . In a way it felt like I was writing about everything. And that was terrifying.

In the midst of that terror, I mistakenly thought—more than a few times—that I'm not cut out for this. I was so afraid. But what I've come to see is that the fear, the intimidation one feels is not only okay, it's necessary. It means you are facing the challenge. What you wind up doing is learning to breathe, to slow down, and to trust in the process. What I taught myself was to stop being afraid, to dive in, to write stuff and then keep going. I had an amazing community of readers around me—my agent, my editor, friends and colleagues, my father—and they all propelled me forward. The better I got at taking the incremental steps of this long, long road, the more I came to trust in the process. It's really important to tune out the voices that we all carry—the voices that tell us we're not cut out for the job, because if we listened to them, no books would get written.

I'm going to follow up with more questions about your process, but I think there are a lot of parallels between this and what you've said about how everyone says having a dog is hard. (NB: Before the interview had started, Elliott and I had spoken about her interest in adopting a puppy, and I had also adopted a puppy a few months before this interview took place.) It's something about those formulas, like, "It takes twice as long in order to do the thing." You have to both embrace the fear, but also not listen to it.

Denial is my friend!

I can promise you that, unless you have the world's worst puppy—and even then, it won't be that bad—it will be easier than writing *Invisible Child*.

I was talking to Chanel [the family matriarch in *Invisible Child*] today about dog names, and we were laughing. Even she said, "You know, Drea, this is a lot of work." I was like, Oh my god, don't be one of the naysayers!

Can you talk a bit about your process and how you went about delivering pieces of the book? Getting parts of it read? When did you switch from reporting to writing? Was that happening all along?

I do best with extreme order. I'm not one of those journalists with a mess on my desk. I have piles, but I know what the piles are. They're usually labeled. My filing system and my note-taking protocols border on obsessive. It's the only way that I can manage multiple streams of information. Among those streams, by the way, is the information—and I think this is the most important thing for authors to pay attention to—that comes from within. These are the observations you're making in the field, or even as you're writing. Revelations, epiphanies, new questions—all the things that shape a book and give it life. That stream, for example, got its own notebook and then it fed multiple folders—"themes" was one, "quotes" was another. There were so many shattering quotes. Even if they never wound up in the book, reading those quotes kept the voices alive as I wrote. And then there was this other tool I consider sacred.

I'll back up from way before *Invisible Child,* to when I was posted in the Bronx. This is twenty years ago. I was covering all manner of things including the courts, and I wound up paired with the great Benjamin Weiser. We decided to try our hand at a story on prosecutorial misconduct, and it was my first stab at investigative work. It didn't turn into much, but I got the great pleasure of learning from him. He's a legendary federal court reporter for *The New York Times.* He is really, really amazing—the kind of person I love to work with, because he's so altruistic and wise. And so one day, I asked Ben for his tricks of the trade. "I want to know how you do it." He looked at me and said, "Every time you start a story—and I don't care if it's a daily, or if it's a two-year project—as soon as you start reporting, create a timeline. And whenever you learn about a new event, or witness something big, plug it into that timeline." It's perhaps the best advice I have ever gotten. Events form the arc of any story. A timeline shows you that progression. It becomes a blueprint for structure. Whenever I feel lost in the writing, I go back to the timeline. That saying, "the chronological is the most logical," is true.

Since then, I have never stopped using timelines. But with the Dasani series, my timeline got unwieldy. It stretched back centuries. So I added a color-coding system. Events that happened to the entire family were marked in yellow, Chanel was red, her husband was green, city policy was gray. And how did this help? Well, Joanie, for example—Dasani's grandmother—I remember plugging in the date she lost her food stamps and then seeing how that coincided with policy shifts at the local and federal level. These events were all connected. That's what a timeline does. It connects the dots.

But my timeline kept growing because there were all these records coming in—boxes of them. And at one point, my editor at the *Times,* Christine Kay, said, "The boxes are driving everyone crazy." We had just moved into our new building, which was designed by Renzo Piano, who did not seem to understand reporter culture. Everything was glass, ostensibly in the name of "transparency." But reporters actually like to hide away and not have everyone in our business. Anyway, they put me in this little glass office that all my colleagues could peer into. And my timeline went up across the entire wall. I have a photo, which I'll send you. And soon, my colleagues were comparing me to this character on a television show I hadn't seen. When I finally watched the show (*Homeland*) I saw that they were talking about the moment when Carrie has a psychotic break while piecing together a terrorist network on her wall. So, they were basically saying, "Are you bipolar?" And, I mean, from their perspective, I get it! Having a huge, color-coded timeline spread across the wall looks crazy. But here's the thing: I think it's crazier *not* to do that. Because otherwise, you're carrying it inside. And you can't possibly—I don't care how big your brain is—carry all of that and think clearly and be efficient.

One person's bipolar is another person's efficient structure for conveying complexity.

I am a visual thinker. The timeline helps, but there are many other tools. For example, in the field, I never rely solely on notebooks. I take video, audio, photos on my iPhone. All of that material, by the time I am writing, brings me back to the moment and makes it come alive. I also like to arrange visual prompts in front of me, on a whiteboard—drawings, song lyrics, maps, a big photograph.

How did you develop your methodology? Was it just going with your own instincts? Were there people you stole from?

What I've learned from people is more about craft. Method is so personal. That doesn't mean you can't learn. I've sought lots of advice from different people, but I've never ended up using their systems because each system is like a fingerprint. It's a reflection of how you think, and each person thinks differently. You can say, "Use Scrivener, it's awesome!" and each person will use it in a different way. Hardware hacks are useful, but how you put it all together is so individual. The first time I organized my book material into a structure, and then divided it into phases of writing—chapters that would keep changing, of course—I remember taking stock of all the material I'd been with from the very beginning and feeling lost.

Let me go back to 2006 when I began to write my imam series [Elliott's series for *The New York Times* about an Egyptian imam serving an immigrant community in post-9/11 Brooklyn]. That is the story that really transformed me into a writer of long-form stories. It was such a gift. But I think back to that first terrifying moment when I sat down with my pile of notes, transcribed from the field, and everything was in chronological order. And I began to sort through it, page by page by page. I'd never written more than a four-thousand-word story. I had no idea. What I found myself doing was forming grids on a legal pad. And then putting scenes, character sketches, themes into these separate grids.

Being able to see it all together, and then determining how each scene or theme connected, then shaping that into an outline, and then from the outline, writing—this was all new to me. I went through countless drafts and had a magnificent editor, Joe Sexton, who taught me a lot about the architecture of good storytelling. I was just happy to see it all come together, a three-part series on A1. I mean, at the time, I was still working the Sunday-night shift in the Bronx. That it wound up winning a Pulitzer was like a bizarre lightning strike. You have to feel so damn lucky to have that happen, especially at a young age. I was in my early thirties and suddenly I went from metro to investigations, where all they did was this kind of work. What a crazy privilege. And I kept learning from the most gifted people, right up until I began the book.

By then, I had my process down. It usually goes something like this: Before writing anything new—a scene, a chapter—I start by gathering all my material, and then I just sit with it, reabsorb it, and pay attention to what moves me. Whether it's a gut feeling or a brain spark, something's happening in my body somewhere, and that's what I try to listen to. Then I start writing, and what a beast. It can flow. It can stop. It can be so frustrating or it can feel like deliverance. It's unwieldy. One thing I've learned is to ease up on myself. If I'm stuck, I move on, go to something else. I don't push. The work is always happening, on some mysterious level. You are never really "switched off" as a writer—the wheels are constantly turning. I learned the most about this from artists in residencies—poets, people who work with their hands, sculptors, painters, and also fiction writers.

The novelist Maxim Loskutoff taught me that there is no such thing as writer's block; there is nothing being blocked. When the writing has paused, it's because something else is happening. It is not ready to come out. It's turning its way through your brain and that is part of the process. Years ago, I would stubbornly stare at the screen. I stopped doing that. When I'm stuck, I pivot. When I'm in the flow, I stay there. I try to yield to the beast.

I really believe that the best work happens in the rewrite. I start by reading it out loud so I can hear it. I hear the lyricism, or I don't hear the lyricism, and I keep rewriting and reading it out loud till it sounds right. Another thing that a fiction writer shared with me— which was salvation—relates not so much to the writing as to the presentation of fact, especially when you feel close to your subject. And that's always a hard road, the challenge of pulling away in order to write about them with the clear-eyed precision and depth that the reader deserves—which is not always the portrait that the person you are following would want to read. I really struggled with this when it came to Dasani's mother. And then the novelist Jennifer Gilmore told me, "Here's a rule: the more you love your character, the less the reader will, and the harder you are on your character, the more the reader will love your character." And maybe that's because when a reader sees that you are being tough, they are like, "Okay, I can trust this because you've shown me some shit. You are no longer standing between me and Chanel. You have gotten out of the way. Now . . . what do I really think of Chanel?" Instead of, "Oh, you are trying to sugarcoat this. It's all about you."

I wanted to end with you talking about teaching. You are teaching now. What has it been like?

What I love the most about teaching is watching people summon bravery. Because this is a really hard thing to do for a living: the amount of bravery, the courage that is required to walk up to someone you don't know, ask them questions, and hopefully gain their trust; the skills you pick up along the way to do that, in order to observe them, which requires a whole new form of bravery; to stay the path of trusting your instincts and your powers of observation, and then figuring out how to translate that to the page. These are all critical things that are hardwired into us by the time we've been at it for twenty years—so much so that we forget how vulnerable we are. Watching my students learn to use these muscles for the first time has been profoundly moving. I also think that teaching has brought me back to my earliest self. It holds up a mirror to all those rookie mistakes I used to make. One thing I had to learn, very early on, was to get out of my own way.

So, how does that manifest?

I'll tell you a story about that imam series. When I sat down with that huge pile, I was out in California on vacation. And that was my vacation, all ten days in a room with this pile, and I was terrified. Finally, I absorbed it, did my first big outline for the three parts, and then wrote my first top. My editor (Joe) told me to "just keep going," which I wrote on an index card. I still have that index card and I periodically put it up next to my screen. It helps when I'm about to try something hard. If I stall, I look at it and keep going. It's become a mantra. So, I wrote the whole imam series, all three parts, and gave it to him. He called me up and said something that, at first blush, struck me as ridiculous. Well, let me back up. At first, he said something great. He said, "Listen, what you have is amazing, Andrea. What you have is a world that people don't know. But the top doesn't work." And I knew that. The top was a deep-in-the-weeds mess. I was trying too hard. But I chose it as the top because it involved this phenomenal moment I had witnessed. The imam was in his mosque in Midwood, Brooklyn—a storefront mosque—up on the second floor, writing out contracts of Islamic law that people signed. Whether it was business deals or marital issues, he had this whole parallel system of justice that he was presiding over in his mosque. It was fascinating. But as the lead? It just didn't work. There were too many things happening at once and it was hard to follow. I think I was overcompensating for my deep insecurities. The *Times* had given me six months to work on this, and I wanted to show them how deep I had gone.

But the reader doesn't care about any of that. There's no more honest relationship than the one between your words and the reader. If the writing works, the readers stay. If it doesn't, they're gone.

I remember Joe looking at me and then saying, "What you have is so special that you could literally just start the story by describing the mosque." And I was like, "Are you kidding me? Describe a mosque? Who is going to read that?" But it was a brilliant move, because what he was really doing was telling me to get out of my own way. It was the most perfect thing an editor has ever done. He was like, "You're off in Shakespeare land. I am taking you back to Dick and Jane. We're not going to do sonnets. I'm going to unburden you of all that pressure, so you can get out of your own way and see what you have."

Okay then—the mosque, the mosque. What could I do with that? Well, what happens outside that mosque? I started asking myself these basic questions. How does the day begin? I knew that the imam arrived there early every morning. So I went with him. And I watched him walk as the sun was rising. "The imam begins his trek before dawn, his long robe was billowing like a ghost through empty streets." That was the first line. I wrote it in one go. It was so simple—an imam walking into a mosque. And that's why it worked. The reader needs an early point of connection, as a way into the story. In that first line, there is something familiar but also mystifying. They've seen that image, maybe on TV, of an imam walking in a robe. But now, as the imam goes inside his mosque, we go in with him. We are climbing the stairs and entering a whole new world that is part ours and part his. We're inside. And that is always where the reader wants to be.

I was in D.C. a few weeks later when Joe read the draft. He calls me. He's like, "Where are you?" I tell him that I'm standing in Trader Joe's. And he says, "I don't know where this is gonna go. I can't promise anything. But, as far as I'm concerned, you just won the fucking Pulitzer." (Joe loves to swear.) "This is so fucking great, Andrea. This is it." Of course, I didn't believe him. But what was so special about that moment was the feeling of breakthrough. I just needed, as Joe told me, to get out of my own way and tell the story that wanted to be told.

And this is the thing I love about teaching. I now get to tell my students to get out of their own way. "What you have is great!"—

I like to be a cheerleader—"but let's just breathe." Or I tell them to put something aside. We're going to use it, don't worry, we do not have "to kill your darlings." We don't have to do that (I hate all these clichés). We just have to slow down and notice, because the hardest thing that we're up against as writers is the transition from observing to writing. It is so hard because, in order to really get inside, you have to go deep, and you have to understand everything in its most granular reality. But then, in order to write about it, you have to pull away. These are opposite motions, like a camera that zooms in and then zooms out. And in the zooming out, you have to remember what the reader doesn't know. You have to hold these two contradictory things at once—intimate knowledge and the reader's lack thereof. They have to work together somehow and it's really, really hard. It can feel impossible, until it doesn't.

WHAT'S NEXT?

After anything you publish, some well-meaning person will inevitably ask you, "What's next?" This is especially true after you publish a book, and there's a good chance, no matter what level of success your book achieves, you'll feel pressure to figure out your answer to this question as soon as possible.

You may also hear advice about the magical moment to write or to sell the next book. Some folks will say you should have something in the queue before your first book actually publishes, as that is the period of time when the publisher is most excited about and focused on you—and before they are able to measure your auspicious potential against actual sales. Others suggest that you begin the next book while waiting for the first one to come out, if only for your own sanity. By this logic, instead of focusing on your book's reception, you'll instead turn to something creatively exciting, and will thus become less of a manic Amazon-ranking checker in the process. I love this idea in theory, and I hope you are reading this chapter while creatively excited. But in my experience, having a book about to come out or having one just published is not the time when the imagination is at its most fecund. Nearly every writer I know can't focus on anything but their book's reception in the months leading up to its publication, and many feel a little out to sea in its aftermath. If this describes you, you're perfectly normal.

If and when you come up with your next book idea, you will have legal considerations to keep in mind. Your book contract likely contains an "option clause," meaning your initial publisher is the first one you must approach with the option to publish it. The option clause comes with certain protections for both parties. First, it stipulates that you can't approach your publisher with your next book while writing your first one. Depending on the contract, you must wait until either your first book is delivered and accepted, or it is published. This prevents you from lobbing book ideas at your editor like you are trying to win a prize at Skee-Ball. The contract also requires the publisher to get back to you about any submission within a reasonable amount of time, usually specified to be somewhere between thirty and sixty days. You are under no obligation to accept any offer, just to give your publisher the right of first refusal. Sometimes authors bristle at a contract's option clause or ask that it be taken out (which is very hard to do). I think the option clause works in the author's favor: it encourages your publisher to think of your book as more than a one-off. The option clause assumes, or at least hopes for, an ongoing relationship between author and publisher. The promise of making a long-term relationship even longer keeps both parties accountable.

Another caveat about your option clause should shape the way you think about your next book. You are not required to submit *every* future book to your publisher, just whichever one you first choose to show them. You can of course submit another idea to them if they pass on your option book, but you are no longer under any sort of contractual obligation to them, nor they to you. That initial option submission is the one they will seriously consider. In practical terms, this means choose your shot wisely. Think of your option clause not as a ticking clock, but as an opportunity. It's okay to take your time and make the most of it. The quality of your submission, rather than its timing, is far more determinative of whether it will sell.

Now that I have covered the necessary bases, I want to underscore that you are likely reading this well before having published your debut, let alone your second, book. Perhaps you have no idea what your first book will be. Perhaps you just decided you might like to be a nonfiction writer. Don't waste a second of your time or brain space worrying about book two. If this book is used as it's intended, you'll be dipping in and out of it as your career progresses and changes course. My parting advice is not to worry too much about steps in your career that are so far down the line from where you are now. This doesn't mean you can't hope and dream and plan and strategize. I hope I have given you guidance for every step of the way, but in terms of focus, decide what is the most immediate task at hand. Perhaps it is pitching your first article. Perhaps it is starting your own writing group. Perhaps it is seeing if you can chat with a few professors at the MFA programs you're applying to. Perhaps it's scouring the acknowledgments of your favorite recent books to find out who represents your favorite writers. Just as with your writing, take your career steps bird by bird.

And when you get stuck? Pick up a book. If the writers I know have anything in common, it's not only that they are voracious readers, but also that many of their best ideas have been sparked by reading others. Read beyond your own subject of expertise and beyond your own genre. Push yourself through a book with which you passionately disagree or whose form doesn't do service to its content, and then spend time thinking about your own reaction—and how you can do better. As for any book you love? I think you know what to do, which is the most generous thing you can: Tell everyone you know all about it.

Contracts 101: Contracts for Short
Work, with Jonathan Lyons

If you manage to sell a piece to a magazine, there are things in your contract you absolutely should vet, which is why I review and sign off on my clients' contracts for magazine pieces, as do many agents. If you are unagented, a lawyer can do this, but realistically speaking, the money you'd spend on a lawyer to review the contract you signed with *The Atlantic* online or *The Paris Review* could be more than either publication would pay you. My lawyer (I love saying that—so fancy!), Jonathan Lyons, of Lyons and Salky Law, specializes in publishing contracts and reviews these kinds of agreements all the time. Here is his advice on how not to sign your life, or more particularly, your subsidiary rights, away when you sell your shorter pieces.

What kinds of contracts are writers typically offered for writing essays and articles?

There are generally two types of agreements offered, a **work-for-hire** agreement and a **license** agreement.

With a license agreement, a writer retains copyright ownership of the piece, but licenses certain rights to the publisher. There can be a variety of different rights granted in license agreements—with the central components being **territory, languages, formats,** and **exclusivity.**

- **Territory:** The territory grant is typically one of the following: United States, North America, or World, and it specifies where a piece can be published.
- **Languages:** The most common grant is for English-language only, but publishers regularly request more, especially if they publish in various languages. For example, *Vogue* has twenty-six international editions. Thus, if you grant *Vogue* "World Rights" in "all languages," you are giving them permission to publish your article translated into Russian, French, Italian, etc.
- **Formats:** The formats granted are typically print or online, or more often both. Publishers may also request audio rights, and sometimes dramatic rights (or perhaps an option on such rights).
- **Exclusivity:** A license can be conveyed to a publisher either **exclusively** or **nonexclusively,** or most often, some combination of the two, where a publisher will have the first exclusive right to publish a piece, and then the nonexclusive right to do so thereafter, or after a certain period of time (e.g., a sixty-day exclusivity period). When an author gives a magazine an exclusive license to publish an article, the author may be restricted from using any of the verbatim text from a magazine article in a potential future book. To be clear, this would not restrict the author from writing a full-length book based on or inspired by the article, they just cannot use the same actual text. If the rights are conveyed nonexclusively or become nonexclusive at a later date, then there is no potential issue with an author repurposing the article.

Work-for-hire contracts, on the other hand, are not licenses. Rather, the publishers own the copyright to the piece, and they are treated as the author of the piece under copyright law. In practice this means the publisher can use the piece in any way they want. The most common example of when work-for-hire applies is when an employee prepares material in the course of their employment. In any situation other than an employee-employer relationship, there must be a written contract that specifically states that the material produced is being done on a work-for-hire basis. Many magazine and newspaper publishers will initially try to obtain rights on a work-for-hire basis if they can, with major newspapers being particularly insistent on this.

Do you think one sort of contract is preferable to the other? If a writer has a choice, or is in a position to ask, should they request a licensing agreement over a work-for-hire agreement, or vice versa?

Wherever possible, a licensing agreement is highly preferable to a work-for-hire agreement. In fact, when a client receives a work-for-hire agreement from a publisher, prior to requesting any changes, I advise that they tell the publisher to send their licensing agreement instead as a starting point for review.

I know from working with you that you often do extensive markups of contracts for original articles and essays. If a writer doesn't have the benefit of working with a lawyer, what are the top things they should look out for in a contract?

- **Scope:** What is the scope of the contract? Is it for one piece, or for any pieces an author writes for a publication? Unless the other contract terms are fully satisfactory, an author should push for the former.
- **Ownership/Grant:** As discussed earlier, is this a work-for-hire agreement or a license? If it is the latter, what territory, languages, and formats are being granted? Generally, an author wants to retain any rights the publisher won't directly exploit (use) themselves.
- **Exclusivity:** What is the exclusivity? Is there a requirement for the publisher to publish within a period of time?
- **Payment:** What fee is being paid (whether by word or for the entire piece), and when? Is there a "kill fee" if the publisher fails to publish the piece? If the publisher has the right to license or otherwise exploit the piece in more than

just print and online formats, is there compensation paid to the writer each time the piece is used?

- **Credit:** Will the writer receive credit for the piece? If so, how will the writer be credited?
- **Approvals:** Can changes be made to the piece without the writer's approval? Does the writer have approval over the piece being licensed outside the original format? Can the piece be bundled with other pieces without the writer's approval? If the right to exploit the piece in other formats has been granted, which may involve an adaptation of the work, does the writer have approval over such adaptation?

What are a few rights that an author should try to retain, if they have some leverage?

I believe that wherever possible you should try to limit the rights granted to the publisher to rights they actually exploit themselves, i.e., print and digital in connection with their publication. This means you would retain film/television rights and book adaptation rights, for example.

Have you ever seen a contract for an article or essay that was so author-unfriendly that you advised the author it wasn't worth publishing the piece? Are there any red flags so egregious one just shouldn't publish the piece?

This very much depends on the writer, the piece, and the publisher. I normally do not recommend a writer to agree to a work-for-hire, but there are exceptions—for example, if a writer is just starting out and really needs the credit; if the piece is highly unlikely to be something the writer would ever adapt into a book (such as an interview, book review, or a how-to list), or for film or television; or if the piece is being written for a major newspaper that insists on a work-for-hire arrangement. I also typically insist that the writer has sign-off on all substantive changes to the piece. Again, however, if this is a major break for the writer, and the publisher has a good editorial reputation, perhaps sign-off on those changes can be skipped. But for any established writer, I wouldn't recommend that.

Authors are often afraid to push back on contractual language with media outlets because they are so eager to get published. Have you ever seen a media outlet cancel an agreement because an author questioned the language in the contract? How much leverage does an author, particularly an unknown one, have in these situations?

Sure, I've seen that happen, but it's rare, and I think in most instances it's a sign the publisher is not a good choice for the author anyway. Most publishers expect writers to ask questions about their agreements. Publishers should be able to explain what their terms mean, and if they can't make a change, a writer has requested they should be able to explain why. Of course, if a writer is asking a thousand questions and demanding unreasonable changes, a publisher understandably may feel it's not worth spending the time negotiating. But so long as the writer does their homework, asks thoughtful questions, and is polite throughout, a publisher will typically respond patiently.

Even an unknown author can have leverage, assuming the piece is highly sought after. Publishers understand that writers feel possessive of their writing and are typically willing to work with them at least a little bit to try to make them comfortable (while, of course, balancing their business interests).

Contracts are full of intimidating legalese. Are there words you see again and again that you think it would be helpful for authors to know?

- **Dramatic rights:** The right to use and adapt a work in connection with the making of a film, television, or theatrical or stage production.
- **Kill fee:** A payment (typically a percentage of the fee they would have been paid) in case the publisher decides not to publish the piece. The range can vary quite a bit depending on the publisher and the stature of the writer.
- **Time is of the essence:** This is a term of art used to emphasize that delivery by the date in the agreement is absolutely essential. In practice, this would mean that if you

deliver even one day late, the publisher may terminate. This term isn't appropriate unless the piece is timely.

- **Noncompete:** A noncompete is a clause in an agreement that restricts a writer from doing certain things. In the context of short nonfiction agreements, this is typically a restriction from publishing another piece that's on the same subject as the piece in question with a competitor of the publisher for a certain period of time. To be enforceable in New York, it needs to be limited in scope and duration, necessary and not harmful to the public, and does not impose an undue burden on the writer. Writers should either delete or limit these as much as possible.

- **Form and content:** This term of art is used around acceptability of a piece, meaning that both the arrangement and actual substance of the piece must be acceptable to the publisher.

- **Warranty:** This is a legal promise in an agreement. Typically, you see publishers request that the author warrant that the piece is original, has not been published before, and will not violate the rights of others. If writing a controversial piece, writers should consider providing caveats to the last, such as "to the best of writer's knowledge."

Contracts 102: The Book Contract, with Jonathan Lyons

What are the basic characteristics of a book contract?

Your standard book contract is a license. This means that the author owns the copyright to the work they have written. The author then licenses the right to use the work to the publisher in certain formats, languages, and countries around the world over a period of time.

The format rights granted by an author to a publisher in a traditional book deal will almost always include the right to publish the book in print and electronic formats, and frequently will include audio rights as well. In the United States, the territories typically granted to a publisher will most often either be exclusively in North America or exclusively throughout the world. This means that the author is granting *only* the U.S. publisher the right to print the book in North America, or in the UK, or in the world. Authors also can grant rights based on language. For example, an author can grant a U.S. or UK publisher English-language rights only, or the right to publish in some or all other languages. Finally, the time period granted in a publishing agreement is the duration of the copyright for the book, and copyright lasts until seventy years after the death of the author. However, in practice the actual term of publishing licenses (assuming the contract hasn't been terminated for reasons provided for in the agreement, such as the book going out of print) is thirty-five to forty years from publication. Under the U.S. copyright act, an author or the author's heirs can terminate the agreement after providing at least two years' notice and do a new deal.

The publishing agreement will also contain details regarding the delivery of the manuscript by the author to the publisher, what the revision process will look like, proofreading the manuscript, and all other steps necessary to prepare the book for publication. It should also include a time period within which the publisher has to publish the book once they have accepted the manuscript.

Book contracts also describe the various items or times during the publication process for which an author must be consulted or give approval. These include both conversations about the appearance of the book itself, such as the title, cover design, and jacket copy, and discussions about how the publisher may exploit the book, such as with abridgments or condensations, who will narrate the audio edition, and sublicenses to other publishers.

Publishing agreements need to detail the financial arrangements between the author and publisher, including the advance and royalties for different editions of the book. There also needs to be an accounting provision reflecting how often payments are going to be made.

All book contracts will require that the author make certain promises (i.e., warranties) with respect to the book, and protect (i.e., indemnify) the publisher if those promises are broken. These typically include that the author actually has the right to enter into the agreement and convey the rights that are being granted to the publisher, that the contents of the book won't violate the law or rights of others, and more.

Of course, these are just the basic characteristics of a publishing agreement. There are numerous other terms that should be addressed, including publicity, copyright registration, out of print, permissions, income splits, nonexclusive territories, noncompete, author copies, governing law, assignment, and more.

What are a few key rights that an author should make sure are being protected in their book contracts?

When granting rights, an author should typically consider two things: First, am I being properly compensated for the rights the publisher wants? Second, is the publisher likely going to exploit the rights they wish to acquire?

When considering compensation, an author (in conjunction with their agent) should consider the potential value of those rights. For example, if a publisher wants the audio rights to a book, does the advance reflect the potential audio sales for that book? Or if the publisher wants foreign language rights, does the advance include the amount of money that an author may have otherwise been able to make in non-English-speaking countries?

As for the ability to actually use such rights, does the publisher have a strong track record of either producing such versions themselves or licensing them to other publishers? As in the earlier example, does the publisher actually create audio editions for each book they acquire audio rights for? What is their track record in selling books in other languages and in other countries that might be similar to your book?

Of course, there are certain rights that almost never make sense to be included in a contract if you have an agent. Most publishing houses do not have a dedicated department for exploiting film and television rights. With only a few exceptions, this is also true for merchandising rights.

Are there words you see again and again in contracts that you think it would be helpful for authors to know?

- **First proceeds:** It's rare that a book is fully completed and acceptable to a publisher when a book contract is signed. As a result, a publishing agreement will spell out a delivery and revision process. But what if the publisher ends up rejecting the book after the revision? The author is almost always obligated to pay back the publisher any portion of the advance they've received. However, publishers recognize that they hold the financial power in this situation, and authors are very unlikely to have the means to pay back that advance immediately. As a result, there is often language in agreements that allows an author to pay back this advance out of the "first proceeds." Basically, the author is given a chance to sell the book elsewhere and repay the publisher

from the advance received by the author from the new
publisher.

- **Reserve against returns:** Booksellers typically aren't
  buying books outright from publishers, but rather on a
  consignment basis. This means that the bookseller can
  return copies they don't sell back to the publisher and
  get reimbursed for such unsold copies. As a result of this,
  a publisher will hold back a percentage of an author's
  royalty money to cover the costs of books returned by the
  booksellers.
- **Premium:** A premium is a special sale to a customer,
  where a book is sold in conjunction with another product.
  Think of children's books that might be sold accompanied
  by a toy. These sales are typically made in bulk and on a
  nonreturnable basis. While these types of sales are almost
  always worth pursuing, authors typically have approval
  since their work will thereafter become associated with that
  product or service.
- **Deep discount:** While you may not see this exact term used
  in publishing agreements, the concept itself is in almost all
  contracts and something to always be on the lookout for.
  Publishers typically sell books to booksellers at a discount of
  the price that a customer sees at a bookstore or online. The
  bookseller will then sell the book to customers and pocket
  the difference between the price they paid to the publisher
  and the price at which they sold the book to the customer.
  Publishers sometimes include language in their publishing
  agreements that provides for a lower royalty to be paid
  to the author when the discount at which they sell books
  exceeds a certain amount. This clause originally applied
  only to sales made on a nonreturnable basis, but now
  some publishers will apply it to any sales, which is a major
  concern for authors and agents.
- **Out of print:** Most publishing agreements in the United
  States are binding for the term of a book's copyright.
  However, there should be a provision in a contract allowing
  an author to terminate an agreement earlier if a book is "out
  of print." This means different things to different publishers,

and so needs to be clearly defined in the contract. Sometimes a book is out of print if it's simply unavailable for purchase (a definition more favorable to publishers), other times it is deemed out of print if sales are below a certain threshold in a given accounting period (a definition more favorable to authors).

What issues are you seeing on the legal publishing horizon that an author may not have to be aware of now, but might want to keep an eye out for by the time this book is published?

Artificial intelligence (AI) is unsurprisingly a hot-button issue in the industry right now. Authors want protections against their work being used to train AI technologies, as well as limitations on the use of AI in connection with the preparation and publication of their books. Publishers want to be able to use AI in the normal course of their business operations, and also want restrictions relating to authors using AI to prepare their works. Compromises have already been reached between some agents and publishers regarding this issue, and I imagine by the time of this book's publication, language will be in place with all major publishers.

Concerns around author publicity, social media, and morality clauses will also likely only increase in the years to come. While publishers are longtime advocates of First Amendment rights, they are still for-profit businesses with a duty to their shareholders. When an author publicly advocates for ideas that are antithetical to a majority of people, and such actions may lead to damage to the reputation and business of that author's publisher, what should the publisher's remedies be? These issues are still up for debate.

Foreign Rights 101, with Rights Director Rebecca Gardner

Though much of what I discuss in this book pertains primarily to the American publishing industry, the United States isn't the only place people read books by American authors. Here to help you understand the mechanics of how American books get published outside the United States is The Gernert Company's rights director, Rebecca Gardner.

What are "foreign rights"?

Foreign rights is the work of licensing a book to international publishers who then sell their own edition of that book in each respective market.

An agent can choose to sell or hold on to foreign rights when negotiating a deal with a publisher on behalf of an author.

- If an agent believes a book has international potential, they may sell "North American" rights to a publisher, keeping control of the foreign rights to sell on the author's behalf. In this case, any money received from foreign licenses is in addition to monies that come from the North American deal.
- If a publisher makes an offer for "World Rights" that the agent feels is strong enough, the publisher handles the foreign licensing, and money from international deals goes

against the U.S. advance until the book earns out. After
earnout, the publisher keeps a percentage (usually 20–25
percent) and pays the rest through to the author via the
regular royalty statement schedule. These terms are outlined
in the "subsidiary rights" section of the publisher's contract
with the author.

- Sometimes a deal is for "World English," which means the
publisher acquires the right to sell or license their edition in
English-language markets around the world and the agent
handles the licensing of translation rights.

How are foreign rights to a book sold?

The big-picture answer is by pitching ideas and submitting material
to editors at international publishing houses who are the most likely
to be interested, would potentially make the strongest investment,
and would have the best vision for how to make a book succeed in
their market.

Who does the pitching and the selling?

Depending on who controls the foreign rights, there are a few options.

If the literary agency holds the foreign rights:

Many agencies have a person (or department) dedicated to foreign
rights who cultivates relationships with international editors and
pitches books on behalf of or in tandem with the author's literary agent.

At some agencies, the foreign team sells directly to foreign publishers, but at others they work with international coagents who are
based in various markets around the world. Coagents bring their local
knowledge to the conversation, come up with a list of editors who
might be interested, handle the mechanics of the submission, and in
consultation with the agency's foreign-rights team, negotiate the deal.
Ongoing relationship management between authors, agents, and foreign publishers is also part of the coagents' role.

Typically, coagents and the author's primary agent each take a 10
percent commission of the gross value of foreign deals. If the agent

sells foreign rights directly, the agent will advise on their commission. Some agents sell directly in particular markets but work with coagents elsewhere.

If the publisher holds the foreign rights:

Publishing houses (all the majors and many smaller presses) have a person or team dedicated to foreign rights. If a publisher buys World Rights or World English rights to a book, its person or team handles the foreign licensing, either selling directly or via international coagents as described earlier.

As noted, the full value of foreign licenses is accounted against the U.S. advance, and after earnout, the publisher keeps a percentage (usually 20–25 percent) of foreign deals and pays the rest through to the author via the regular royalty statement schedule. These terms are outlined in the "subsidiary rights" section of the publisher's contract with the author.

Many U.S. editors have relationships with international editors and love to discuss and promote books they've acquired. They don't handle the actual selling, but a recommendation from one editor to another can be very effective. These editorial connections exist regardless of whether the publisher controls the foreign rights or not.

How is the pitch made?

In-person or virtual meetings are a great way to seed early interest in a project, but official submissions are made primarily via email, first with a proposal or a submission manuscript and then with subsequent versions of the material. Updates and reminders containing pertinent news about the author, U.S. publication plans, international deals, film or television options, and other helpful ammunition are shared along the way.

How does a foreign deal actually happen, once it's clear someone wants to bid?

The ideal scenario is for multiple editors to be interested, leading to a competitive bidding situation, but the ultimate goal is to find one editor at a good house who really gets a project and is moved to offer for it.

The rights holder/coagent can conduct the same sorts of auctions that may happen in the United States, with editors making successive rounds of bids, presenting editorial letters and marketing plans to showcase their vision along the way. An author might be in the lucky position of having to choose between two or more best bids in any given foreign market, but ultimately, and more commonly, if there's only one bid from a particular place, as long as it's from a quality publisher, it's a win in that the author's book will reach readers in another part of the world.

It's common for the rights holder to discuss foreign offers with authors before accepting them, but an author should clearly state if they want approval or consultation over foreign deals before the selling begins. Usually authors are presented with the advance, currency, payout schedule, royalties, territory, length of term (deals in translation normally range from three to ten years, and can be renewed for a fresh advance), along with information about the editor and publisher who is offering, plus additional context about the market.

What is the timeline for selling foreign rights? And for foreign publications?

The beauty (and sometimes frustration) of selling foreign rights is that there is no singular moment when it happens. Foreign interest can come from the very first moment a literary agent submits a project in the United States, but can also develop at any stage of a book's publication.

If a project has especially strong foreign potential, sometimes the material sent to U.S. editors is submitted internationally at the same time. It's exceptional, but occasionally an international deal can happen before a U.S. deal closes.

While some markets are open to acquiring books at the proposal stage, it's more common for international editors to wait for a copyedited manuscript or later stages before considering something seriously. In many instances, international editors wait until a book has launched in the U.S. to see its full publication story. If a book hits the bestseller list, wins a prize, or a film or television series is made, these things can inspire fresh interest months or even years after a book has first published.

UK deals often happen first as British publications tend to coincide with U.S. release dates. Online media coverage can often be viewed from anywhere, so British publishers ideally want their edition to benefit from U.S. publicity that may reach UK readers.

Typically, translated editions hit shelves anywhere from six months to two years after a deal is done, and there are many factors that might impact that timing. Publishers aim to hire the best translator they can for any given project and may need to work around a translator's schedule. Once the translation is ready, a foreign publisher has to do all the same preparation and marketing work as a U.S. publisher and wants to ensure that a book launches at the best possible time in its market. If a book is particularly newsworthy or time sensitive and a "global publication" is planned (where all or most foreign editions release at the same time as the United States), international publishers can ready translations quickly, but they need strong coordination from the rights holder to get finished material in hand early.

What happens when a foreign deal is agreed?

Once a foreign rights offer has been accepted, the rights holder/coagent drafts or reviews the contract, organizes signatures, and collects the money.

Once the contract is signed, the rights holder/coagent ensures international publishers have all the material and information they need for their publication, including:

- Final material to give to translators (who are hired by the foreign publisher)
- Polished catalog copy, publication date, word count, and illustrations
- News of blurbs, reviews, U.S. marketing and publicity, and sales in other markets
- U.S. and international jacket designs to consider for their use
- Author photo and biography

The rights holder/coagent acts as the primary point of contact for the author throughout the international publishing process, sharing jacket art, marketing plans, translation questions, and publicity requests, as well as troubleshooting issues with foreign publications along the way.

How does the money for a foreign deal compare to that for a U.S. deal?

The UK is often the biggest customer for U.S. books because it's a lively, English-speaking market with a strong publishing tradition. Some people subscribe to a rule of thumb that a British advance should ideally represent 10 percent of a U.S. advance, reflecting the relative size of each market, but this isn't always the case. UK advances can represent a much larger percentage of a U.S. advance when a book excites British editors. When a British advance seems tiny in comparison with a U.S. advance, some authors wonder, "What is the point of having a British edition since the book already exists in English in the U.S.?" A British publisher will develop a cover that works for the market, pursue local media coverage, and has a sales force and marketing team focused on UK retailers, influencers, and readers. This can give a book a better chance of reaching English-language readers outside the United States in a way that wouldn't necessarily happen if a U.S. edition simply existed on Amazon UK. [NB: Most deals with UK publishers are for "UK and Commonwealth rights," which means their edition is also sold in countries such as Australia, New Zealand, South Africa, India, and many more. You can learn more about Commonwealth countries here: https://thecommonwealth.org/our-member-countries.]

In the smallest translation markets, such as Turkey, Ukraine, or Slovenia, as of this writing advances typically range between $1,000 and $3,000. Smaller advances also exist.

In larger translation markets, such as Germany and China, or markets where a book has a particularly strong resonance, six-figure deals can happen. Achieving an advance at this level is rare these days, but when the subject, writing, and timing are right, it's possible!

Translation offers are made at every level in between, but generally, if a book inspires a foreign advance of $25,000 or more, today that is considered quite good.

Is there anything authors can do to help with selling foreign rights or generating international interest in a book? Is this something that should begin in the writing process (in other words, using international examples on the page, addressing an audience wider than an American one), or only after the book is complete?

If a book is written in a way that doesn't feel limited to an American audience, that can help generate foreign rights interest. If an author incorporates international information (examples, statistics, case studies, trends), it is more likely that international publishers will want to take a look, but the mere existence of that material doesn't guarantee foreign sales. Depending on the topic, foreign publishers may prefer that it is addressed by a local author—often because of perspective, but also ease of access, homegrown connections, and language fluency when it comes time to promote the book. If having an international component naturally adds to what a book is trying to achieve, that's great, but international research shouldn't be pursued if it feels forced, manufactured, or just outside an author's or the project's purview.

If an author is fluent in another language; is from a particular country; went to university or worked abroad; has a significant international social media following, professional connections, or media interest; travels consistently to a particular place; and for any other reason has notable international experience or insight, it can be helpful to include that information in the foreign submission, so be sure to highlight it for your agent. It's also helpful for international editors to know if the author is willing to write an extra chapter, a bespoke introduction, travel for publicity, or facilitate a local endorsement. Any of these things can help, but as is the case with content, no single thing can guarantee or predict foreign sales.

ACKNOWLEDGMENTS

I never would have written this book without the encouragement, guidance, and kindness of my agent, colleague, and friend Meredith Kaffel Simonoff. I can't think of Meredith without thinking of the other witches in our agency's coven; thank you to Anna Worrall, Joy Fowlkes, and Nicole Tourtelot for the magic of your friendship.

Thank you to my mother, Johanna Habib Czarnecki, and my step-dad, Joe Czarnecki, for your belief in me. I love you both.

I wrote this book during a very difficult period in my personal life. I never would have gotten through it without the love and support of my best friends Adrienne Calo and Jackie Cheney.

Thank you to the lovely and brilliant Maria Goldverg for acquiring this book for Pantheon and for your useful early feedback. Deepest thanks to the amazing Denise Oswald for taking over as my editor, for your sharp eye and steady hand, and for making this book your own. I'm deeply grateful to the entire publishing team at Pantheon and Doubleday for your excellent work on publishing *Take It from Me,* including publisher Bill Thomas, assistant editor Shanna Milkey, production editor Amy Brosey, managing editor Lisa D'Agostino, copy editor Jane Cavolina, jacket designer Emily Mahon, designer Roderick Mills, text designer Michael Collica, publicist Rose Cronin-Jackman, and marketer Julianne Clancy. Thank you to Cristobal Riego and Heather Radke for your early feedback, to Mo Crist and Kevin Lind for your research assistance, and to Jana Cholakovska for fact-checking.

Thank you to everyone at The Gernert Company for being the best colleagues anyone could hope for, especially to my boss David

Gernert, who was endlessly and selflessly supportive of my writing a book and even came up with my title! Special thanks to Rebecca Gardner, Seth Fishman, Sarah Burnes, and Chris Parris-Lamb, all of whom I quoted in these pages. As is so often the case in my work life, I knew I could turn to you when I got stuck.

Thank you to my authors. Every day, you give me new reasons to be grateful and to be proud. I promise to always have your backs.

Thank you to my generous interview subjects and those who granted permission to reproduce your work: Anastasia Berg, Andrea Elliott, Andrew Miller, Anne Helen Petersen, Ben Purkert, Beowulf Sheehan (who also took my beautiful author photos), Brettne Bloom, Caren Zucker, Catherine McCarthy, Chloé Cooper-Jones, Chris Jackson, Clint Smith, Courtney Naliboff, Dan Gerstle, Dan Kois, David Patterson, Dorothy Brown, Eamon Dolan, Elyse Cheney, Emma Berry, Farley Chase, Hanif Abdurraqib, Harrison Hill, Heather Radke, Isaac Butler, Isaac Fitzgerald, Jake Silverstein, Jeff Goldberg, Jelani Cobb, Jenisha Watts, Jennifer Weaver, Jofie Ferrari-Adler, John Donvan, John Maas, Jonathan Lyons, Judy Batalion, Jynne Dilling Martin, Karen Han, Karen Kelsky, Kathy Belden, Kathy Huck, Laura McGrath, Lauren Oyler, Lauren Wein, Leigh Stein, Lena Little, Leslie Jamison, Linda Villarosa, Mark Greif, Mark Krotov, Meghan O'Rourke, Meredith Talusan, Merve Emre, Michael Cader, Michael Goldsmith, Molly Turpin, Niki Papadopoulos, Nikole Hannah-Jones, Rachel Syme, Rachel Wiseman, Rebecca Gardner, Ruth Ben-Ghiat, Ruth Macy, Sam Freedman, Sanyu Dillon, Steve Vladeck, Tom Mayer, Vanessa Mobley, Vann Newkirk, Wendy S. Walters, Wesley Lowery, Whitney Peeling, and Yaniv Soha.

Finally, thank you to Christopher Iannini. You are the greatest good fortune in my fortunate life. I love you so much.

INDEX

Page numbers in *italics* indicate images and tables.

Alia Hanna Habib is a vice president and literary agent at The Gernert Company, where she represents MacArthur Fellows, Pulitzer Prize–winning journalists, National Book Award finalists, and numerous *New York Times* bestselling authors. She joined The Gernert Company in 2017 after starting her publishing career as a publicist at Houghton Mifflin Harcourt and working as an agent at McCormick Literary. She is a graduate of Barnard College and has earned an MA in English Literature from Rutgers University.

A NOTE ABOUT THE TYPE

This book was set in Adobe Garamond. Designed for the Adobe Corporation by Robert Slimbach, the fonts are based on types first cut by Claude Garamond (ca. 1480–1561).

Composed by North Market Street Graphics
Lancaster, Pennsylvania